SHOWTIME DOCUMENT FILMS

P9-BYS-080

THE FULL TRANSCRIPTS OF

THE PUTIN INTERVIEWS

WITH SUBSTANTIAL MATERIAL
NOT INCLUDED IN THE DOCUMENTARY

OLIVER STONE
INTERVIEWS
VLADIMIR PUTIN

FOREWORD BY ROBERT SCHEER

HOT BOOKS
an imprint of Skyhorse Publishing, Inc.
New York, NY

Hot Books books may be purchased in bulk at special discounts for sales
promotion, corporate gifts, fund-raising, or educational purposes. Special
editions can also be created to specifications. For details, contact the
Special Sales Department, Hot Books, 307 West 36th Street, 11th Floor,
New York, NY 10018 or info@skyhorsepublishing.com.

Hot Books is an imprint of Skyhorse Publishing, Inc.®,
a Delaware corporation.

www.skyhorsepublishing.com

10 9 8 7 6 5 4 3 2

Library of Congress Cataloging-in-Publication Data is available on file.
ISBN: 978-1-51073-342-8
eISBN: 978-1-51073-343-5

Cover design by Brian Peterson

Printed in Canada

THE PUTIN INTERVIEWS

ALSO BY OLIVER STONE

Snowden: Official Motion Picture Edition
By Oliver Stone and David Talbot

The Untold History of the United States
By Oliver Stone and Peter Kuznick

On History: Tariq Ali and Oliver Stone in Conversation
By Oliver Stone and Tariq Ali

Scarface: The Movie Scriptbook
By Oliver Stone

A Child's Night Dream: A Novel
By Oliver Stone

Table of Contents

Foreword 1

First Interview

    Trip 1—Day 1—July 2, 2015 5
    Trip 1—Day 2—July 3, 2015 28
    Trip 1—Day 2—July 3, 2015 50
    Trip 1—Day 3—July 4, 2015 61
    Trip 1—Day 3—July 4, 2015 78

Second Interview

    Trip 2—Day 1—February 19, 2016 102
    Trip 2—Day 2—February 20, 2016 125

Third Interview

    Trip 3—Day 1—May 9, 2016 153
    Trip 3—Day 2—May 10, 2016 165
    Trip 3—Day 3—May 11, 2016 177
    Trip 3—Day 3—May 11, 2016 198

Fourth Interview

    Trip 4—Day 1—February 10, 2017 208

End Notes..248

Index 273

PUBLISHER'S DISCLAIMER:

The following is a transcript of a series of interviews conducted between Oliver Stone and Vladmir Putin, on four separate trips to Russia for a total of nine days between July 2, 2015 and February 10, 2017. Since Putin's words were translated from Russian, we took the liberty of fixing grammar, unclear language, and various inconsistencies. And because the interviews took place over a two year period, we edited out some repetition. In all cases, we did the very best we could to ensure that the intent and meaning of what was said was accurately reflected in the transcript.

Foreword

Thirty years ago, as a *Los Angeles Times* correspondent, an assignment led me to the inner sanctum of the Politburo, that darkly mysterious and all-powerful center of the Soviet Union, as its leader Mikhail Gorbachev was initiating his ambitious drive for openness and change. His *Perestroika*, or restructuring of the Soviet government, would inevitably—if inadvertently—end the brutal Communist experiment to mold a brave new world of disparate ethnicities, cultures, and religions spanning one-sixth of the planet's land mass.

My interview was with propaganda chief Alexander Yakovlev, the Politburo's most liberal member and a close Gorbachev ally, while down the hall I would later knock on the door of Gorbachev's No. 2 man, Yegor Ligachev, depicted most often as the strongest opponent of *Perestroika*. I didn't encounter the less-defined figure of Boris Yeltsin, who would become Russia's first president when the Soviet Union collapsed four years later. Yeltsin would come to appoint former KGB lieutenant colonel Vladimir Putin, part of the reform faction, to join his administration, and on December 31, 1999, when Yeltsin resigned, he named Putin acting president. The following year, Putin would be elected to the office, soundly defeating the Communist Party candidate.

In a historic and immensely important series of interviews filmmaker Oliver Stone has conducted with Putin, which is the subject of this book and a four-part *Showtime* documentary, Putin states he believed that with the Soviet Union's collapse, the Cold War was over, and with it the endless threats of confrontation. But that was not to be.

Although Putin discarded Communism as an ideology and indeed embraces the traditions of Russian Orthodox Christianity, he remains a fervent nationalist, determined that Russia be granted the respect he strongly believes it deserves. That means deference to its historic concerns over its borders and the treatment of Russian-speaking people who, with the collapse of the Soviet Union, suddenly found themselves thrust outside newly drawn borders, Ukraine being a prime example.

In his discussion with Stone, Putin credits Gorbachev with recognizing that profound change was required in a failing Soviet system, but he faults him for his naïveté regarding the immense obstacles to that change at home and, more importantly, in the United States. Putin is dismissive of Gorbachev's belief that reason would triumph, since both sides of the Cold War—each possessed of the capability to destroy all life on this planet—desired peace.

The central query in the Stone-Putin interviews is how matters devolved to the current state of tension. Thus they are compelling as a key text for understanding this dangerous time. The intermittent conversations between July 2, 2015 and February 10, 2017 occurred during a period when relations between the world's two most formidable military powers degenerated to a point of suspicion and hostility not witnessed since the end of the Cold War more than two decades ago. And as Stone reminds in several pointed exchanges, the tendency of power to corrupt rulers of any country in the name of a false patriotism should be of concern in any nation, Russia most definitely included.

The discussion is respectful, and as Stone states at the conclusion, it gives Putin a chance "to state his side of the story;" but that is a story the film director-journalist questions energetically, considering the continuing controversy over Russia's role in the world, ranging from its support of the Assad regime in Syria to charges of interference in the 2016 US presidential election. Stone knows much about futile wars and the lies told about them, having served two combat tours in Vietnam, a story he documented in his Academy Award-winning movie *Platoon* and the two others in his brilliant Vietnam trilogy, *Born on the Fourth of July* and *Heaven and Earth*. He explored the subject convincingly in his 2012 ten-part revisionist history for Showtime, *The Untold History of the United States*, and its 750-page companion volume, which challenges the conventional US Cold War narrative that provides an essential backdrop for this current work.

Putin is no less familiar with the subject, having come to power in Russia on the ashes of a Soviet Union that, despite surviving the immense horrors of the German invasion and fifty million dead, unraveled in the wake of a pointless invasion of Afghanistan. He leads a society that retains enormous military power but is far less successful in its peaceful economic achievements.

These men share a conviction that militaristic hubris is fatal, and both express wariness of ideologies in their respective societies that historically supported imperial adventure. But this is not a conversation of equals, for Stone is very much the questioning artist eager to pursue contradiction and oddities of thought, while Putin makes amply clear that, as guarded as he appears, he is highly mindful of his position as the commander-in-chief of the world's second most awesome military power, and that his words have consequences far beyond the requirements of interesting filmmaking. Still, there is clearly a mutual, if wary, respect between the two that makes for a candid glimpse into the minds of the powerful, both the ruler and the artist.

For Stone, filmmaking provides a natural outlet for his scorn of the perceived wisdom of his nation's foreign policy establishment. For Putin, the task is more complicated, being the leader of a nation in profound transition from Soviet Communist ideology to a new Russian national identity that attempts to bridge "a thousand years" of Russian history, spanning eras of the czars to the powerful oligarchs, the Russian version of our crony capitalists.

Putin emerges here as the prophet of a wounded Russian nationalism that, while capable of posing a potent threat, should not be confused with the Communist ideology that preceded his rise to power, and which he clearly views with considerable distaste. That tension provides the leitmotif of this rare glimpse into the workings of Putin's mind and, in a larger sense, of the quandary of Russia's place in a much-changed world. The interview begins at a time when few expected the US victory of a populist rightwing candidate who trounced a dozen leaders of the GOP establishment in the primary and went on to defeat the anointed candidate of the Democratic party leadership. By the end of the transcript, less than a month after Donald Trump's inauguration as president, the lengthy interview comes to an end that is both illuminating and depressing.

In that last session, Stone strenuously pushes Putin to complete the interview in a manner the intellectually aggressive documentarian believes will answer some unanswered questions. That includes controversial aspects of Putin's twenty-four years as head of the world's largest nation, by land mass. Is Putin addicted to power? Does he see himself as the indispensable agent of Russian history? Has the largely unchallenged power he wields corrupted his vision? This is not the first time these topics have been broached, but whereas Stone's earlier probing seemed welcomed by Putin, there is now a weariness that, he makes clear, is borne not so much from assuming his ideas are unappealing to a Western audience, but rather that they simply will not be heard.

Now facing his fourth American president, and ironically one he is widely accused of having helped elect (which he denies), Putin seems worn down by the effort to break through to any American leadership. He asserts that it, and more importantly the bureaucracy that informs it, inevitably views Russia not as a partner, a word he uses frequently to refer to the United States, albeit with a lacing of sarcasm, but as a convenient scapegoat for its own failures.

At the third interview's conclusion, Putin asks Stone if he has ever been beaten. Stone assures him, "Oh, yes many times," to which Putin responds, referring to the projected release of the documentary: "Then it's not going to be anything new, because you're going to suffer for what you are about to do."

It is a painful but perhaps accurate prediction, given the current climate of widespread condemnation of yet unproven claims of Russian interference in the US election. Stone replies: "I know, but it's worth it . . . to try to bring some more peace and consciousness to the world."

—Robert Scheer

Trip 1 — Day 1 — July 2, 2015

ON PUTIN'S BACKGROUND

OS: I think a lot of Western people don't know much about you except for the news. We'd like to know about your background and where you came from. I know that you were born in October, 1952, after the war. That your mother was a factory worker and your father had been in the war. But I don't know what he did after the war. And I know that you lived in a collective apartment with other families as you grew up.

VP: My mother didn't work at a factory. She was a worker, however, but she did different jobs. But I was an only child. They had lost two children before me. One during the Siege of Leningrad,[1] during the war. And they didn't want to give me up to an orphanage. And that's why my mother was working as a warden—

OS: Because she did not want to give you up?

VP: Yes, that's correct. And my father was working at a plant—a factory.

OS: Doing what exactly?

VP: He was an engineer. He graduated from college. He had a vocational education and he was working in a factory.

OS: Steadily or was it stop-gap work? Did he work on a steady basis?

VP: Yes. Yes. On a steady basis. I would say. And he'd been working for a very long time. And then he retired and he still worked until he was 70 or so.

OS: He was wounded in the war, though?

VP: Yes, he was. When the war started he was serving in a special unit. There were small intelligence groups which were sent to the area guard of the enemy to perform different actions. There were 20 people sent in such a group and only four survived.

He told me of that and later, when I was president, I got the archives and I received a confirmation of what had happened. It's quite curious. It was. And then he was sent to the armed forces to one of the most dangerous areas of the Leningrad front. It was called the Nevsky Pyatachok—the bridgehead. There were hostilities on the Ritneva River. The Soviet army managed to create a small bridgehead two by four kilometers.

OS: Going on, your older brother died within a few days, I believe it was, or within a few months of your birth?

VP: No, he died during the Siege of Leningrad. And he was less than three years old. And back then in order to save children, children were taken from their families to support them, to save their lives. But my brother got ill and he died. And our parents were not even informed where he was buried. Quite curious, just recently there were some interested people and they managed to find something in the archives. They used the surname, the father's name, and the address from whence the child was taken. And they managed to find some documents about his death and about where he was buried and the orphanage where he was sent. And last year was the first time that I visited his burial place. It's in Memorial Soundry in St. Petersburg.

OS: Well, considering the casualties from World War II, I would imagine your father and mother were not broken by these tragedies. They must have looked to their third son as a new hope.

VP: Well, indeed they were not broken. But the war ended in 1945, and I was born only in 1952. And that was a very difficult time for ordinary people who believed in the Soviet Union. And yet they decided to have another child.

OS: And tell me . . . I hear you had a bit of . . . a bit of a juvenile delinquency problem. You were a bit of a wild child until, I heard, you studied Judo at the age of 12.

VP: Yes, indeed. My parents tried to pay attention to my upbringing but still . . . I lived in freedom and I spent much time in the courtyard and the streets. And certainly I was not always as disciplined as some would have liked me to be. And since I started going into sport on a systemic basis, started to do Judo, this became a changing factor in my life for the better.

OS: I also heard that your grandfather on your mother's side was a chef at times for Lenin and for Stalin.

VP: Yes, indeed. It happened. It's a small world as it were. It's true. Before the 1917 revolution he worked at a restaurant in Petrograd, in Leningrad. He was a chef, a cook. I don't know how he got to work for someone of Lenin's stature. But later, indeed, he worked in the countryside where Stalin lived and he worked for Stalin. He was a very simple man—a cook.

OS: Did you hear him tell any stories?

VP: No, he didn't. He didn't tell me anything, but to be honest, part of my childhood I spent in the Moscow Oblest. We lived in St. Petersburg, which was called Leningrad back then. But in the summer we went for a few weeks to visit my grandfather—he was a retiree. But he still lived where he used to work. He lived in one of the State dachas. And my father told me how he went to his father when Stalin was still alive. And my grandfather showed him Stalin from afar. That's the only thing I know.

OS: We have something in common—my mother who's French, her father—my grandfather—was a French soldier in World War I. He was a chef also in the trenches. And he told me many stories about World War I and how tough it was.

VP: Yes, my mother told me also about the first World War, from what had been told to her by her father. He also participated in the first World War.

One curious story from the human side. It was a war in trenches. And my grandfather got back and he told one story. He saw that one of the Austrian soldiers—I believe that was the Southern front—was aiming at him. But my grandfather was first, he shot first and the Austrian fell. And then my grandfather saw that the Austrian was still alive. But his disposition was like that—he was the only person there apart from the Austrian—and the Austrian was bleeding to death. He was going to die. And my grandfather just crawled to him. He took his first aid kit and bandaged his wounds. Quite curious. He told his relatives, "I wouldn't have shot first if I hadn't seen that he was aiming at me." But whatever country you are from—we are all the same, we are all human beings and those people are also just ordinary people, just workers as we are.

OS: The French war was as bloody as the Russian war. In World War I, one-half, 50 percent of the population of young men between 17 and about 35 were killed or wounded in that war.[2]

VP: Yes, that's true.

OS: You graduated from high school and I believe you went directly to law school. That's the Russian system?

VP: Yes, that's true. I graduated from high school, secondary school, in Leningrad and I directly entered Leningrad University and started to study law.

OS: And graduated in 1975? That's pretty good—as a lawyer and met your first wife there—I mean your last wife—your only wife.

VP: That was later. That was after seven years.

OS: And then you joined the KGB right away in 1975 in Leningrad.

VP: Yes, as a matter of fact, there was this system of distribution of jobs in the Soviet higher education institutions. So when you graduated from a higher education institution, you were supposed to go where you were sent.

OS: Oh, so you had no choice?

VP: Well, I'm going to tell you. So I was taken right away—by job distribution I was obliged to go there—but I also wanted to. Moreover, I entered law school because I wanted to work for the KGB. And still when I was a pupil at school I went to the KGB office in Leningrad by myself. And I asked them what I had to do in order to work for the KGB. And the worker there told me that I had to have a higher education and better legal education. And that's why I entered law school.

OS: Oh, I see.

VP: But you know, since that moment no one remembered me of course, and I hadn't had any contact with the KGB. And when the time came for the distribution, it was quite unexpected that the KGB found me and offered a job.

OS: And you had romanticized, of course, the Soviet films about the KGB and intelligence work.

VP: Indeed. That's exactly the case.

OS: Their names were Tikhonov and Georgy . . . Starring Tikhonov and Georgy . . . Movie actors.

VP: There were books, there were films. That's quite correct—you formulated it quite aptly.

OS: Yeah. And you went to Dresden from 1985 through 1990, but for the first 10 years you were mostly in Leningrad?

VP: Yes. Exactly. In Leningrad and also in Moscow at special schools.

OS: And you were rising, you were doing very well.

VP: Yes. On the whole, yes.

OS: East Germany from 1985 to 1990 was pretty dismal.

VP: Well, not exactly dismal. Back then, in the Soviet Union, there were these processes which were related to *Perestroika*.[3] Well I don't think we're going to elaborate on that—there were many issues related to *Perestroika* but there was still this vein—this spirit of innovation. And when I came to Eastern Germany, to the Republic, I saw no spirit of innovation at all.

OS: That's what I meant.

VP: And I had this impression that society was frozen in the 1950s.

OS: So Gorbachev—you didn't know him, I mean, you didn't really have . . . A sense of reform was going on but you were not in Moscow to feel it. It was a strange time. Did you go back to Moscow? Did you experience *Perestroika*?

VP: You know, it was quite understandable to Gorbachev and to his entourage that the country needed changes. Today I can say with all confidence that they didn't understand what those changes were and how to achieve them.

OS: Right.

VP: And that's why they did many things which dealt great damage to the country. Even though they were reacting for the sake of good and they were right to think that changes were required.

OS: But Gorbachev—I met him several times—he came to the United States and I also met him here. But he has a resemblance to you in the sense that he came up through that system. Very much humble beginnings. He was an expert in agriculture. He studied the documents, he worked very hard and he seemed to recognize early, in his memoir, that there were many difficulties that would not work in the economy. Things were not working.

VP: We all have something in common because we're human beings.

OS: Yeah, but what I'm saying is that he was a worker. He was specific and he was asking questions—how do we fix this?

VP: I was not a worker and I think it is exactly this specificity, this concreteness, which many of the former Soviet leadership were lacking. Gorbachev included. They didn't know what they wanted or know how to achieve what was required.

OS: Okay. But there was a coup d'état in 1991 in August,[4] and you resigned on the second day of the coup. The coup being from the Communist Party.

VP: Yes, there was an attempt at a coup d'état. And back in those days—I don't remember if it was the second day or the third day—indeed I resigned. Because when I returned from Germany I worked at the university for some time. And I was still an officer of the KGB—external intelligence service. And afterwards the former mayor of St. Petersburg, Mr. Sobchak, offered me a job.[5] And that was quite a curious conversation because I used to be his pupil and he invited me into his cabinet.

OS: But that was afterward. Why did you resign? I mean this is your career.

VP: I'm going to tell you everything. So when Sobchak invited me to work for him, I told him that I was very much interested in working with him. But I thought that it was impossible. And that it was not the right thing to do. Because I was still an officer of the external intelligence service of the KGB. And Sobchak was a prominent Democratic leader—a politician of the new wave. And I told him directly that if someone were to know that I worked side by side with him, as a former KGB worker, it was going to do damage to his reputation. And back then the country was witnessing very acute political strife. But I was very much surprised at Sobchak's reaction when he told me, "Oh that's nothing to me." And I worked for him for a short time as his adviser. And afterwards, when the coup d'état was attempted, I found myself in a very ambiguous situation.

OS: In August, '91?

VP: Yes, the coup d'état was attempted with the use of force. And I could no longer be an officer of the KGB while remaining a close adviser to the democratically elected mayor of St. Petersburg. And that's why I resigned. Sobchak made a telephone call to the president of the KGB of the USSR. And he asked him to let me go. And he gave his consent just a couple of days later for the decree and my resignation to be issued.

OS: But in your mind, did you still believe in communism? Did you still believe in the system?

VP: No, certainly not. But at the beginning I believed it and the idea is a good one and I believed in it. And I wanted to implement it.

OS: When did you change?

VP: You know, regrettably, my views are not changed when I'm exposed to new ideas, but only when I'm exposed to new circumstances. It became clear that the system was not efficient and the system was at a dead end. The economy was not growing. The political system was stagnating. It was frozen and was not capable of any development. The monopoly of one political force, of one party, is pernicious to the country.

OS: But these are Gorbachev's ideas, so you were influenced by Gorbachev.

VP: These are not ideas of Gorbachev. These ideas were put forward by the French socialist Utopians,[6] so Gorbachev has nothing to do with these ideas. Gorbachev was responding to the circumstances. I reiterate—his merit is that he felt this need for changes. And he tried to change the system. Not even change, he tried to renovate it, to overhaul it. But the problem is, this system was not efficient at its roots. And how can you radically change the system while preserving the country? That's something no one back then knew—including Gorbachev. And they pushed the country towards collapse.[7]

OS: Yeah, that must have been traumatic. The Soviet Union collapsed, and the Russian Federation was formed under Yeltsin. But I was in St. Petersburg in early '92 and I met with Sobchak. I think I may have met you—who knows, if you were an assistant to him back then.

VP: No, I don't remember, but I want to tell you that Sobchak was an absolutely sincere, wholesome man. From an ideological point of view, he was a Democrat, but he was categorically against the disintegration of the Soviet Union.

OS: He was against the disintegration. Yes, it was a wild time, it was exciting. It felt like it was a birth of something new and no one knew where it was going. There were gangsters, there were—people were different. They were wearing new clothes. I had been in the Soviet Union in 1983 during the Brezhnev era and was very depressed by it. So when I came back seven or eight years later it was unbelievable to me. Sobchak took us to a fancy restaurant and we had a wonderful time with him.

VP: But back then, at the same time, when the fancy restaurants appeared, the Russian social security system was destroyed completely. Whole branches of the economy stopped functioning. The healthcare system was in ruins. The armed forces were also in a very depressive condition, and millions of people were under the poverty line. And we have to remember that as well.

OS: Yes, that was the other side of it. You moved to Moscow in 1996 and became the head of the Federal Security Service for 13 months.

VP: No, not right away. I moved to Moscow and at first I was supposed to work for President Yeltsin's administration. And I started to work in the office of the administration of President Yeltsin. I was in charge of legal matters. And afterwards I was transferred to the administration. And I was responsible for the Oversight Directorate. This Department was overseeing the government and the regional administrations. After that I became the director of the Federal Security Service (FSB - Federal'naya Sluzhba Bezopasnosti).

OS: Right, so in that role you must have seen what a mess this was, I gather. It was a nightmare of chaos.

VP: Yes, certainly. I often hear criticism addressed to me. They say that I regret the collapse of the Soviet Union. To start with, the most important thing is that after the disintegration of the Soviet Union, 25 million Russians—in a blink of an eye—found themselves abroad. In another country.

That's one of the greatest catastrophes of the 20th century. People used to live in one country; they had relatives, work, apartments, and they had equal rights. And yet in an instant they found themselves abroad. And there were certain signs and then full-fledged civil wars. Yes, I saw that all personally, especially when I became director of the Federal Security Service.

OS: And in 1999 you worked your way up to be the acting Prime Minister. And Yeltsin resigned in 2000. Obviously, just looking at press conferences and film of Mr. Yeltsin, he was clearly alcohol diseased. His brain seemed to be—the way he spoke and the way he stared at the camera, the way he moved—he looked like he was catatonic.

VP: You know, I do not think that I have the right to give any assessment—either about Gorbachev, or the personality of Yeltsin. Well, I told you that Gorbachev didn't understand what had to be done, what the objectives were and how to achieve them. And yet he was the first to make a step towards giving the country its freedom, and that was a historical breakthrough. Quite an evident fact—and the same thing goes for Yeltsin. Just as any one of us, he had his problems, but he also had his strong side and one of those advantages was that he never tried to avoid, to shirk responsibility, personal responsibility. He knew how to assume responsibility. Even though certainly he had his demons. But what you said is true. It's no secret. It was also the reality.

OS: Just out of curiosity, because I know the Khrushchev story, having to drink with Stalin—did you have a drink with Mr. Yeltsin at night sometimes?

VP: No, never. I was not as close to him as you might suspect. I never was one of the closest advisers either to Gorbachev or to Yeltsin. And it was a complete surprise when he appointed me head of the Federal Security Service. That's the first thing. Secondly, I never abused alcohol. But even when we met, it was also always in a businesslike manner. And I never saw him drunk when he was at work.

OS: A hangover maybe?

VP: I never checked. I never tried to smell him. I'm quite sincere. I never went with him to hunt, I never spent time with him. I met with him at his office. And that's it. I never drank a shot of vodka with him.

OS: Wow. So here you are—many prime ministers come and go and all of a sudden—you're the acting prime minister. Now what?

VP: Yes, you know that's a curious story. You see, I came from Leningrad to Moscow in 1996 just as you said. And on the whole in Moscow I didn't have any strong support, any contacts. In 1996 I came, and on January 1, 2000 I became acting president. So it's an incredible story.

OS: Yeah.

VP: But I have to tell you that indeed I didn't have any special relationship either with Yeltsin or his team.

OS: Maybe some other prime minister had been fired and he just said, "Well you take the job now."

VP: I don't know. Probably he was trying to find someone because he had decided to resign. And indeed several prime ministers had been appointed, then resigned. I don't know why he chose me. Before me there had been very talented prime ministers and recently just one of them has passed away. But when Yeltsin offered this job to me for the first time I refused.

OS: You refused? Why is that?

VP: Yes. I told him—it was in the adjacent office—he invited me in and told me that he wanted to appoint me as prime minister and then wanted me to run for president. I told him that was a great responsibility and that I had to change my life for that. And I was not sure that I was willing to do that. And he told me, "Well, we'll get back to this conversation later."

OS: Changed your life in what way? I mean, you had already been a bureaucrat in the government for a long time.

VP: Well it's quite a different story still. It's one thing when you're a bureaucrat—even a high level bureaucrat—you can live almost an ordinary life. You can go to see your friends, go to the cinema, to the theater, to talk to friends freely. And not assume such personal responsibility for the fates of millions of people for everything that's going on in the country. And to assume responsibility for Russia back then was a very difficult thing to do. And, moreover, in August 1999, when Boris Yeltsin offered my candidature as prime minister and the parliament supported that decision. And the second Chechen War started in Russia in August.[8] And that was an ordeal for the country. And frankly speaking, I didn't know back then President Yeltsin's final plans with regard to me. But the situation was just like that. I had to assume responsibility for this situation. And I didn't know how long I would endure. Because at any second President Yeltsin could tell me, "You are dismissed." And there was only one thing I was thinking about back then: Where to hide my children?

OS: Oh really? And what would you do?

VP: Well, what would you think? The situation was very acute—just imagine if I were dismissed. I didn't have any bodyguards and what would I do? How to secure my family? And back then I decided if that was my fate, then I had to go to the end. And I didn't know then that I was to become president. There were no guarantees of that.

OS: May I ask, were you ever in meetings with Yeltsin and any of the oligarchs?

VP: Yes, certainly.

OS: So you saw the way he handled it?

VP: Of course. It was quite official, very pragmatic. He met them not as oligarchs but as representatives of large enterprises—as people on whose work the fates of millions of people depended and large labor forces.

OS: Did you sense that Yeltsin was being pushed around?

VP: Yes, but he didn't understand that. Boris Yeltsin was a very distant man. If he is to blame for anything with regard to this oligarchic system of governance, it's that he was very trusting. And he had no relations whatsoever with oligarchs. And he never got any benefits from those oligarchs personally.

OS: Did you ever meet Berezovsky or people like that?[9]

VP: Yes, certainly. I was acquainted with Berezovsky even before I came to Moscow.

OS: In what way? Was it friendly?

VP: No, we didn't have any friendly relations. I met him because I was working in St. Petersburg and there was a request from Moscow to receive someone from the US Senate, if I remember correctly. That was a senator flying from Tbilisi and he wanted to meet Sobchak and, since I was in charge of external relations of the city, I was asked to organize that meeting. I reported to Sobchak. He agreed and we met that senator, that gentleman who came from Tbilisi and Berezovsky came with the senator—he was accompanying him. And that's the way I met him. And Mr. Berezovsky fell asleep during the meeting.

OS: Well, Berezovsky is a smart man, he must have summed you up—looked at you wondering how he can handle you or deal with you, right? I mean, it's going both ways.

VP: No, you see I was just an assistant to Sobchak. If he was thinking about something he was thinking about how to foster his relationship with Sobchak, not with me.

OS: Okay, well we're in 2000 now. This is a dark time. Now you've become president. The vote was 53 percent. You're not expected to last. You're president of a country which is in a dark time—the Chechen War is going on. It looks very bad and the oligarchs . . . Privatization is everywhere. You push back. I've seen the documentaries and I can show the footage of that fight. There was the greatest struggle it seems to me—one of the darkest times of your life.

VP: Yes, that's . . . exactly the case. But those difficult times came not in 2000 but much earlier. I think it was in the early 1990s, right after the collapse of the Soviet Union, and by 2000 . . . In 1998, we had a crisis—a very large economic crisis. In 1999, the second Chechen War was resumed and I became acting president and the country was in a very difficult situation. And that's the truth.

OS: And did you wake up at four in the morning? Did you ever sleep? What were the dark nights like?

VP: No, I never woke up at 4 a.m. I went to sleep at midnight and I woke up at seven or so. I always slept for six to seven hours.

OS: Very disciplined. No nightmares?

VP: No.

OS: Really? This is a discipline from the military, from the KGB experience?

VP: I think that's thanks to sport and to military service as well.

OS: You have a lot of discipline, sir.

VP: The thing is, if it's not done then it's really difficult to work. If you're not disciplined then you will not have enough strength to address the current issues. Let alone strategic ones. You always have to keep fit.

OS: Yeah, but did you see your children during this period? And your wife?

VP: Yes, certainly. But only for a very short time.

OS: Regular basis? You'd have dinner at home or did you have dinner with them? Did you see them on a nightly basis?

VP: I came home very late and I went off to work very early. Well, of course I saw them but very briefly.

OS: And when did your parents die? In this period?

VP: My mother died in 1998 and my father in 1999.

OS: That must have been very difficult—among all these other difficulties.

VP: For the last two years my parents were in a hospital. And every Friday, I flew from Moscow to St. Petersburg to see them. Every week.

OS: And for the weekend, and come back on Sunday, or . . . ?

VP: No, I went just for one day. I saw them, and then I came back to Moscow.

OS: Were they proud of you?

VP: Yes.

OS: Your mother and father couldn't believe it, right?

VP: That's indeed so. My father didn't live two months to see me appointed as prime minister. But even before I became prime minister, when I saw him, when I came to see him, he always told the nurses, "Look—here's my president coming."

OS: That's nice. That's nice. You're credited with doing many fine things in your first term. Privatization was stopped. You built up industries—electronics, engineering, petrochemical, agriculture, and many others. A real son of Russia—you should be proud. You raised the GDP, you raised incomes, you reformed the army, you resolved the Chechen War.[10]

VP: Well, it's not exactly like that. I didn't stop privatization. I just wanted to make it more equitable, more fair. I did everything so that state property was not sold for free. We put an end to some schemes—manipulation schemes—which led to the creation of oligarchs. These schemes that allowed some people to become billionaires in the blink of an eye. With all due respect to Wassily Leontief, the American of Russian origin and Nobel Prize winner in economics. And when he was alive I met him and I attended his lectures and I listened to him talk. He said that property could be distributed freely for one ruble. But in the end, this property was supposed to get into the hands of people who deserved it—that's what he thought. I think that in our conditions, in the Russian conditions, it led to the legal enrichment of a whole category of people. And it also led to a situation where the government either lost control of strategic industries or just led to the destruction of those industries. So my goal was not to stop privatization, but to make it more systemic, more equitable.

OS: I saw the footage of you with the oligarchs in 2003-4. It was an interesting meeting. But did you have head-on collisions with Berezovsky and people like that, with Khodorkovsky.

VP: No head-on collisions. I just told them that they had to be equidistant from the government. That was the fashionable term back then. And I told them that if they acquired their property within the framework of law, then we would not seek to take that property from them. But today laws are changing and they have to conform to the new laws. I assume that any attempts at revisiting the outcome of privatization can do more damage to the economy of the country than the privatization itself. And that's why we're going to continue with the privatization on a fairer basis and do everything in our power to secure these properties, these titles, but everyone has to un-derstand that everyone has to be equal before the law. And no one objected back then.

OS: You cut the poverty rate by two-thirds?

VP: That's correct.

OS: Respect for the old people. Pensions.

VP: Yes, many fold.

OS: In 2000, 2,700 rubles was the average income. In 2012, 29,000 rubles.

VP: Yes, that's correct.

OS: Immensely popular in 2004—you're reelected with 70 percent of the vote.[11]

VP: A little more than that.

OS: And 2008, because only two terms are allowed, you would become the prime minister. A force behind the throne. And in 2012 you run for presi-dent and you win. By 63 percent, I believe 63 percent in 2012.

VP: Yes, that's correct.

OS: So yes, three times president. Maybe, some people would say a fourth term like Roosevelt—you've outdone Franklin Delano Roosevelt.

VP: He was president four times?[12]

OS: Yes, he didn't complete his fourth term, but he obviously was immense-ly popular. And obviously you're criticized for many things. And we can get into that later, but you're criticized for cracking down on the press, among other things, but I'm not going to get into that tonight. I realize that you have been president now for almost 15 years. Which is unbelievable.

VP: No, just first two terms—that's eight years—four and four. And now starting from 2012—it's 10 years.

OS: Okay. Well you worked hard when you were prime minister, too.

VP: Yes, I worked hard and quite successfully too on the whole. But back then, Russia's president was a different person. I know the assessments given to this period abroad. I have to tell you that President Medvedev performed independently all his functions. There was this division of functions according to the Constitution. I never interfered within his domain.[13] There were certain issues when he deemed it possible to consult me on this or that matter. But that was quite a rare occurrence. He did almost everything as he deemed necessary. Furthermore, I can tell you a curious story. During the inauguration of President Medvedev,[14] we met here—just a handful of those who were close to him—and one of the Russian dignitaries said some kind words to me. And he said, "We all understand everything—that you're still our president," he told me. And I told everyone, "Thank you for the kind words, but please, do not send false signals to society. Only one person can be the president of the country—the one who is elected by the people."

OS: Fair enough. Five assassination attempts, I'm told. Not as much as Castro, whom I interviewed—I think he must have had 50—but there's a legitimate five that I've heard about.[15]

VP: Yes, I talked with Castro about that and he said to me, "Do you know why I'm still alive?" I asked him, "Why?" "Because I was always the one to deal with my security personally." Unlike Castro, I do my job and the security officers do theirs and they are still performing quite successfully. I was quite successful in performing my functions and they in theirs.

OS: So you are saying you did not follow the Castro model?

VP: I don't see there is a need for that.

OS: In other words, you trust your security and they've done a good job.

VP: Yes.

OS: Because always the first mode of assassination, from when the United

States went after Castro, you try to get inside the security of the president to perform assassination.

VP: Yes, I know that. Do you know what they say among the Russian people? They say that those who are destined to be hanged are not going to drown.

OS: What is your fate, sir? Do you know?

VP: Only God knows that. Only God knows our destiny—yours and mine.

OS: To die in bed, maybe?

VP: One day this is going to happen to each and every one of us. The question is what will we have accomplished by that time in this transient world and whether we'll have enjoyed our life.

OS: I have about 10 more minutes of questions and then we can wrap it for tonight.

In a Russian documentary I saw about you, they described the Iceberg Theory, which is in foreign affairs most people see one-seventh of the iceberg, the top only, they don't see the six-sevenths below the surface of the water. And that all foreign affairs are very treacherous and different than what they appear to be.

VP: That's very complicated.

OS: Well, I'd like to go there tomorrow and the next day. I mean it's almost impossible to tell what's going on in the world unless you look below the surface.

VP: You know, it's sufficient just to closely monitor what's going on in the world always and then you'll understand the logic behind what is going on. Why do ordinary people often lose touch with what is going on? Why do they consider these things complicated? Why do they think that something is concealed from their eyes? This is simply because ordinary people live their lives. On an everyday basis they go to work and earn money, and they are not following international affairs. That's why ordinary people are so easy to manipulate, to be misled. But if they were to follow what's going on in the world on an everyday basis, then despite the fact that some part of diplomacy is always conducted behind closed doors, it's still going to be easier to understand what's going on and you'll be able to grasp the logic behind world developments. And you can achieve it even without having access to secret documents.

OS: I've read about your prodigious work habits. You read, you study. And I wanted to tell you a story that I recently read about John Kennedy. He was an exciting and glamorous president, but he also worked very, very hard. His brother Robert Kennedy wrote a book, *Thirteen Days*, about the crisis in Cuba between Khrushchev and Kennedy and in the book it was amazing that Robert Kennedy described that his brother read every document, every speech by a foreign leader that he could. He knew what the speech was, he didn't take the extract of the information from the CIA, from this intelligence agency, because he didn't trust them. And as a result, he was able to reach his own conclusions with Khrushchev and solve this crisis.

VP: I do not read abstracts. I always read documents—the original ones. I never use analytical materials provided to me by the intelligence services. I always read separate documents.

OS: It's interesting, I had that feeling. Your theory of life they say is summed up in the philosophy of Judo?

VP: Yes, more or less. The main idea—the flexible way, as it were—that's the main idea in Judo. You must be flexible. Sometimes you can give way to others. If that is the way leading to victory . . .

OS: And at the same time there's a rat story, which you told Mike Wallace, where you chased a rat, when you were a young boy I guess, with a stick, and the rat turned on you.

VP: It didn't bite, but it tried to jump at me. And then I was the one to run from the rat. And there were the stairs, and there was a landing, then another flight of stairs. So it was like that—one leading down, then the landing, then another stairs. Even though I was very small I was still able to run faster than the rat. I had the time to run down the stairs, then the landing, and then down the other stairs. And do you know what the rat did? It jumped from one set of stairs to the other from above.

OS: Well, you pissed off the rat with the stick, right?

VP: Yes, I think that was the case.

OS: So in your philosophy with Judo it would be don't push too hard some-times—your opponent may look weak, but your opponent may turn on you.

VP: Well, I didn't go into Judo back then. And the conclusion, I think, is somewhat different here. You know there is this famous saying: you should never corner a rat. And that's exactly what I did. No one should be cornered. No one should be led to a situation which ends in a dead end.

OS: The oligarchs underestimated you. When you became president, they didn't think you would last.

VP: You see, oligarchs are different. And that's true. Among them there were those who were willing to conform to the system of relationship with the government that was being proposed to them. And they were told that no one was trying to infringe upon their property. They were told that the government would protect their property. Even if the previous laws had been unjust. The law is always the law. But that's another rule to be observed.

OS: The law is always the law, unless it changes. People protest. In America, there was civil rights legislation. Many good things come out of protest—dis-obedience to the law.

VP: That's also true, but our situation was different. I believe that the pri-vatization laws at the beginning of the 1990s were not just. But if we were to conduct de-privatization, as I said before, it would have been even more damaging to the economy and to the lives of common people. And that's what I told the big business leaders, that was a frank discussion. I told them that the previously-existing schemes were to be phased out of existence. I told them that laws were supposed to become fairer and more just. And I also told them that business was to assume more social responsibility. And many businessmen, the overwhelming majority of them, conformed to the new laws. Do you know who was not happy about the new laws? Those who were not true businessmen. Those who earned their millions or billions not thanks to their entrepreneurial talents, but thanks to their ability to force good relationships with the government—those people were not happy.

They didn't like the new laws. But there was just a handful of those. On the whole our relationship with business was good.

OS: Just to close on a note about Stalin. You know, you've said negative things about Stalin, and of course he's widely condemned in the world. But at the same time we all know that he was a great wartime leader. He led Russia to victory over Germany, over fascism. What do you make of that ambiguity?

VP: I think that you are a cunning person.

OS: Why? We can discuss it tomorrow if you want.

VP: No, I'm ready to answer. You know, there was one prominent politician of the past, Winston Churchill. He was very firmly against Sovietism, but once the Second World War started, he was a great advocate of working together with the Soviet Union, and he called Stalin a great war leader and revolutionary. And after the Second World War, as is well known, it was Churchill who initiated the Cold War. And when the Soviet Union made the first nuclear test, it was none other than Winston Churchill who announced the need for a co-existence of two systems. He was a very flexible person. But I think that deep down in his heart, his attitude toward Stalin never wavered, never changed.

Stalin is a product of his era. You can try to demonize him however much you like. We try to talk about his merits in achieving victory over fascism. As to his demonization, there was such a person in history as Oliver Cromwell—he was a bloodthirsty man who arrived in power on the wave of a revolution and he turned into a dictator and tyrant. And monuments to him are still scattered all across Great Britain. Napoleon is deified. What did he do? He used the surge of revolutionary zeal and arrived in power. And he not only restored the monarchy, he pronounced himself Emperor. And he led France to a national catastrophe, to utter defeat. There are many situations, many people like that—more than enough in world history. I think that excessive demonization of Stalin is one of the ways to attack the Soviet Union and Russia, to show that the Russia of today has something originating from Stalinism. Well, of course we all have these birthmarks.

What I'm saying is Russia has changed radically. Well, of course something probably has remained in our mentality, but there is no going back to Stalinism, because the mentality of the people has changed. As to Stalin himself, he arrived in power with wonderful ideas that he was propounding. He was talking about the need for equality, fraternity, peace . . . But of course he turned into a dictator. I don't think that in a situation like that anything else would have been possible. I'm referring to that particular situation in the world. Was it any better in Spain, or in Italy? Or in Germany? There are many countries where the government was based in tyranny.

But of course this doesn't mean that he was not capable of bringing together the people of the Soviet Union. He managed to organize resistance to fascism. And he was not behaving like a Hitler. He was listening to his generals. And he even conformed himself to some of the decisions which were offered to him by his generals. This doesn't mean, however, that we have to forget all the atrocities Stalinism committed—the destruction of millions of our compatriots, the extermination camps. These things are not to be forgotten. And he is an ambiguous figure. I think that at the end of his life he was in a very difficult position—a very difficult mental situation, I believe. But that requires an impartial study.

OS: And your father and your mother admired him, right?

VP: Yes, certainly. I think the overwhelming majority of the former Soviet citizens admired Stalin. Just as the overwhelming majority of the French admired Napoleon in the past—and many still admire him.

OS: I would like to just end on a quick, lighter note. I saw footage of you—it's unbelievable—where you have learned . . . You obviously were not trained as a young man in these skills but you've learned how to play the piano. I saw that.

VP: Certainly. Recently a friend of mine taught me to play with two fingers a couple of very popular melodies.

OS: I mean, it's still amazing that at your age you wanted to learn something new and I also saw you skiing. You had never been skiing before.

VP: I started skiing when I was a student. And I just recently started skating.

OS: Yeah, I saw that—in hockey.

VP: When I started skating, my first thought was—that's just two years ago—I thought that I was never going to learn how to skate. And my first thought was: how to stop, how do I stop?

OS: Yeah. So are you worried about breaking an ankle? Or you're not worried about injuring yourself, are you?

VP: Well, if you keep thinking about these things then probably you should stay at home.

OS: Well, hockey is a rough sport.

VP: Well, I didn't expect it to be so rough. I thought that Judo was the roughest one, but it turned out that hockey was very athletic in its nature.

OS: Are you still playing?

VP: Yes, this morning I played hockey.

OS: Really? Unbelievable. And do you have any plans to conquer a new sport?

VP: No, not yet.

OS: But you've learned French?

VP: No, actually just a couple of phrases.

OS: Well, you went to Guatemala—that was enough to get the Winter Games.

VP: One of the International Olympic Committee members told me that I had to say at least a couple of words in French. That was a must he said.

OS: Oh, it was just a couple? You cheated.

VP: He said it was a token of respect. Not to the French, but to the Francophone African countries.

OS: Well thank you Mr. Putin for a wonderful beginning.

VP: Thank you. We're going to continue tomorrow.

Trip 1—Day 2—July 3, 2015

ON YELTSIN AND THE GULF WAR

VP: There were many economic advisers from the United States working with the Central Government and the administration of President Yeltsin. And since we were in St. Petersburg we had little to do with it.

OS: But you joined with Yeltsin in '95, right?

VP: 1996, to be more exact. I'd like to draw your attention to the fact that I was working in the office of the administration of the president and we had to deal with domestic matters. And I personally was in charge of legal affairs. But certainly later when I worked at the office of the administration and when I was working in St. Petersburg, we closely followed all these matters. And we saw the discussions between the American School of Economics and the Europeans, the majority of whom were not entirely approving of the recommendations which we were given by the Americans. I refer in particular to the privatization of state property. And to be frank we couldn't interfere within this process and we didn't. But what the Europeans told us back then, I thought that was quite objective, quite just. But what the American experts promised us looked much more attractive.

OS: Now, looking back at it, was this a private effort or did you feel the presence of the American government as well?

VP: I think both. Both the private sector and the government. Certainly the private sector was taking an active part in this process. But no doubt under the control of the central government.

OS: Did Mr. Yeltsin ever express dark thoughts about American interests here?

VP: No, never.

OS: Never?

VP: Never. Well, he didn't express those thoughts but he didn't go deep into economic issues. He trusted the government on the whole. He trusted those people who work around him. Those people whom he thought to be the new generation.

OS: And the Europeans were telling you what?

VP: Europeans thought that unchecked privatization that was conducted in Russia wouldn't lead to raising the efficiency of the economy. Particularly as far as privatization in the key branches of the economy was concerned. As a matter of fact they proposed a softer way to us. Two words: market economy. And I believe that would have been much more efficient now that I look back at that time. And it wouldn't have led to such acute social consequences. But we have to admit and to give credit to those who took the decision back then—they were bold enough to take steps without which no transition towards a market economy would have been possible.

OS: And who would that be?

VP: Yegor Gaidar, primarily. Chubais, from the economy ministry. Andrei Nechaev.

OS: So you're saying you agree with the policy, but it was implemented too quickly?

VP: I agree with the objectives which they put forward. But I do not agree with the methods which they employed.

OS: As a young man, did you see anything wrong when Gorbachev made his deal with Reagan and brought back the troops from Eastern Europe? Did you see anything wrong with the United States intervening in Iraq in January of 1991?

VP: Publicly, I spoke about that, as far as the first part of your question is concerned. As to Eastern Europe, I think it would be senseless and damaging if the Soviet Union itself was to impose on other peoples and other nations their rules of conduct. Their vision of how society was to develop, how the political and state system of those countries was to be constructed. And that approach didn't have any future. And it was quite evident that one way or another that had to end. People cannot always put up with decisions which are imposed on them from outside. Apart from that, Eastern Europe and Europe on the whole had their own political traditions and that couldn't be neglected.

OS: Let's lay it on the line here. I mean, I was in the Vietnam War. We sent 500,000 troops to Vietnam. That was outrageous and condemned by the whole world. After the détente with Gorbachev, Reagan and the United States put 500,000 troops into Saudi Arabia and Kuwait.

VP: I know that you are very critical of the American government in many dimensions. I do not always share your point of view. Despite the fact that, with regards to the American leadership, we do not always have the relationship we would like to have with them. Sometimes decisions have to be taken which are not entirely approved of in some parts of society. But it's better to make some decisions than make none.

OS: So you don't disapprove of the US sending 500,000 troops to the Middle East all of a sudden?

VP: You know, I think it's erroneous and wrong to impose on other nations and peoples one's own standards and models. I'm referring in particular to democracy. Democracy cannot be imported from outside, it can only be born within society. And society should be helped to follow this path, but trying to impose it by force from outside is senseless, it's counterproductive, it's damaging. And as to the use of force, including ground force, sometimes it is necessary. Certainly it's better if it's done at the invitation of the governments concerned or in accordance with international law, and based on a decision by the UN Security Council.

OS: Yeah. Okay. Well, I mean Gorbachev makes a supreme effort for peace. And within a few months of the Berlin Wall falling, the US is sending troops into Panama illegally—not supported by other nations, condemned by the Latin American countries.

VP: Well, certainly there is nothing good about that. Besides, Gorbachev, before taking any unilateral steps should have thought about how his partners would respond. Steps can be taken towards your partner, but you have to understand what's going to follow. You asked me about Iraq. I think that was a mistake. Sending troops to Iraq, overthrowing Saddam Hussein.

OS: That was later. I'm talking about the beginning of this thing in 1991, when they invaded Kuwait.

VP: Back then the United States didn't go further—they didn't overthrow the government in Iraq. I know there are discussions on this matter and some say they should have gone further and overthrown Saddam Hussein. And others say that everything was done correctly, they had to stop at the right moment. And President Bush was quite right to do what he did, he was cautious. He responded to aggression and then stopped when the time was right.

OS: Okay, I understand your point of view. I don't agree with it, but I understand. For the United States to send 500,000 troops anywhere in the world is to establish a major, major interest. And once you send that many US troops into an area, it changes forever the dynamic in that area. There is no way now that the United States would leave the Middle East.

VP: Yes, I think so, probably. The most depressing thing is the attempt to change regimes in that part of the world with the hope that the next day everything is going to sort itself out. And that American-style democracy will emerge. But that's impossible and we're witnessing what is happening in that region right now. Where did ISIS come from? There were never any terrorists there before. And now they have a beachhead there and they are in control of two thirds of Iraqi territory. And the same is happening in Syria. Libya, as a territorially integral state, has ceased to exist.[16] And remember how happy they were when Gaddafi was killed, but there were no reasons to be happy.[17] The standard of living there was quite high—near the average European level. Did they have to fight for democracy? Yes, they had to, but not using these means which they resorted to. You see the result—it's a catastrophe.

OS: I understand. I think you're getting a little bit ahead of me.

ON 9/11

OS: I wanted to go first of all to the growth of this issue, which is the second Bush . . . W. He came into office and in 2001 he met you. And he said, in Slovenia I believe, "I looked into his eyes and got a sense of his soul."[18]

VP: Yes, that's exactly what he said. He's a very decent person—a good person.

OS: What did you sense when he was saying that—what did you feel?

VP: I felt that here was a person we could come to agreement with—a person we can deal with—at least that's what I hoped.

OS: And on 9/11, you were one of the first to call him and offer condolences?[19]

VP: Yes, we had planned military exercises of our new strategic forces for the next day. And I canceled those exercises and I wanted the president of the United States to know that. Certainly I understood that heads of state and governments in such a situation need moral support. And we wanted to demonstrate this support to President Bush.

OS: And when President Bush invaded Afghanistan, you cooperated with the invasion and set up bases in the Caucasus in Eurasia in order for the Americans to have a supply line for the war in Afghanistan?

VP: Well, it's not exactly like that. We didn't set up any military bases specifically for that purpose. Since the Soviet Union, we have had a division in Tajikistan which we later turned into a military base specifically to protect this direction, which is dangerous from the terrorists' point of view—in Afghanistan. We supported the United States.[20] And we allowed them to use our territory to supply weapons and other cargo.

OS: And continued to do so until recently.

VP: Yes. We believe that this cooperation is in our national interest. This is a field where we can and should put our forces together. We provided our American partners with additional information including intelligence information, as far as it was possible.

OS: Russia has a long history of intelligence in Afghanistan. Of course you know a lot about it. How come you guys did not figure out where bin Laden was and what was really happening with bin Laden? Not just where he was, but how weak the Al Qaeda base was at this point in Afghanistan.

VP: Al Qaeda is not the result of our activities. It's the result of the activities of our American friends.[21] It all started during the Soviet war in Afghanistan. When the American intelligence officers provided support to different streaks of Islamic fundamentalism, helping them to fight the Soviet troops in Afghanistan. So it was the Americans who nurtured both Al Qaeda and bin Laden. But it all spun out of control and it always does. So they're to blame.

OS: I understand. Although Bill Casey, Director of the CIA under Ronald Reagan, made it a special effort—this is documented—to excite the Muslims in the Caucasus in Central Asia against the Soviet Union.[22] His plan was bigger than just to defeat the Soviet Union in Afghanistan. He was hoping for regime change in the Soviet Union.

VP: You see, the thing is, these ideas are still alive. And when those problems in the Caucasus and Chechnya emerged, unfortunately the Americans supported those processes.[23] Not the official forces, not the democratic government of Yeltsin. They didn't support that. Even though we counted on American support. We assumed that the Cold War was over, that we had transparent relations with the United States, with the whole world, and we certainly counted on support. But instead we witnessed the American intelligence services support terrorists. And even when we confirmed that, when we demonstrated that Al Qaeda fighters were fighting in the Caucasus, we still saw the intelligence services of the United States continue to support these fighters. There was one episode, I told President Bush about that, and he said, "Do you have any concrete data who specifically does what specifically?" And I told him "Yes, I do have such data," and I showed him, and I even named those persons of the American intelligence services who were working in the Caucasus, including in Baku. And those officers didn't just provide some general political support—they also provided technical support, they helped transfer fighters from one place to another. And the reaction of the American president was the right one—very negative. He said, "I'll sort this all out." There was no response, by the way. And weeks had passed—

OS: What year was this?

VP: 2005 or 2004. Some time had passed and we received a response from the American intelligence services. The response was quite peculiar. They wrote to us: "We support all the political forces, including the opposition forces, and we're going to continue to do that."

OS: They sent a letter to you in 2005?

VP: Yes, the CIA sent us a letter.[24] They sent this letter to their counterparts in Moscow. And to be honest, I was much surprised—especially after my conversation with the American president.

OS: Did you speak to him after that?

VP: Yes, certainly. You know, politics is a strange area. I'm quite confident that President Bush has always been a person with integrity. But all this bureaucracy, which still clings to the ideas that you've talked about—namely the possibility to use fundamentalism to destabilize the situation. Well, these ideas are still alive. And despite the fact that the situation has changed radically in Russia itself—the Soviet Union ceased to exist. I'm going to say something very important, I believe. We are now quite confident—we had a very confident opinion back then. But our American partners were talking about the need to cooperate, including in fighting terrorism, but in reality they were using those terrorists in order to destabilize the internal political situation in Russia. And frankly speaking, we were much disappointed.

OS: I suppose you want us to go over to the Palace.

VP: Yes, it will be easier there.

OS: Two big dreams.

VP: You were flying in one?

OS: Yes, I try to remember the dreams. I wake up, I write them down, it's a habit I've gotten into.

VP: Very interesting.

OS: Yeah, it's important. That's why I was surprised when you said you didn't pay attention to dreams or didn't remember them.

VP: Sometimes I remember my dreams but for a very short time and then I forget.

OS: I make an effort to get up in the middle of the night to remember them, because I know I'm going to forget them when I go back to sleep.

VP: And where do you live most of the time?

OS: Between New York and Los Angeles. And I travel a lot.

VP: Do you have an apartment or house, an apartment in New York and a house in Los Angeles?

OS: I have places in both. But I spent the last six months in Munich.

ON THE WAR IN IRAQ AND AMERICAN EXPANSION

OS: Okay. So you're involved in the Afghanistan war and the cooperation with the United States. They're in Central Asia now. You know more and more about their support of terrorism—Islamic terrorism—against the Soviet Union. But now they are fighting terrorism and they're looking for bin Laden and putting a huge amount of money into hunting Al Qaeda—although I'm told that Al Qaeda forces in Afghanistan reached as low a level as 100 fighters. There were only 100 Al Qaeda left when we were still fighting there.[25]

VP: Regrettably, the general principle in some countries is to support people who have extreme views in order to get their help fighting people who are seemingly their enemies. The thing is, the greatest problem is, distinguishing between these people is impossible. Because these people also evolve and change. They conform to conditions and it's impossible to understand who is using whom—whether the intelligence services of the United States is using Islamic radicals. The radicals understand that the intelligence services want to use them to fight for their own interests and they get money, they get support, they get arms, and then they deal a heavy blow to their benefactors. Or they transfer part of their money, weapons or equipment to other armed units and are involved in activities which are not welcomed by the benefactors or those who support this or that country's unit. The same is happening with ISIS right now. Exactly the same thing. When there is this talk about the need to support the opposition in Syria—the normal opposition, they are given money, they are given weapons, and then it turns out that some of them defected to ISIS. And our partners recognize that. But it's a systemic mistake which is repeated always. This is the same thing which happened in Afghanistan in the 1980s. And right now it's happening in the Middle East.

OS: I know we discussed it before, but please tell me again whether you believe the United States was involved in any way with supporting the Chechens in the first or second war.

VP: Yes. We're 100 percent sure that we have objective proof of that.[26] You see you don't have to be a great analyst to see that the United States supported financially, provided information, supported them politically. They supported the separatists and terrorists in the Northern Caucasus. And when we're asking our partners, "Why do you receive them at the official level?" they responded, "We're not doing that at a high level—it's just a technical level—the level of experts." But that was just ridiculous. We were seeing that they were granting them support. Instead of trying to pull forces together to fight a common threat, someone is often trying to use the situation to their own advantage and short term interests. But in the end, they're the ones who get damaged by those people they support. That is what happened in Libya when the US ambassador perished.

OS: Are you talking about arms to the Chechens? Are you talking about money, about Saudi Arabia contributing, too?

VP: Saudi Arabia at the state level didn't grant them any support. We have always had good relations with Saudi Arabia—with the late king and with the current leadership of the country. We do not have any proof that the official government supported terrorism in any way. There is another thing. There are many private funds and physical persons who provided support and we know about that. That was also a source of concern to the royal family of Saudi Arabia. They were always preoccupied with this threat of a surge in terrorism. Bin Laden is a Saudi. But Saudi Arabia is not our ally, it's the ally of the United States in the first place.

OS: But the US support was covert—you say you have evidence that they were supporting the Chechens?

VP: Yes, certainly. I've been telling you about that. As to information and political support, no proof is required. That was evident to everyone, because it was done publicly, openly. And as to the operative support and the financial support, we have this proof and moreover some of this proof we submitted to our American counterparts, and I've just told you about that. And you know the response—I've told you about it as well. There was this official letter and they told us that, "We support all the political forces including the opposition forces and we're going to continue to do that." And it was evident that they were not just talking about the opposition forces. They were also talking about the terrorist organizations and structures. Nevertheless, they were painted just as regular opposition.

OS: In your mind, what was the most dangerous moment in the Chechen wars—the first one, the second one, what years?

VP: You know, I find it difficult to name a particular moment. The so-called Second Chechen War started with the attack of international armed gangs from the territory of Chechnya on Dagestan, and it was a tragedy.[27] The thing is, it all started with the federal forces opposing the terrorists. It started with common citizens in Dagestan, and Dagestan is also a Muslim republic. They took up arms and they organized resistance to the terrorists. I remember those days very well. I remember well when Dagestan was not just urging us, they were crying to us: "If you don't want to protect us, Russia, then give us arms and we'll do that ourselves." And back then I had to be actively involved in sorting out this issue. Back then I was acting prime minister.

OS: Meanwhile the United States, while they're in Afghanistan, invades Iraq in March 2003. What was your reaction to the build-up to the war, as well as the invasion?

VP: We understood that the developments, which were nascent in Afghanistan, were related to the attacks of terrorists against New York. And we had this information saying that there was a terrorist cell—the concentration of terrorists in those territories. And we said right away we would contemplate providing support to the United States. As to Iraq, I told you already. We believed that, in the end, that would lead to the disintegration of the country, to the disappearance of structures which were able to resist terrorism, which in turn would lead to large scale regional problems. We put forward proposals to cooperate in this direction, but they were left unanswered. The United States prefers to make these decisions unilaterally. Incidentally, you know that not all NATO allies of the United States supported their action. France and Germany were against that decision. Moreover, there was this unique situation—both France and Germany, not we, formulated their own position on Iraq and they tried to convince us to support the European position.

OS: I'm sorry if I didn't understand, but you were saying that the Russians had evidence that there were terrorist cells related to the attack in New York in Iraq? Is that what you're saying?

VP: No, it was in Afghanistan.

OS: Right, but I thought you said Iraq. So you knew that there was no link between the New York attacks and Iraq, you knew that?

VP: Certainly, there was no link whatsoever. There was a link with these terrorist groups which were in parts of the Afghan territory. But Iraq had nothing to do with that.

OS: But that was put forward by the Bush administration, particularly by Richard Cheney, the Vice President—that there was a link.

VP: We didn't have any proof of that.

OS: So you knew this was a manufactured theory.

VP: Concocted in some way where probably the official government of the United States used some information which was not entirely correct. I do not think that I have the right to put forward any accusations. But that was a great mistake, as we are witnessing right now.

OS: The weapons of mass destruction—I presume you had a similar reaction.

VP: Yes, absolutely the same. Moreover, we had exact data that there were no WMDs whatsoever in Iraq.[28]

OS: You never discussed this with Mr. Bush?

VP: Yes we discussed it, but our American partners thought that they had enough proof and that was sufficient. That's what they thought.

OS: Well, so from your viewpoint—and you've talked to many world leaders—Mr. Bush is a decent man, he has integrity, and yet he's misled time and again by his experts, his specialists.

VP: Well, not always—not all the time. Secondly, after the terrorist attack in New York, President Bush certainly thought how to protect the United States and to protect the citizens of the United States. He thought how to do that. And it was easy for him to believe the data he was provided with by the intelligence services. Even though that data was not entirely correct. There are attempts at demonizing Bush, and I don't think that's the right thing to do.

OS: Okay. Okay. So Mr. Bush did continue to expand NATO during his presidency, after Clinton had started to re-expand NATO.

VP: That was another mistake.

OS: Okay . . . How did you feel? I mean from what I've heard from Mr. Gorbachev, as well as read from American officials including James Baker, there was a deal with the Soviet Union not to expand NATO eastward.

VP: Yes, I talked about that publicly—including in Munich. And when the decision was made on the reunification of Germany, and back then, the dignitaries both in the United States and the United Nations Secretary General, and the representative of the Federal Republic of Germany. They were all saying there was one thing that the Soviet Union could be sure of—that the eastern border of NATO would not be extended any further than the eastern border of the German Democratic Republic.

OS: So this was a clear violation.[29]

VP: It was not enshrined on paper. It's a mistake, but that mistake was made by Mr. Gorbachev. In politics, everything has to be enshrined on paper because even something which is enshrined can be violated often. And he just talked and he decided that that was enough. But that's not the case. And after that there have been two waves of NATO expansion. Incidentally, I remember President Clinton and his last official visit here. We met in the adjacent room with him and with his delegation. And I told him—half-seriously/half as a joke—"probably Russia should think about joining NATO." That's what I told him. And his response was, "Why not? I think that's possible." But when we saw the reaction of his team, we understood that they were somewhat bewildered or even frightened by this idea.

OS: Did you really mean it?

VP: I said that I said it half-seriously/half as a joke. And what I really meant, I think I would rather not divulge it right now. But that's what I told him and the reaction of his delegation was very cautious. And I can tell you why— because NATO, as far as I am concerned, is a remnant of the past. This organization emerged during the Cold War—between two systems. And as of now, NATO is a mere instrument of foreign policy of the United States. It has no allies within—it has only vassals. And I have a fairly good impression of how work is done within NATO. Someone can argue about some secondary issues. But as far as any serious issues are concerned, there is no discussion whatsoever within NATO. There are only two opinions in NATO—the American opinion and the wrong opinion.

OS: Well, it seems that you're taking this change in the wind seriously.

VP: Just a second—I'd like to add something. Just imagine if Russia were part of NATO. Certainly we wouldn't behave like that, because we have an opinion of our own on a great number of issues. And we would defend our opinion.

OS: So there is an advantage to joining it because you're able to vote "no" on something.

VP: [laughs] I think that's exactly what the delegation of the United States didn't like about that idea.

OS: Well, I believe under the rules of NATO you'd have to share all your nuclear information with the United States.

VP: You see, our openness to all our partners—including towards the United States—after the disintegration of the Soviet Union, and after the change in our political system, was so great that it even covered our nuclear forces. We had almost no secrets back then. The American monitors were at one of our largest factories producing components for nuclear weapons. And those monitors were stationed there on a permanent basis. You see? We were open enough. And there were no additional threats to us.

OS: It's clear at this point in time that you're missing the signals in the wind—there were a lot of signals coming, including Mr. Bush's withdrawal in 2002 from the anti-ballistic missile treaty of 1972.[30]

VP: No, that's not the case. We were most actively discussing this issue with our partners. And there is one curious thing—the presidents of your country change, but the policy doesn't change—I mean on principled issues. I refer in particular to the withdrawal of the United States from the ABM Treaty.[31] It's the goal. That treaty was the cornerstone of the system of national security as a whole. It was the foundation of international security. And first President Clinton tried to persuade me to support the United States withdrawal from this treaty.

OS: On what basis?

VP: No foundation, no basis at all. He was saying that there was a threat emanating from Iran. Then the same attempt was undertaken by President Bush. We tried to convince him, to show him, and that was not entirely fruitless, that it was a threat to us. And at a certain stage our American counterparts at the defense ministry level, at the state secretary level, said that they understood our concerns. And I have to say that we proposed that we should work together on an ABM system—the United States, Europe, and Russia. But in the end, even though quite sadly our partners refused to follow up on that proposal, they suggested that we should handle our concerns—technically. But they refused to follow up on their own proposal. In this regard we spent very much time on this matter and we were saying that we would not develop our ABM system because that was very expensive and we didn't know whether that would lead to anything at all. But to preserve the crucial element of international security and stability, namely the strategic balance of power, we would be obliged to develop our offensive capabilities—missiles capable of surmounting any ABM systems. And their response was quite simple. They told us they were not building up that system against Russia. And they told us, "Do whatever you like, because we'll assume it's not against the United States." And I said, "All right, let's do it this way." And that's what we're doing. And I find it strange that now when we announce that we are renovating our nuclear capabilities without overstepping the limits of treaties on the reduction in our nuclear arsenal, it always leads to a very nervous reaction on the part of our partners. We were not the first to start this race and we told them in the first place what we were going to do—what we would have to do.

OS: Two quick questions—so, Bush did this without consultation? He just did it?

VP: We had had many discussions, many negotiations on that matter and the United States made this decision to withdraw from the treaty unilaterally.

OS: Right, with Clinton there were discussions, but with the Bush people it didn't work?

VP: We had discussions both with the Bush team and the Clinton team.

OS: Okay, so no rules—new rules. American rules.

VP: Probably our partners thought that the armed forces of Russia, the economy of Russia, the technological capacities of Russia were such that we would not be able to face the challenge. But as of now I think everyone has understood that Russia is not just capable of that. Russia is doing that and meeting the challenge.

OS: Now, but not then?

VP: Back then I believe there was this understanding that Russia would not be able to do that.

OS: Can I ask—this is a technical question: Did Russia back then have any ability to monitor the US systems, or could the US have cheated anyway?

VP: We had these capabilities and we still have them. First we agreed on reductions. Both we and the American partners followed them and stuck to those agreements. There is a reservation on these agreements—if one of the parties decides that this treaty goes contrary to their national interests, then any party to the treaty has the right to withdraw from it unilaterally. So you see there has been a great deal of discussions on this matter. I just do not think that I have the right to talk about certain things because they are of a confidential nature. But sometimes I found those discussions just ludicrous, because everyone understood everything. First they feigned not to understand something and when everything was sorted out, they've gone through all the details, they recognized our concerns, but they proposed that we should remove our concerns this way or that way and then they withdrew even that proposal. By the way, the whole ABM system—the very idea of an ABM system—is based on the following. It's based on the idea of nuclear threat emanating from Iran. Right now we are coming to an agreement with Iran. We are placing under outside control all of its nuclear program. There are even talks about lifting sanctions from Iran. What does this mean? It means that we are all admitting that there is no threat, missile or nuclear, whatsoever emanating from Iran. So it has to be done right now? All these ABM programs have to be cancelled?

OS: Cancelled?

VP: Yes, so why do that? If the whole idea of an ABM system is based on a threat from Iran and now this threat is gone, are there any reasons to continue with this program?

OS: Correct me if I'm wrong—I had the impression that the Russians were ahead technically in creating an anti-ballistic missile program.

VP: Not entirely like that. We have more sophisticated air defense systems. But as to anti-ballistic defense, the thing is we have to talk about protecting ourselves from ballistic missiles and ballistic missile strikes with a cosmic velocity. And another type of system is required to counter this threat. These anti-ballistic missiles are just a part of a greater anti-ballistic missile system, and these missiles are usually placed on the periphery of the country. This system is very complicated, very large, it requires information support, space support. But to Russia two threats exist—the first threat is the placement of these anti-ballistic missiles in the vicinity of our borders. In Eastern European countries, these count as part of our missile compounds which are located in the European part of the country. And the second threat is that the launching pads of these anti-ballistic missiles can be transformed within a few hours for offensive weapons to be placed in those launching shafts. And both these threats are quite real. And we now have a situation—if these ballistic missiles are placed in Romania or Poland, if those missiles are also placed on the water using ships patrolling the Mediterranean Sea and the Northern seas, and in Alaska—where Russian territory is encircled by these systems. So, as you can see, that is yet another great strategic mistake made by our partners.[32] Because all these actions are going to be answered by Russia adequately. And this means nothing else but a new cycle of an arms race. And our response is going to be much cheaper than the antiballistic missile system. Well, of course our response can be rougher, not so sophisticated, but our systems which we're going to build are going to be efficient. And we're going to preserve the so-called strategic parity. And I think that not just the citizens of Russia and the United States are interested in that—the whole world is interested in that. Balance is of the utmost importance.

OS: Right.

VP: You remember how the nuclear project developed? When the United States created the nuclear bomb and the Soviet Union entered the race and started to actively develop the nuclear program. Russia had both Russian scientists working, and foreign scientists, Germans primarily. But our intelligence also received a whole bunch of information from the United States. Suffice it to remember the Rosenberg spouses who were electrocuted—they were American citizens . . . [33] The Rosenbergs didn't acquire that information—they were just transferring that information. But who acquired it?

OS: Klaus Fuchs.[34]

VP: The scientists themselves—those who developed the atomic bomb. Why did they do that? Because they understood the dangers. They let the genie out of the bottle and now the genie cannot be put back. And this international team of scientists, I think they were more intelligent than the politicians. They provided this information to the Soviet Union of their own volition to restore the nuclear balance in the world. And what are we doing right now? We're trying to destroy this balance. And that's a great mistake.

OS: So stop referring to them as partners— "our partners"—you've said that too much. You're being euphemistic. They're no longer partners.

VP: But dialogue has to be pursued further.

OS: Yes, but "partners" is a euphemism. "At one point . . . " you could say that. Yeah, sometimes understatement doesn't work. But in this period, the withdrawal from the ABM Treaty, the invasion of Iraq, expansion of NATO. . . . It must be clear that your view of US intentions has to have become more suspicious certainly and that Russian policy has to change. And in 2007 in Munich you made a statement that there was indeed a new attitude in Russia.[35]

VP: I didn't want to say that the policy would be different. I was just saying that I thought it was unacceptable what the United States was doing. And I said we saw what was happening and that we had to take measures. I was saying that we would not let ourselves be dragged to the slaughter house and applaud that at the same time.

OS: Right. With that speech and others, you've talked very eloquently about international sovereignty of countries. You've talked about the violation of sovereignty in Libya, in Iraq, in Syria. Would you like to add any other countries?

VP: No, I just want to emphasize that that approach is dangerous. When we had the walk through the garden I told you that democracy could not be exported. It cannot be imported from outside. It has to emerge from within society. And this work is more promising even though it is more difficult; it requires patience, it requires much time, and it requires attention. Certainly it's easier to send bombers. And what then? What comes next? And then a surge of terrorism and the need to take the next step to fight terrorism. Take ISIS. Where do they recruit new members? There are many countries sending people there. And what about the armed forces of Saddam Hussein? They have been dismissed, but they are in the streets, and right now they are in charge. They take cannon fodder from all across the region and the leadership already exists and they're well-trained.

ON US-RUSSIAN RELATIONS AND THE COLD WAR

OS: The US attitude toward the old Soviet Union—the moment the revolution happened in 1917. It was hostile, the US troops came to Siberia, along with 16 other armies to destroy the revolution. Woodrow Wilson sent those troops—he was a liberal. From that point on, it was very difficult for the Soviet Union to accept that the United States was not its enemy. Until Franklin Roosevelt recognized the Soviet Union finally in 1933. The United States and the allies did nothing to help the Soviet Union when the Soviet Union was warning the world about the fascist threat in Spain and throughout Europe. In fact, many US politicians—including Harry Truman at one point—said to let the Germans and the Russians kill each other. And despite the alliance, at many times during the alliance Stalin felt that he was not being supported by Churchill or by Roosevelt. And the Soviet Union was bleeding enormously in order to fight the German war machine. The US and England entered the war against Germany late—much later than the Soviet Union needed, and basically did not commit a lot of troops to the struggle until 1944.[36]

At the end of the day, by Churchill's own admission, it was the Soviet Union that destroyed the guts of the German war machine. Five out of six German soldiers were killed on the Eastern Front.

Russia was basically impoverished after the war, had nothing, and was promised aid by Roosevelt, and by Britain—they were promised something like 20 billion dollars to be split 50/50.

But Roosevelt died in April of '45 and Truman took over. Truman had a different viewpoint about the Soviet Union. The Cold War started in that period. And the blame was put always on the Russians in the American history books and in the West. And as you said last night, they used the tyranny of Stalin as a justification and an excuse.

US bases circle the world now—we don't know exactly—800 to 1,000, maybe more bases. US troops are in 130-plus countries, military missions, and sometimes treaties. Has this ever stopped? Has this attitude of the US ever stopped that they had an enemy in Russia, whether it was communism or Putinism, or any form—it was just the concept of an enemy?[37]

VP: Well, I think everything flows, everything changes. After the Second World War a bipolar world order emerged, and I think that was a strategic mistake the Soviet Union made. Certainly it's good to have allies. But it's impossible to first force someone to be your ally. We have good examples. We fostered our relations with Central European countries. The Soviet Union troops left Austria—and that's it. And now Austria was preserved as a neutral state. It was an asset and the same goes for Finland. And to tell you the truth, if such a structure of relations were preserved then we would have been able to preserve our influence there on a civilized basis. We would have been able to cooperate with them. We wouldn't have had to spend enormous resources to support their inefficient economies. We probably would have been able to have military treaties with them.

But the Soviet Union was acting quite straightforwardly, primitively, and they gave an excuse to the United States to create NATO and to launch a Cold War. Well, the Cold War was not initiated because of that, it was because the Soviet Union started its atomic bomb project and it created an atomic bomb quite quickly. I think that when the United States felt they were at the forefront of the so-called civilized world, and when the Soviet Union collapsed, they were under the illusion that the United States was capable of everything and they could act with impunity. And that's always a trap, because in this situation, a person and a country begin to commit mistakes. There is no need to analyze the situation. No need to think about the consequences. No need to economize. And the country becomes inefficient and one mistake follows another. And I think that's the trap the United States has found itself in. But there is an understanding that controlling everything, commanding everything is impossible. But there is also a need for a society to understand reality in the same fashion, because if society is dominated by these imperialist notions, then society would push the political leadership—especially in an electoral campaign—to follow this rationale.

OS: In the US?

VP: Yes, certainly. If there is this imperialistic notion in society, and if the whole of society believes that they are sinless, that they are the righteous ones, then the political leadership has to follow the same logic as society.

OS: Well, what we have basically in the US is a bipartisan foreign policy which is creating military bases everywhere and intervening in other countries, and basically trying to guide the policies of those countries. Right now we are facing problems, obstacles in China, Iran, and Russia. And they keep talking about these three. What I'd like to talk about next time is this pursuit of world domination. What are the obstacles to it and where does Russia fit into this program?

VP: Well, let's agree on something. I know how critical you are of the United States' policies. Please do not try to drag me into anti-Americanism.

OS: I won't. I'm just trying to talk about the facts of what happened. And I want to do it honestly because the old Soviets were always very realistic about American policy. They always tried to understand the intentions of the Americans. I don't know if those think tanks still exist here, I would imagine they do, and that you get very accurate assessments of what United States intentions are.

VP: Yes, certainly, I do get those assessments. We understand that. I've told you already, I believe that if you think that you are the only world power, trying to impose on the whole nation the idea of their exclusiveness, you then create this unrealistic mentality in society which in turn requires an adequate foreign policy which is expected by society. And the country's leadership is obliged to follow this logic of imperialism. And in practice this might go contrary to the interests of the American people. That's my understanding of how things stand, because in the end it leads to problems, to deficiencies in the system. And it demonstrates that it cannot be in control of everything—that's impossible. But let's talk about that later.

OS: Okay, thank you.

Trip 1—Day 2—July 3, 2015

———

OS: So can we talk on the way? I don't want you to crash. [laughs]

VP: Neither do I.

OS: No traffic—I love summer nights. I met you the first time when I was finishing the Snowden movie here in Moscow early in the summer of 2015. You were at a play, written in the 1960s, celebrating the Russian Folk tradition of the villages.

VP: I was invited to this play a long time ago by the head of the theater. One of the very famous and very popular Russian artists—Alexander Kalyagin. He played in many popular films. And that is his theater. Several years ago I attended the ceremony of the inauguration of this theater. He's also the head of the Association of Theatrical Actors.

ON SNOWDEN

OS: I want to talk about Snowden a bit. In 2012, this is a long time ago now, and you've said you were good with Bush. Presumably you were good with Obama. You were dealing with him on Syria. You were dealing with him on Iran. There was no break. I don't remember anything melodramatic about your relative positions with the United States. And then out of the blue you gave asylum to Edward Snowden in 2013.

VP: Not exactly like that. On the whole, the relationship dampened because the United States supported terrorist groups in the Caucasus. That has always been a problem in our bilateral relations. Not just with the President, but also with Congressmen—they were saying that they were supporting us but in practice we saw that their actions were completely contrary to what they were telling us. And then our relations were dampened even further because of Iraq.

There were other issues as well which were of concern to us. For instance, the unilateral withdrawal of the United States from the ABM treaty.

OS: Yes, but that was during the Bush era—now Obama's come in.

VP: Yes, but still that issue persisted in our relations, and continued to be part of our relationship. Indeed after we granted asylum to Mr. Snowden it didn't lead to improvement of our relationship; on the contrary, it aggravated it.

OS: I want to go back. We know that Bush supported the Georgian offensive in 2008.[38]

VP: Not exactly—yes and no. We were surprised when we saw that the aggression by President Saakashvili was not just supported by Bush. They tried to paint the picture that Russia was the aggressor, when it was quite evident that it was Saakashvili who decided to launch the aggression.[39] Moreover, he declared that publicly. And he made a TV address. There was just some surprise at how everything could be turned upside down. And they even tried to shift the blame on Russia next door. So even without Snowden there were many issues dampening our relations. So that when the Snowden factor came up it was an additional factor aggravating our bilateral relations.

OS: But can I say, after Russia took a strong position against Saakashvili—a very strong position and made it clear that there was a red line so to speak in Georgia—let's say at that point there was no new dramatic conflict after the Georgian situation. It seemed to me that Obama accepted those conditions.

VP: To start with, I'd like to clarify. You see, we were very cautious with those unrecognized republics. I, personally, as president of Russia, never met the leaders of those two unrecognized republics. And in my personal contacts with President Saakashvili, I told him many times that we would facilitate the restoration of the territorial integrity of Georgia. But I was telling him that he had to accept the realities and acknowledge them and understand that the problem they were facing had just arisen until recently. The tensions between these groups had deep historical roots. After the first World War, after the so-called October Socialist Revolution—back then Georgia declared that it wanted to be an independent state. And Ossetia declared it wanted to be part of Russia. And back then in 1921, Georgian troops undertook two punitive actions against these factions. And all that is part of the historical memory. Something had to be done about that. We had to gain the trust of the people if Georgians wanted to preserve the territorial integrity of their country.

OS: But I repeat, I don't remember there being anything major, loud, between Obama and you up until the Snowden story . . .

VP: That's true, but if you'll allow me, I'd like to say just a few more words about Georgia. Many times I told Saakashvili, if he wanted to restore the territorial integrity, he had to be very cautious with regards to the population of Abkhazia and South Ossetia. And I told him we're willing to help you, and moreover I think George [Bush] can confirm that. I told him that he had to avoid potential aggression because if he were to launch hostilities against Abkhazia and South Ossetia, then the ethnic composition of the Caucasus being what it was—there were people living in adjacent regions in the Russian Federation who couldn't have stayed outside that conflict. And we wouldn't have been able to prevent them from engaging in that conflict. Just have a look at South Ossetia—a small republic. And in the north there is North Ossetia, as a constituent entity of the Russian Federation. And the same people live in both South Ossetia and North Ossetia. And it would have been impossible to prevent them from dashing to help their compatriots. And Russia would not have been able to stay outside that conflict. And our American partners were telling us, "Yes, we understand it." It all led to the war which was started by Saakashvili. His actions dealt a great blow to the Georgian state. As to Snowden, indeed, at that time we seem to have had good relations with the United States. And the Snowden affair pushed our relations to deterioration.

OS: So here we are in June, 2013. You get a call, I suppose, and hear that Snowden is on the way via Moscow. I'm sure you get calls from the US, including Obama. How does the situation devolve and how do you handle it?

VP: Our first contact with Mr. Snowden was in China. We were told back then that this was a person who wanted to fight for human rights and against violations of human rights. And that we had to do that together. I'll probably disappoint many people, probably even you, but I said we wanted nothing to do with that. We didn't want to do that because he had quite difficult relationships with the United States as it was, and we didn't want to aggravate those relations. And Mr. Snowden didn't want to give us any information, he was just urging us to fight together and he has to be credited with that. But when it turned out that we were not willing to do that yet, not ready, he just disappeared.

OS: He just disappeared?

VP: But then I got a report that Snowden's on a plane bound for Moscow and that he was supposed to get on another plane and fly to Latin America, if I'm not mistaken. But it turned out that the countries he wanted to fly to were not quite happy about receiving him. Secondly, this is not our information, this information comes from other sources and that information was leaked to the press while he was on the plane. And it turned out that he could not continue his journey. And he was stuck in the transit area.

OS: But the US revoked his passport in midair which they have never done before.[40]

VP: I didn't remember that, but anyway, it was quite clear that he could not continue his journey. He's a courageous man, probably even foolhardy. And he understood that he had no chance. He stayed in the transit area for 40 days. And then we provided him with temporary asylum. But of course the Americans asked us to extradite him. It's quite understandable that we couldn't do it.

OS: Why not?

VP: Because back then we were talking about concluding a treaty on cooperation on legal matters. That was our initiative. And that also would have stipulated mutual extradition of criminals, but the United States refused to cooperate with us.[41] And they also refused to sign the agreement which we put forward. And according to our law, Snowden didn't violate any law—he didn't commit any crime. That's why in the absence of this agreement on mutual extradition, given the fact that the US has never extradited any criminals to us who sought asylum in the United States, we had no choice. It was absolutely impossible for us to unilaterally extradite Snowden as the United States was asking us to do.

OS: Did Obama get on the phone with you?

VP: I should not like to discuss this in the film because it's of a confidential nature.

OS: Let me ask you—I'm sure you must have, as an ex-KGB agent, you must've hated what Snowden did with every fiber of your being.

VP: No not at all. Snowden is not a traitor. He didn't betray the interests of his country. Nor did he transfer any information to any other country which would have been pernicious to his own country or to his own people. The only thing Snowden did he did publicly. And it's quite a different story.

OS: Right. Did you agree with what he did?

VP: No.

OS: Do you think the National Security Agency had gone too far in its eavesdropping?[42]

VP: Yes, certainly, I think so. Well, in that matter Snowden was right. But you asked me and I gave you a direct answer—I think he shouldn't have done it. If he didn't like anything at his work he should have simply resigned—that's all. But he went further. I'm not acquainted with him personally, I only know of him from the press. If he thinks that by his actions he can prevent some threat to his country, I think he has the right to do it. That's his right. But since you are asking me whether it's right or wrong, I think it's wrong.

OS: So you're saying that he should not have whistleblown—which is an expression we use, "to whistleblow"—and he should have resigned in principle, somewhat like you did when you resigned from the KGB.

VP: Yes, I think so. I had not given it thought, but I think yes.

OS: You resigned because—I gather from yesterday, that it was in part because you did not want to serve in a government if the Communists controlled it.

VP: I resigned because I didn't agree with the actions undertaken by the Communists in the attempted coup d'état against Gorbachev. And I didn't want to continue to be an intelligence officer during that time.

OS: So you do agree the NSA went too far. And how do you feel about Russian intelligence activities in their surveillance.

VP: I think they're working quite well. But it's one thing to work well within the framework of the existing legislation. And it's quite another story if you violate the law. Our intelligence services always conform to the law. That's the first thing. And secondly, trying to spy on your allies—if you really consider them allies and not vassals—is just indecent. It's not done. Because it undermines trust. And it means that in the end it damages your own national security.

OS: But the US surveillance no doubt has been heavily surveilling Russia?

VP: And they are still continuing that surveillance. No doubt. That's what I always assume.

OS: Right. In a scene in the movie we show where Snowden shows his colleagues a heat map in Hawaii where it shows that the United States is collecting twice as many billion phone calls in the United States as it is in Russia. Russia is number two. The US is number one.

VP: Yes, I think that's quite true. Regrettably, that's an existing practice of how the intelligence services work today. Well, I am a grown up now and I understand how the world works. But spying on your own allies? That's just unacceptable.

OS: Would you call the US an ally?

VP: Yes, sure. But it undermines trust among allies. And it destroys relations. But I'm just telling you that as an expert.

OS: Well you must be spying on the US because if the US is spying on you . . . I mean the Americans are going to say I'm sure you're spying on us.

VP: Yes, sure. I don't have anything against their spying on us. But let me tell you something quite interesting. After radical changes—political changes—took place in Russia, we thought that we were surrounded by allies and no one else. And we also thought the United States was our ally. And this former president of the KGB, of the special services of Russia, all of a sudden he transferred to our American partners, our American friends, the old system of eavesdropping devices at the US Embassy in Moscow. And he did it unilaterally. Just all of a sudden on a whim—as a token of trust symbolizing the transition to the new level.

OS: Was that Yeltsin?

VP: No, it was the head of the Russian intelligence service. It was under Yeltsin. And many named him a traitor. But I'm quite confident that he thought it had to symbolize a new character of our relations. So we were willing to stop the activities of the special services. But we never witnessed any step from the United States toward us.

OS: The Snowden affair, in terms of the US-Russia relationship, seemed to turn—was a big deal for the neo-conservative movement in the US. And the neocons seemed to focus in on Russia once again. It wasn't too long afterward that the Ukraine issue came up.

VP: Yes, that's true. Probably we can talk more about it tomorrow. But as to Snowden I think I've elaborated on our position.

OS: As a realist, as a political realist, I think I would consider Snowden a pawn in the game.

VP: I think you're mistaken. He would have been a pawn if he had been a traitor. And he's no traitor. Well, listen to my position as to what he has done. I think he's still a personality and he has a position in his own right and he's fighting for this position. He's defending it. And he spares no effort in this fight.

OS: So under these circumstances, in this three-year period that you have given him asylum, you would not return him under any circumstances to the United States?

VP: No, under no circumstances. Because he's no criminal.

OS: In your law he did not break the law?

VP: Our American partners say he has violated the law. But in Russia, he has violated no laws. And there is no inter-governmental treaty between the US and Russia on extradition because our American partners refused to sign this agreement. When criminals who had committed crimes in Russia fled to the United States, the US refused to extradite those criminals to us. We are a sovereign state and we cannot decide on extradition without reciprocity.

OS: Are you saying that if the US signed that agreement then Snowden would come under consideration to be returned?

VP: Certainly, we have such an agreement with Armenia, and one of our military men committed a crime in Armenia. And in accordance with this treaty, he would have to stand trial in Armenia.

OS: So if the United States wanted Snowden badly enough they would sign an extradition treaty with you?

VP: They should have done it earlier. It's too late now. Because the law cannot be retroactive. So if we sign this treaty in the future, this law will only be effective with regards to cases that arise after this treaty has been signed.

OS: Okay—one last question. They revoked his passport in the air.[43] They knew he was going through Moscow. Many people believe that it was the intention of the United States to stick Snowden in Russia because this would be the best place for him to be reviled and to be called a traitor.

VP: I don't believe that. Nor do I believe that the American intelligence service were the ones to organize the terrorist attacks in New York.

OS: I didn't say that. I'm just saying—

VP: I know you're not saying that. I'm just saying that I do not believe this version of events. Nor do I believe that they organized Snowden's flight to Moscow.

OS: No, that was organized by WikiLeaks. WikiLeaks did a very good job. They had, I'm told, 25-plus tickets to come out of Hong Kong so that they didn't want anybody to know he was going. When he was in the air, I believe it came out from the Hong Kong authorities, or possibly Wikileaks, that Snowden was going to Moscow. And at that point he did have a safe passage to Ecuador and to Cuba. And he was welcome in Venezuela, as well as in Bolivia. So he had a destination. It would have worked. The question remains to me—why didn't the US authorities let him go through Moscow to Latin America? If they wanted to snatch him in a commando raid they could have done a far easier job of it in Venezuela or Bolivia probably than in Russia.

VP: They just acted unprofessionally. I don't think they did it on purpose. They were acting under emotions. And they were very nervous, very anxious. And in such cases with intelligence matters you should never be nervous. You should keep calm. They should have let him climb on a plane and then make this plane stop at one of the airports on the way.

OS: You think they could have?

VP: Yes, sure, why not. They managed to stop the plane of the Bolivian president.[44]

OS: Stunning.

VP: It's just outrageous. They're acting with impunity. And yet they were bold enough to do it. Just imagine if they hadn't revoked his passport. They could have let him climb on a civil aircraft and while it was flying over Europe, according to some technical matters, they could have made the plane stop.

OS: Unless they wanted him here in Moscow to embarrass.

VP: I don't think so, because that's too subtle for them.

OS: Really?

VP: I don't think so. And besides, he's sitting here. And what is he doing? He's not doing our bidding—he's doing everything he does of his own volition.

OS: Yes, and he's been effective in the United States and in Europe as well. Congress has looked at reform. Our courts have looked at the laws and have struck some down. That's not to say they're being carried out, but several courts have judged them illegal. This illegal bulk surveillance. So he has been effective.[45]

VP: If they had detained Snowden somewhere on his way to Latin America, this never would have happened. That's why I'm quite confident that the American authorities were just acting under the pressure of circumstances and they have made many mistakes.

OS: Okay, fair enough.

VP: Their mistakes are what saved Snowden because otherwise he would be in prison now. He's a courageous person and I give him that. And he has character. I don't know how he's going to continue with his life. I just don't understand that.

OS: Well, one thing is clear. I think the only place in the world where he's safe is here in Russia.

VP: I think so too.

OS: And there's a great irony in this. In the old days, the Russian defectors would go to the United States. And this is a reversal.

VP: But Snowden is not a traitor.

OS: I know he's not.

VP: That's the first thing. And secondly, there's nothing strange about that today, because however much they try to demonize Russia, Russia is a democratic country and also a sovereign country. There are risks to that, but also a great advantage to that as well. Because there are just a handful of countries who can really wield their sovereignty. And the other countries are burdened with so-called allied obligations. In reality, they have limited their own sovereignty of their own volition. That's their decision.

OS: Okay, sir. Thank you. Tomorrow we'll start off with Ukraine.

VP: Sure, whatever you say. And I will go work a little bit more.

Trip 1—Day 3—July 4, 2015

OS: Hello, Mr. Putin. How are you today?

VP: Fine, thank you.

OS: Right now, I'm fine. I have water and Coca Cola. You're not going to drink anything? You don't drink very much or take a lot of water.

VP: Well, you're doing the right thing when you drink a lot of water.

OS: When I wake up in the morning I have three big bottles.

VP: In the morning, I also drink a bottle of water like that one.

OS: So, by the way, just to finish last night, I checked and Mr. Snowden was on an Aeroflot plane coming from Hong Kong to Moscow. So I don't think the United States would have intercepted an Aeroflot plane. I'm not sure.

VP: Oh, that wouldn't have been a problem for them.

OS: Really?

VP: To start with, they could land any plane due to some technical reasons in any airport, anywhere in the world, under the pretext of the need to check the aircraft. They could have made all the passengers disembark anywhere. And then separate the passengers. And within 10 hours Snowden would have been in prison in the United States. But the thing is, he was flying by Aeroflot just to Moscow and then he was supposed to embark on another aircraft, on another airline. He was supposed to change aircraft in Moscow.

OS: But you would not have objected strongly to the grounding of an Aeroflot plane?

VP: What does it have to do with the Russian territory? He would have been downed when he was flying to Latin America.

OS: I thought because it was a Russian plane, it was considered Russian territory.

VP: No, Russian territory is only considered that way when it's a military vessel, military aircraft, or a merchant ship in neutral waters.

OS: Okay. I'd like to talk about Ukraine.

VP: Just a second—if our aircraft were landing in some transit country between Russia and Latin America, I wouldn't have known about that in the first place. No one would have reported it to me. It's just a transport procedure—a standard one which has nothing to do with any politics. And if Snowden had flown from Moscow further, then I wouldn't have known about it either. So it has nothing to do with us. It has to do with what the former bosses of Snowden were trying to do to him.

ON UKRAINE

OS: Okay, Ukraine. I want to say first of all that I interviewed Mr. Yanukovych here in Moscow a few months ago. And he told me his version of events.

VP: The thing is, here is an objective sequence of events. These events can be assessed differently, and you can name these events using different words, different formulas. But it's quite evident you can follow what was happening day after day. And then you can give the people a chance to make an assessment of their own of what has really happened.

OS: Well, I would like your perspective on it from November to February 20th, 2013 into 2014. During those three months, there was quite a bit of protest in Ukraine. You must have been aware of it.

VP: Do you want to know what was happening in Ukraine starting from the early 1990s? What was happening there was the systemic robbery of the Ukrainian people. Right away after independence, Ukraine started an even wilder privatization and robbery of state property, which led to the deterioration of the standard of living—right after Ukraine gained independence. Whatever powers came into force, nothing changed for the lives of ordinary people.

And certainly the people were fed up with all those arbitrary actions and that crazy corruption, the impoverishment and the illegal enrichment of other people. That was the root of the discontent the people were feeling. And certainly people were thinking that exiting in any way to the EU would liberate them from the terrible conditions they had found themselves in starting from the beginning of the 1990s. I think that was the driving force behind the developments in Ukraine.

And the crisis was sparked, as is well known, when President Yanukovych said he had to postpone the signing of the association agreement with the European Union. That was the starting point. And our partners in Europe and the United States managed to mount this horse of discontent of the people. And instead of trying to find out what was really happening, they decided to support the coup d'état.[46]

And now let me tell you how it unfolded and what our position was. Mr. Yanukovych announced that he had to postpone, not cancel, the signing of the association agreement with the European Union because, at that moment, Ukraine had already been a member of the Free Trade Area of the CIS (Commonwealth of Independent States).

Ukraine itself was the engine behind the establishment of the free trade area in the CIS space. And it was the force that led to the creation of this zone. As a result of this, and the fact that the economies of Russia and Ukraine were emerging as a united economy and had unique economic relations, many of our enterprises could not exist independently. There was very deep co-operation between those enterprises.

The markets of Russia were absolutely open to imports from Ukraine. We had and still have a zero tariff barrier. We have a single energy system and a single transportation system. There are many other elements which bring our economies together. For 17 years we have been in negotiations with the European Union on the conditions of Russia's accession to the WTO, and all of a sudden, it was announced to us that Ukraine and the EU were signing an association agreement. And that meant the opening up of the Ukrainian markets. It meant that the technical standards and trade regulation and other elements of the economic policy of the EU were to be implemented in Ukraine, and that was happening very fast without a transition period. At the same time, our customs border with Ukraine was absolutely open. And the EU was able to enter our territory with all of their goods without any negotiations, despite the agreements—principled agreements—which we had reached with them before, during those 17-year talks on our accession to the WTO.

Certainly we had to respond to that. And we said that if Ukraine had decided to act like that it was its choice. And we respected that choice. But this didn't mean that we had to pay for that choice. Why do people living in Russia today have to pay for this choice the Ukrainian leadership has made? That's why we told them that we would have to take protective measures, and those protected measures were nothing special and they were not discriminatory. We were just trying to extend the regular trade regime to the territory of Ukraine which in international private law is called most favored nation status. So we're just going to withdraw the preferences. But without preferences, the Ukrainian enterprises would not exist too long in the Russian market. And we proposed that we hold talks with our European partners in a trilateral format. But there was a flat refusal. They told us that we had better stay out of it. They told us, if we are talking to Canada, you would not interfere, right? If you are in talks with China, we are not interfering with those talks—that's what they told us. And they asked us not to interfere in their relations with Ukraine.

And we said, those situations are quite different—Canada, China, and Russia/Ukrainian relations—these are different stories. But we told them, if you think like that then we're not going to interfere. But in that case, we ask them to respect our right to undertake protective measures and to continue this economic policy. I would go even further, talking about the economics, and after the coup d'état, after the leadership changed in Ukraine, and Mr. Poroshenko arrived in power, at the request of our American partners and the request of the Ukrainian side, we did not implement protective measures.

Whereas the Ukrainian leadership signed the association agreement with the European Union. And they ratified this agreement, and after that they postponed that agreement from entering into force until January 1st, 2016. So you're now shooting this documentary in mid-2015, and as of now, this association agreement between Ukraine and the EU has not yet entered into force.

That's exactly what I had proposed to Mr. Yanukovych. He had proposed that the signing should be postponed. So the question is what was the reason for the coup d'état? Why did they drive this country into chaos, into civil war? So what was the sense behind all that? And now as to the unfolding of the political situation, indeed you have now mentioned the fact that there were riots and a coup d'état was perpetrated.

Let me remind you that before that, on February 21st, 2014, if my memory serves me correctly, three foreign ministers from European countries arrived in Kiev. They took part in the meeting between President Yanukovych and the opposition, and they agreed that early elections were to be held.[47] They agreed on the future of relations between the president and the opposition.

And the following day, President Yanukovych went to the second largest city of Ukraine, Kharkov—he went there to participate in a regional conference. And once he departed, his residence was seized, his administration was seized, and the government was seized as well with the use of force. What would you call that? And the Prosecutor General was shot at, one of his security officers was wounded. And the motorcade of President Yanukovych himself was shot at. So it's nothing more than an armed seizure of power. Naturally, someone supported this coup d'état. Where I started from this—not just personally against Yanukovych, but against the government itself because people were fed up with the chaos of what was happening. The poverty, they were fed up with it, as well as with corruption. After power was seized, some people liked it. But others didn't like it. People were frightened by this surge of nationalism, radicalism.

The first thing the newly-arrived in power started to talk about was the need to adopt a law limiting the use of the Russian language.[48] The Europeans prevented them from doing that. But the signal had already been sent to society, and people understood the direction the country was moving towards in such places as Crimea, where the overwhelming majority of people are Russians by nationality. Whereas Ukrainians who live in those places, as a whole, believe their native language to be the Russian language. Certainly, people in Crimea were especially frightened by this situation.[49] Furthermore there were threats made against them directly. And all that led to the circumstances which are well known. I've elaborated on them on many occasions, so if you are interested, I can repeat. But something like that started to happen in the southeastern part of Ukraine on the whole. In the territory which is called Donbass, there are two large cities, and people didn't accept the coup d'état there either.[50] First there were attempts at arresting them using the police, but the police defected to their side quite quickly. Then the central authorities started to use special forces and in the night people were snatched and taken to prison. And afterwards there was the tragedy in Odessa.[51] And people who were unarmed took to the streets for peaceful protests and they were pushed into a building and were massacred atrociously. Even pregnant women. That is a catastrophe. But still no one is going to investigate it. Certainly not people in Donbass. After that they took up arms.

But once hostilities started, instead of engaging in a dialogue with people in the southeast part of Ukraine, after they used Special Forces, they started to use weapons directly—tanks and even military aircraft. There were strikes from the multiple rocket launchers against residential neighborhoods. We repeatedly appealed to the new leadership of Ukraine, asking them to abstain from extreme actions. They started hostilities once, they were put to rout, they stopped, then elections took place, then this new president arrived in power. I talked to him [Poroshenko] on many occasions. I tried to persuade him not to resume hostilities.[52] And he had an opinion of his own about what was happening. He always referred to the losses his forces had sustained to two or three as people during the hostilities with the militia. Certainly that was a tragedy. It is always sad when people die. But when he resumed the hostilities, thousands of people died. And the official forces suffered another defeat. Then they started hostilities for the third time. And once again they were defeated. After that, the latest Minsk Agreements were signed. They agreed that these agreements would be adhered to by both parties. Unfortunately, we're not witnessing that, and I think the official authorities in Kiev are not willing to engage in any direct dialogue with Donbass. They refuse to be engaged in direct dialogue. Up to now. All the provisions of the Minsk agreements stipulate directly that issues related to amendments to the Constitution, issues related to the adoption of the law, on municipal elections, issues related to this special status of Donbass—all these issues have to be coordinated, that's what it says. But nothing like that is happening.

Right now, the Kiev authorities are trying to make amendments to the Constitution. But according to the information I have—just yesterday I received new information—there is no contact, no negotiations with Donbass. Moreover, the Minsk agreements say directly that the law which had already been adopted by the Verkhovna Rada should enter into force. This is along with the special status of Donbass. Unfortunately, just several days ago President Poroshenko announced that no special status would be granted to Donbass. I have to talk to him. I have to understand what it means. Does it mean that the Kiev authorities refuse to adhere to the Minsk agreements?[53] There are other considerations at work here. One of the provisions of the Minsk agreements says that it's necessary to adopt a law on amnesty. But the law has not been adopted yet. How can you talk to people in Donbass who are threatened with criminal prosecution? Another provision—the economy and the social sphere of Donbass have to be restored. But instead the authorities are strengthening the blockade of these territories.[54] And all things boiled down to one thing—they are saying that Donbass is fighting against them and that's why they're not going to pay them anything. And I say there are pensioners who are entitled, according to the law of Ukraine, to a pension, that there are people with disabilities who are not fighting anyone. They are just victims of this situation—hostages. I asked them, "Do you consider them to be citizens of your country? Well in that case you have to take care of them." Their response was quite simple—"We do not have money and we're not going to pay them anything." We are supplying energy. Ukraine has refused to pay for that energy.

So on the whole, it's a full-fledged, very tough blockade. Many people criticize Israel for the blockade of Palestine. I'm not going to elaborate on that, I'm not going to talk about that because it's a different story entirely. But the same thing is happening here and everyone seems not to notice what is happening. There is not enough food there, not enough medicine.[55] Nothing. And that is a serious issue. We assume that there is no other way to find a solution to this issue, other than adhering to the Minsk agreements—they have to be implemented.

We always hear appeals that we have to influence somehow the leadership of these unrecognized republics. Just recently, the leaders of these republics announced publicly that they were willing to go back to the Ukrainian state under certain conditions—if the Minsk agreements were observed. But these agreements were not implemented. And Donbass is not to blame for that. Let me reiterate, I believe that there is no other way to settle this crisis. And the Minsk agreement is the only way toward that end.

OS: Well, obviously there are problems with it. What if the people in Donbass came across the border to Russia? That would be their only hope if things got really bad.

VP: Do you mean that the best way to solve this issue is to push these people from their homeland?

OS: I'm not saying that, I'm saying if they have no water, no food, and they can't go on living, the only way you can travel is on your feet. I mean we're talking about major migration.

VP: Yes, many people have already resorted to these means—two and a half million Ukrainian citizens are in Russia.[56] The overwhelming majority of them are men who are under conscription. They're eligible for conscription. But in these territories there used to be four and a half million people. Right now estimates are around three million people are left there.[57]

OS: So what if they come?

VP: Well, they are already doing that. They are coming. But once the situation quiets down, they go back to their homes.

OS: Yes, I understand. Of course the Kiev government would claim that the Russian army or the Russian government has intervened already in Ukraine with the annexation of Crimea. And the troops—they're saying there are paratroopers or whatever you want to call them, contractors, soldiers and arms dealers helping them or helping the separatists.

VP: As to Crimea, I'd like to ask you, what is democracy? Democracy is a policy which is based on the will of the people. And how do we know the will of the people? In a modern world we use the voting procedure. People came to a referendum and there were no whips, no machine guns. And you cannot use these means to make a person come to a polling station to vote. People came, the turnout was more than 90 percent. And more than 90 percent voted in favor of re-unifying with Russia.[58] The choice of the people has to be respected. And you cannot try to conform international law to your political interests against the principles of democracy.

OS: Nonetheless, the United States would say that you have violated international law—and that's been a theme that has been repeated again and again by the EU. And you yourself acknowledged that the US had done that in Iraq, so it's a question of course, at the end of the day, of power, isn't it?

VP: Yes, that's correct. As to armed forces of the United States coming to Iraq. And there were no elections there. No elections were held. As to Crimea, yes, we created conditions for people to be able to come to polling stations. But we were not engaged in any hostilities there, no one was shooting there, no one was killed.

OS: But literally the US would argue that elections were held eventually in Iraq.

VP: In the end, yes, but before that there was a war. And there was no war in Crimea. That's the first thing. Secondly, there is another criticism addressed to Russia. They are saying that international law was violated. I have already talked about that but I'd like to emphasize that in the course of the Kosovo crisis, the International Court of Justice considered very cautiously this situation and the ICJ arrived at a conclusion saying that when the issue of self-determination of a nation is concerned, in accordance with Point Two of the United Nations charter, if my memory serves me correctly, the concerns of the central authorities of this or that country on this matter are not required.[59] And thirdly, since you are preparing this documentary and you have time, I'd like to ask you to do something—have a look at what was said on that matter by the representatives of the United States, and the representatives of certain European countries—Germany, Great Britain—what they said in those matters when they were talking about them with the ICJ. All of them were saying that no consent from Belgrade was needed, and they were saying that everything was done in accordance with the United Nations Charter. I was always wondering if Kosovars were allowed to do it, why is that not allowed to Russians, Ukrainians, Tatars, and Crimeans? There is no difference whatsoever.[60] Moreover, the decision on the independence of Kosovo was adopted by the decision of the parliament. Whereas, in Crimea first the parliament voted in favor of independence, and afterwards they held a referendum and during that referendum the people said that they were willing to go back to Russia. Every step has a reason behind it.

OS: Was there any UN condemnation of the annexation of Crimea?

VP: No, I don't know anything of that.[61]

OS: Can we talk a little bit about the airplane that was shot down in July—the Malaysian Airliner [MH17]?

VP: Yes, certainly.

OS: Thank you. I've heard both sides. I know Russian intelligence has claimed there were two planes in the air, or at least two planes, and there was a possible shooting down of the airplane from another aircraft. Is that correct?

VP: There are two principal versions. The first version is that this plane was shot down by the Buk air defense system of the Ukrainian armed forces. And the second version is that the same system, the same system of arms—the Buk systems that are produced in Russia—was employed by the militia, the separatists.[62] Primarily, let me say that in any case it's a terrible catastrophe. And that is simply atrocious. And in this regard, let me say something. That would not have happened if the leadership of Ukraine had listened to us and had not started full-fledged hostilities. It was the Ukrainian authorities who started to use all kinds of weapons systems in Donbass.

Now as to the aircraft, the planes which were in the air—as far as I know, right away after this terrible catastrophe, one of the Ukrainian air controllers, I think he was a specialist originating from Spain, announced that he had seen a military aircraft in the corridor assigned for civil aircraft.[63] And there could have been no other military aircraft than the one controlled by the Ukrainian authorities. Certainly that needs to be investigated. I'm not saying that this plane was shot down. I do not say that this military aircraft shot down the civil aircraft, but the question is what was that plane doing in the corridor because that is against the existing rules of the international flights of civil air aviation. As for the Buk air defense systems, which can send missiles from Earth—according to our specialists and experts, and not just our intelligence services but also our ballistic experts—the reports that I've received say that the strike hit the tail of the aircraft. And if that is the case, then that is exactly where the air defense system of the Ukrainian armed forces were stationed. So I don't understand what they were doing there in the first place. Why were they there and why were they pulled out of there so quickly? In any case, that requires a thorough and de-politicized investigation.

OS: Do you believe the American intelligence has any information about this, because wouldn't they be watching this situation after the coup? Wouldn't they have intelligence from satellites and whatever?

VP: I'm confident that that is exactly the case. But regrettably, there is no proof from the partners that we've received.

OS: But they have not shown much?

VP: No, that's quite understandable, because we understand their position on Ukraine. And certainly they all wanted to shift the blame on the militia fighters in Donbass and indirectly Russia, who supports the militia.

OS: So if they had contrary information they don't want to release it?

VP: Yes, if this information is contrary then they will never reveal it.

OS: Can we talk about outside influences in this Ukraine story now?

VP: Yes, certainly.

OS: We know about the NGOs that were operating in Ukraine. We know that Victoria Nuland, the Undersecretary of State for Eastern Europe I believe, was very active supporting a change in government. We know that Senator John McCain visited and was seen at rallies with extremist leaders, including some neo-Nazis. We know that America and the National Endowment for Democracy, which is also a very influential private nonprofit NGO was very active, very active here. Paul Gershman, who was the president of it made very strong independent speeches—he wanted an independent Ukraine. And we know that the Hungarian billionaire hedge funder George Soros was also very involved in supporting the groups in Ukraine.[64]

VP: Yes, all that is true. You know I do not always understand the rationale behind the actions of our partners. I already said that sometimes I fall under the impression that they've got to control or enforce some discipline in their Euro-Atlantic camp. And to that end they need some external enemy. And despite all the concerns they have, Iran at this point cannot fulfill this need.

OS: In other words, the United States can keep a united pro-American Europe and NATO with an external enemy such as Russia.

VP: I can say something definitely—that is true. I know that, I feel that. Without this internal discipline, the Euro-Atlantic cause is destabilized. This is not the Cold War we're living in. Several years ago, certain leaders told me that our American friends were asking me to frighten them. But they said that they were not afraid. They understood that the world had changed. And that external threat—it is impossible to enforce this strict discipline. And in that regard, that is probably in the interests of someone, but I think that is the wrong logic. Because this logic is looking back into the past. But you have to look into the future. You have to understand that the world is different now. There are new threats arising, strategic threats included. You cannot freeze it as if we were still living through the Cold War. I told you about the ABM system, about the ABM treaty, about the fight against terrorism. Regrettably, I have to say that all our attempts at fostering a relationship with the United States were met either with the lack of understanding or total indifference. But this situation cannot persist.

OS: I'm surprised. I've always had great respect for Russian intelligence services and their knowledge of the West, but in this situation I was surprised by their lack of, it seems, information of what was going on in Ukraine. It's been said that you yourself were surprised by this takeover, and that you were paying attention to the Sochi Olympics and you weren't paying attention to what was going on in Ukraine. What happened to your intelligence service?

VP: No, that is not true. I had a fairly good picture of what was happening within Ukrainian society. And there is no doubt about that. This take-over could have happened at any time. There was a takeover when Kuchma was leaving office.

OS: And a pro-Western group came in, is that what you're saying?

VP: Yes, and Yanukovych was the one to win the elections. But the street did not agree with that outcome of the election, and a third round of elections was proclaimed in violation of the Constitution. So it was also a quasi-coup d'état. Back then I thought they had made a grave mistake. Even though pro-Western politicians arrived in power, people very soon lost their confidence in those leaders as well. Because those politicians continue to do everything that had been done before them by the previous leaders of the country. And that's why they were defeated in the subsequent elections. Unfortunately, President Yanukovych didn't manage to change much in the country either. And the same thing happened to him. The very paradigm has to be changed of their relation to the people. They were talking about the need to get rid of the oligarchs. And now the oligarchs are in power. So nothing has changed really. They were talking about the need to get rid of corruption. What has changed? Nothing. The governor of the Odessa region is now former President [of Georgia] Saakashvili.[65]

OS: Yeah, I know.

VP: That's just a spit in the face, an insult to the people of Odessa and to the whole of the Ukrainian people. I do not want to give any assessments of Saakashvili, I think that would be the wrong thing to do. Whatever person he is, he was president of a nation [Georgia]. And it is up to the Georgian people to give him assessments. And besides, we are personally acquainted with him. He was not even granted a working visa in the United States. The investors he tried to get did not want to give him a permanent job. But quite strangely, he can act as the governor of the Odessa region [in Ukraine]. Are there no people with integrity, people from Ukraine who can do this job quite as well? It's just ridiculous. And it's an insult to the Ukrainian people.

OS: I have three specific questions about Ukraine, then perhaps we can take a walk? During the Maidan massacre, did you get any intelligence of what was going on? It's the strangest massacre. Because of the number of casualties of policemen, and the civilians who were killed, and the policemen not firing back, they were retreating and called back by Yanukovych. And during that it seems like there was a sniper force that was definitely aiming at the policemen and civilians to create the chaos necessary for the takeover.

VP: To start with, that is absolutely correct. Yanukovych didn't give an order to use weapons against civilians.[66] And incidentally, our western partners, including the United States, asked us to influence him so that he did not give any orders to those weapons. And President Yanukovych said that he couldn't imagine any other way of dealing with this situation. He couldn't sign an order on the use of weapons. And when both the police and the protesters were shot at, it's correct what you've said—the goal was to sow chaos. And certainly President Yanukovych was not interested in the expansion of this chaos. He was interested in containing the situation. But I have to say that the so-called protesters were very aggressive.[67]

OS: Some of them, yes.

VP: Some of them centered in the office of the party of regents which was headed by President Yanukovych. And they burned it down. And technical workers came out and they said we are not members of the party. There was one electrician. And he was shot and they were thrown into the basement and then everything was burned. And that was even before the takeover. So Yanukovych was not interested in chaos, he did everything he could in order to quiet the situation, to restore calm.

OS: Well, who are these snipers?

VP: Well, who could have placed these snipers? Interested parties, parties who wanted to escalate the situation. I do not have any data on who precisely those snipers were, but elementary logic tells me.

OS: Have you heard any reports about the training that was going on in other cities, in Minsk and so forth, of battalions and the Right Sector—hardened people of the right?[68] There were 100-man units that came to the city, I am told, in the days before the Maidan massacre.

VP: No, not in Minsk, but we have information available to us that armed groups were trained in the western parts of Ukraine itself, in Poland, and in a number of other places.

OS: I see. Have you heard of the Azov battalion?[69]

VP: Yes, certainly. There are certain armed formations which are not accountable to anyone, nor are they accountable to the central authorities in Kiev. I believe that is one of the reasons why the current leadership right now cannot put an end to these hostilities. That is simply because they are frightened that these uncontrollable armed forces will return to the capital.

OS: My second question—Mr. Obama, during this period, what kind of communications did you have with him?

VP: We were in constant contact. Well, I can say it was almost on a permanent basis. And Mr. Kerry and Mr. Lavrov, they had personal meetings months ago and they also had telephone conversations. And myself and the president of the United States, we both had a great deal of regular telephone conversations.

OS: Obviously you didn't agree.

VP: Yes, we had different assessments as to the causes of the Ukrainian crisis and its unfolding.

OS: Are you still talking to him?

VP: Yes, just a couple of days ago I had a telephone conversation with him. We talked about our bilateral relations, the Middle East situation, and also the Ukrainian situation. But I have to tell you—I think that there is some understanding on a number of issues—despite the differences in our assessments. There is some common understanding.

OS: Would you say relations or the dialogue is cordial?

VP: No, but they are businesslike. And quite even.

OS: Do you see each other visually when you talk?

VP: No, but I can tell you that this dialogue is a dialogue of interested parties. So there is no confrontation behind it. I think that President Obama is a thinking person, he assesses the real situation, with some things he agrees, with others he disagrees. But we also manage to find points of common understanding on a number of complicated issues. And this is a fruitful dialogue.

OS: This is a just a trivial question, but I've always been curious, do you call each other Vladimir and Barack?

VP: Yes.

OS: You call him Barack or Barry?

VP: Barack.

OS: You do—first name, that's great. Last question—Sebastopol and the meaning of it. It was your major submarine base, I believe, on the Black Sea. And it has obviously been a major defense facility. And you had an agreement with Crimea to have troops there—it was a base that was agreed to. I don't know exactly when the treaty was made. How, when this was going down, obviously this is important in your mind—if the United States or NATO troops are able to take over this base, what are the consequences of that?

VP: I was thinking that this never was supposed to happen. Well, there is the subjunctive mood as we say, but there can be no subjunctive mood in politics—the "what if."

OS: Hypothetical.

VP: And this treaty with Ukraine was supposed to be enforced until 2019. And after that it was supposed to be prolonged even further, I don't remember—another 20 years probably. But in response to that we reduced the price of Russian natural gas for Ukraine. We gave them a large discount. And I'd like to draw attention to the fact that even though Crimea is right now part of the Russian Federation, this gas discount for Ukraine has not been withdrawn.

OS: Right. The consequences of a US seizure of the base or a NATO base?

VP: Those consequences would have been very grave, because, well this base per-se doesn't mean anything—no significance, but if they had tried to station either ABM systems or offensive systems in those territories, that would no doubt have aggravated this situation in the whole of Europe. Incidentally, that is what is happening in Eastern European countries. I already talked about that. I just wanted to tell you about one nuance—why we are responding so acutely to the expansion of NATO? Well, as a matter of fact, we understand the value—or lack thereof—and the threat of this organization. I know this organization is a loose one and it's not viable, even despite Article 5 of the treaty. What we're concerned about is the practice of how decisions are made there. I know how decisions are made there. And the experience of previous years of work has given me full information as to how decisions are made. When a country becomes a member of NATO, bilateral talks are held on this country and it's quite easy to deal with this country on a bilateral basis, including on the placement of weapons systems that are threatening to our security. Once a country becomes a member of NATO, it is hard to resist the pressure of such a large presence as the United States, and any weapons system can be stationed in this country all of a sudden. An ABM system, new military bases, and if need be, new offensive systems. And what are we supposed to do in that case? In this case we have to take countermeasures, and that means that we have to aim our missile systems at facilities which, in our view, are becoming a threat to us. And the situation becomes more tense. And who needs that, and why?

OS: You said that the base in Crimea didn't mean anything in itself. Does that mean to say that you would have built another naval base on the Black Sea elsewhere?

VP: We already built such a military base.

OS: Oh, where's that?

VP: In the city of Novorossiysk. And it's more modern, more sophisticated than the last one.

OS: Interesting. What province or region?

VP: It's the Krasnodar region between Sochi and the Crimea.

OS: I see, good to know.

VP: So it's also the Black Sea coast. Right. Thank you very much.

Trip 1—Day 3—July 4, 2015

OS: You should wish me a Happy Fourth of July, being an American.

VP: And I congratulate you.

OS: It's our Independence Day, so to speak.

VP: Yes, I know that.

ON WAR

OS: I'd like to talk about war for a few minutes.

VP: Yes, sure.

OS: Not Cold War, but Hot War. Yesterday you talked about Russia rebuilding its military infrastructure and refreshing its nuclear facilities and adding to it. I think you're building 40 ICBMs, I believe—they're TOPOLs.

VP: We are changing them, substituting them. Introducing new missiles which replace the obsolescent ones—the ones whose term of use are expiring.

OS: And new anti-ballistic S-300s and S-400s and you're working on S-500s too.

VP: Yes, but these are different weapons systems. These are air defense weapons systems.

OS: And other things? I'm also told that most of Russia will be protected by these anti-ballistic missiles from exterior attack. It'll be a missile shield around Russia in 2017, if you stay on target.

VP: Yes, on the whole that's correct.

OS: So, let's talk about the possibility of—the "madman" possibility of war, where the US and Russia go at it.

VP: We are covering almost all of the Russian territory, and along the perimeter of all of its borders.

OS: So, in a Hot War is the US dominant—yes or no?

VP: No.

OS: So it would be a case of Russia surviving it?

VP: I think that no one would survive such a conflict.

OS: Even with the missile shield?

VP: As of now the shield of missiles wouldn't protect the territory of the United States. Just remember the current State Secretary John Kerry once spoke against the so-called Star Wars program which was put forward by Ronald Reagan.[70]

OS: Right.

VP: And why was he speaking against it? You can ask him. Back then, this attempt at protecting so large a territory as the United States from potential military strikes was impossible. And today, despite the modern weaponry, despite the new generation of technologies—information technologies, space technologies, radars, and interception means, information systems—despite all that, I think that as of now, and in the midterm, strategic anti-ballistic missiles will not be efficient enough. And I think there is an element of threat to that. And the threat consists of the fact that there might be the illusion of being protected. And this might lead to more aggressive behavior. And in that sense, we believe that there are more problems than advantages with that, apart from everything else. We are developing systems capable of surmounting these anti-ballistic missile defense systems. And these systems, they bring down the possibilities of antiballistic missile protection even further. And that's why this attempt at unilaterally creating a protective shield, as I believe, is both inefficient and dangerous. And besides, this ABM system is not just a protective system, it is an element of strategic forces which can only be efficient if it works together with offensive weapons systems. And that's why the philosophy behind the use is quite simple—especially given the fact that there are now precision-guided munitions. First you have to make the first strike against the command and control system, then you make a strike at strategic facilities. You protect your own territory as far as it's possible. You can even combine weapons, both strategic and ballistic weapons systems and use other weapons systems. You also use cruise missiles. This all increases the defense capabilities of a country. But at the same time it is no guarantee of security.

OS: Can I ask you also just briefly—space warfare. I know the United States has been working very hard to develop space as a weapon.

VP: Yes, certainly. We know about that as well. That's why it is so important to prevent unilateral actions. That's why we proposed that we should work jointly on the ABM system. What would that mean? That would mean that we would establish the missile dangers and where they emanated from. We would have equitable access to the control system of these systems. And we would also search jointly for solutions to other operational issues related to technological development. I believe such an approach of working together in order to find solutions to these existing challenges and threats would create a far more stable condition, and the world would be a safer place.

OS: This was originally proposed, you know, by John Kennedy with Nikita Khrushchev in 1963.[71]

VP: If you are getting back to the past now, let me remind you from whence the Cuban Missile Crisis started. I'm not an admirer of Khrushchev, but placing Soviet missiles on Cuba was prompted by the stationing of American missiles in Turkey, from the territory of which those missiles could easily reach the Soviet Union. And that's why Khrushchev responded by stationing missiles in Cuba. Cuba was not the one who initiated the Cuban missile crisis.[72]

OS: No, I know. It was a crazy time. Stanley Kubrick, a filmmaker I much admire, made a wonderful film called *Dr. Strangelove: Or How I Learned to Stop Worrying and Love the Bomb*.[73] Have you seen it?

VP: No.

OS: Oh, you must see it. Really, it's well worth it—a classic. Because Mr. Kennedy was dealing with the military's system that had been growing and growing since World War II and the generals, at that point, knew that the Soviet Union did not have the capacity to match them. And many of them said, "This is a time to hit the Soviet Union." So there was a desire for a unilateral strike against Russia.[74] Kennedy said, "You're crazy," and then as other situations developed in Berlin and Cuba it became more dangerous. But honestly, there was a desire to strike first. I fear that still in the United States. I fear the neo-conservative element as being so hungry, pro-war, to make their point, to win their case, that it's dangerous.

VP: And I fear them too.

OS: Knowing that the United States is in this Cold War mode, would you, therefore, at any point in the near future go to war for Ukraine?

VP: I think that would be the worst-case scenario.

OS: If the United States pushed more weapons onto Ukraine, and the Ukrainian government became more and more aggressive in Donbass, it is inevitable that if the Russians decide to fight for the Donbass region, there would be a conflict.

VP: I don't think that anything is going to change. Well, I told our American partners about that. There would be more victims. But the result, the outcome will be the same as it is today. Conflict of such kind—conflicts like Donbass—cannot be resolved via weapons. Direct talks will be required. Why wait, one way or another? And the sooner our friends in Kiev understand that the better it would be. But the western countries—Europe and the United States—have to help the Kiev authorities to understand this reality.

OS: Yes, let's hope so. If you look at the candidates who are running for office in 2016 in the United States, if you look at the Republican side—every one of them made Russian statements—aggressive statements.

VP: That's the logic of internal political strife within the United States.

OS: Well, the United States has become more right wing since the Ronald Reagan era. And now we have Hillary Clinton on the left—the supposed left—she's the Democratic challenger, probably will be, making very aggressive statements also about Ukraine and comparing you to Hitler.[75]

VP: Nothing new to us, in this situation. We are personally acquainted, she is a very dynamic woman. Well, we could make also such a comparison, but due to the level of our political culture, we try to abstain from extreme statements.

OS: Yes, you could make those statements, but you don't. You have maturity, and you've suffered for war. But the United States has never really had a war on its own homeland. And to many people, who are very important people, war is somewhat of a game.

During the Missile Crisis, the head of the Air Force, Curtis LeMay, who had led the firebombing of Tokyo and been in charge of dropping the atomic bomb on Hiroshima and Nagasaki, called on Kennedy to wipe out the Soviet Union. "Now," he said, "before they get too strong."[76]

VP: Yes, we know about that. And we knew about that back then.

OS: Well, I hope you understand that the American temperament is volatile at times and cowboy-ish, and it might come to a situation where they might call for your resignation personally because they will personalize it.

VP: [laughter] Well, they've already done that—they've already personalized it. But unfortunately for them, to them who want that, Russia is a country that is guided by the will of its own people—not directions coming from outside.

OS: Right.

VP: And that's our advantage.

OS: I know how you're going to answer this, but I'm going to ask it anyway. If you were the difference—if you were able to resign and pacify these people in the United States, and it would prevent a nuclear war, would you resign?

VP: I don't think that anyone would push for nuclear war, and people with extreme views in the United States, they should remain calm whoever is chosen as the head of the Russian people. They should be guided by the profound interests of their own people—the American people. And I think the fundamental interests of the American people are consistent with having good relations with Russia.

OS: So do I, but the corporate media is calling for Cold War and it's been very anti-Russian.

VP: The problem is not with persons or personalities. The problem consists in the fact that the current American leadership would not suffer any other opinion than their own. They do not need countries who have sovereignty. Our partners are not willing to be engaged in a dialogue on equal footing. And so removing any leader in Russia is not going to lead to the pacification or to the improvement of bilateral relations without the willingness of one of the parties, including the United States, to see their partners as equal partners.

OS: We're going to walk inside?

VP: Yes, we can. But I don't think there is anything interesting to see inside. But we have no secrets there, so I can show it to you. What would you like to see? It's my gym inside.

OS: Sure. I hear you work out almost every day or five times a week.

VP: Every day.

OS: Seven days? No.

VP: Yes.

OS: That's too much. I like ping-pong.

VP: You want to play?

OS: Yeah, if you want. You're very competitive, huh?

VP: Yeah, but I don't know how to play. Unlike you.

OS: Well, first I have to get used to the table.

[playing ping-pong through the following exchange]

OS: I didn't sleep enough. The ball is too heavy.

VP: Well, that's exactly the case.

OS: What if I win?

VP: Friendship is going to win.

[playing stops]

OS: There's the gym. Beautiful. No treadmill? All ellipticals. Do you do all of them variously?

VP: Yes, all of them. Do you like it?

OS: Yes, I would come here more often. Do you have a trainer?

VP: No, I'm my own trainer.

OS: Well, you will live a long time if you keep doing this.

VP: Well, only God knows how long I'll live.

OS: Yeah. It's beautiful. Swim first, then gym? Then you relax the muscles. It's a beautiful gym. Do you think when you swim, do you get ideas? From the unconscious, do you find it to be meditative?

VP: No, just absurd things come into my mind when I swim.

OS: You don't believe much in dreams. This is for badminton or what?

VP: For tennis.

OS: I play paddle tennis. You don't play tennis?

VP: No. This statue is the founder of Judo. Do you like it?

OS: Very much. Beautiful, well done. Every day, though? That's tough.

VP: I'm just accustomed to it.

OS: Do you watch television news while you're doing it?

VP: No, I don't.

VP: Do you like horses?

OS: Yes, I used to have a big place in Colorado that had horses.

VP: How many?

OS: Eight or nine horses and about a thousand acres. Beautiful riding. I used to ride, gallop, and all that. I was very free.

VP: And what kind of horses did you have?

OS: I bought them at auction in Colorado—you know, no Arabians, no big deal, just riding horses. Western saddle.

VP: You see the horses?

OS: Yes, Arabian horses?

VP: Yes, mostly.

ON RELIGION

VP: Do you want to see our church?

OS: Yes. When you come here, where do you sit, if you sit? Are there any chairs? Do you sit down?

VP: No, there are no chairs in a Russian Orthodox Church. The mass is served while you stand.

OS: I see.

VP: It's the traditions of the Russian Orthodox Church.

OS: People don't pray kneeling, they pray standing.

VP: Well, you kneel, but you don't sit on anything while you pray. Do you know where this icon comes from? I brought it from the United States. The patriarch of the Russian Church abroad presented it to me while I was staying in the United States.

OS: Was this one of your major problems with communism, that it was atheistic? You didn't feel that it appealed to the people?

VP: Well, I think that happened at a certain moment when I understood it. You see, it's St. Elizabeth. She was the wife of the Governor General of St. Petersburg, and when he died at the hands of terrorists, she founded a monastery. And then she took her vows. After the 1917 revolution, the Bolsheviks executed her, and the Russian Orthodox Church abroad announced her as a saint. When I was staying in the United States, I was presented with this icon from the patriarch of the Russian Orthodox Church abroad. And I brought this icon here, to my home. And all of a sudden I understood that she got back to her home, because it used to be her home in the past.

OS: I was talking about your adoption of Orthodox religion back in the Russian system. You've been a proponent of that.

VP: Well it's quite simple really. When I was a child my mother baptized me.

OS: Legally?

VP: Yes, well they tried not to speak about that publicly. But that was absolutely legal. She went to church and she asked to have me baptized.

OS: But bringing this back and making it frontal in Russian life has made you very popular with most of the population?

VP: I was not the one to do it, to make it this central element. It was done by the Russian people themselves.

OS: Okay, I understand. But there's been a renaissance.

VP: This renaissance is due to the fact that the communist ideology ceased to exist. And in reality there was some sort of an ideological vacuum. And this vacuum could be filled by nothing else but religion.

OS: Right. I see.

VP: You asked me about the baptism. I can tell you an interesting story. Recently I was talking to the patriarch of Russia and Moscow, Kirill. I asked him how he had come to this church. And he told me that his father was a priest. And I asked him where. And he told me in Leningrad. I asked him in what church he was serving. And he named the church. And I also asked him during what years he was a priest there. And he named the years. And it turns out that I was baptized exactly at that church during those years. I asked him, "What was the name of your father?" He said, "Nicolau." "And were there any other Nicolaus apart from your father at that church?" And he said, "No." "Do you know," I'm telling him that, "your father was the one to baptize me. Because my mother told me that the name of the priest who had baptized me was Nicolau."

OS: So this is your dacha, your ranch?

VP: This is the official state residence.

OS: And you come here on weekends?

VP: Well, I almost live here. Partly here and partly in the Kremlin.

OS: Oh, I see. So it's about 25 minutes, 20 minutes from Moscow?

VP: 20 minutes or so.

OS: For example, this weekend you have guests come over for the weekend?

VP: Right now?

OS: This weekend, for example?

ON FAMILY

VP: Right now my daughters are here. They are staying here and we agreed to have dinner together after our meeting with you.

OS: That's nice—not too early, I hope. The two daughters are married and they bring their husbands, so you meet your sons-in-law on the weekend?

VP: Yes, they have their own family life and we meet, of course.

OS: So are you a grandfather yet?

VP: Yes.

OS: Do you like your grandchildren?

VP: Yes.

OS: So are you a good grandfather? Do you play with them in the garden?

VP: Very seldom, unfortunately.

OS: Very seldom. Do the sons-in-law argue with you? Do they have different opinions, do they give you sort of gossip?

VP: Well, sometimes their opinions are different, but we're not arguing—we're having a discussion, so to speak.

OS: Daughters too?

VP: Yes, them too.

OS: That's nice.

VP: But my daughters are not into politics and they're not into large business. They are into science and education.

OS: They both studied to be professionals.

VP: Yes, they graduated from university. They are now writing their theses.

OS: You're a very lucky man. Two good children.

VP: Yes, I'm proud of them.

ON CHINA

OS: You've talked much about the multipolar world and the importance of it. Balances of power. But you haven't said anything about China.

VP: China can speak for itself.

OS: But it is a very important regional power and world power, now.

VP: Yes, no doubt about it. It's a world power.

OS: Right. And naturally if the US is the dominant world power they are going to run into issues not only with Russia, but with China.

VP: I think it's always about global leadership—not arguments about some second rate regional issues. And the competition is primarily among the world powers. That's the law. The question is what are the rules by which this competition is developing. I would very much like common sense to accompany any competition like that.

OS: I know that Russia has grown closer to China. Your trade agreements. I don't know if you've had military agreements.

VP: Russia doesn't need any special agreements to get closer with China. Russia and China are neighbors. We have the longest joint border in the world, I believe. So it's quite natural that we should maintain good neighborly relations. So there is nothing strange about that. On the contrary, I think that's very good, both to the people of China and to the people of Russia. And to the whole world. We are not trying to build any military blocs.

OS: I understand.

VP: But our trade and economic ties are developing dynamically.

OS: But China has made it clear that it wants to avoid confrontation with the United States, as does Russia.

VP: Well, that's good. That's the right thing to do. We also want to avoid confrontation. We don't want any confrontation with the United States, because we have our issues to attend to.

OS: I understand, but Ukraine has brought you into a direct, potential conflict.

VP: The problem is, we were not the ones to initiate that conflict. We are not responsible for organizing or supporting a coup d'état. And we're not the ones to blame for the fact that part of the Ukrainian people didn't agree with that.

OS: Could the US have a strategy here? A long-term strategy saying, "We know China is going to be this economic global power, we know Russia is— can we start to attack this problem by dismantling Russia?"

VP: I don't know anything about that. You'd have to ask them. I wouldn't want to think that is the case. But that would be the wrong way. The right way is to build equal relationships and to achieve mutual respect. Russia doesn't need any expansion. We have an enormous territory—the largest one in the world. We have vast natural resources. We have wonderful people. We've got a profound system for developing and renovating our own country—any conflict just diverts us from this strategic goal.

OS: I totally agree, I'm just looking at the alternatives, which is that China is building up its nuclear capacity.

VP: Yes, and China is going to continue to do that—that's quite logical.

OS: With Russian cooperation, or not?

VP: We are not cooperating in the nuclear military field. We are developing joint projects in peaceful nuclear energy. And solely for peaceful purposes. But we have a huge military/technical cooperation, but it has no nuclear elements to it.

OS: You recognize that China would not have guaranteed Snowden asylum?

VP: I cannot comment on that. You have to ask our Chinese friends.

OS: I notice they haven't let RT—the Russian television network—into China.

VP: Well, I don't know anything about that. I don't think that Russia Today is operating in the Chinese language—not yet. But I don't think that's a problem of our bilateral relations. It's just a matter for discussion, for negotiations.

OS: I saw the head of RT, Margarita Simonyan, and she was telling me that China would not let them in yet.

VP: And yet, negotiations have to take place—I believe this is a matter of business.

OS: Like the apricots from Greece? I heard the story when Alexis Tsipras was here, that you wouldn't give Greece some kind of import license for apricots?

VP: No, it's not that. We cannot make any exemptions for the countries of the European Union. But to all countries of the European Union we can offer cooperation and establish joint enterprises. And if these joint ventures are created in Russian territory, then they can partly import produce for their own purposes.

OS: Well, China has talked about wanting to create the Silk Road again through Eurasia. We know that Russia signed an oil and gas deal with China—a huge one. So there's a new business renaissance here in Eurasia, with Russia, China, and all the Eurasian countries.

VP: There is nothing new about that.

OS: I know.

VP: We've been long pursuing that purpose and the so-called sanctions introduced by the West, they simply pushed this process forward. Apart from what you know, we also have plans for developing the so-called Trans-Siberian Railroad, the Baikal Railroad, and it all corresponds well to the Chinese plans of reviving the Silk Road. So, on the whole, we have very harmonious relations which are complimentary to each other.

OS: Yes.

VP: Let's have a look at the horses.

[walking into the stables]

OS: Ah, beautiful—nicely done.

VP: You like it?

OS: Well, so far, yeah. That's a beauty—wow. What is this, a race horse?

VP: I'll have to ask.

OS: Wow. Looks like a thoroughbred. Is he one? Looks like he's fast.

VP: Yes, he's very fast.

OS: You ride them all?

VP: Seldom, unfortunately.

OS: Well, if they throw you, these are big horses.

VP: Yes, once I fell and flew over the head of the horse.

OS: Yeah, that's dangerous. I must've fallen off five or six times. Many concussions. And here's a tiny one.

ON BIN LADEN

OS: Did you read the article recently—there was a big break by the investigative reporter Sy Hersh in London, he's an American reporter, on the bin Laden raid?[77]

VP: No.

OS: It's an amazing story and makes sense to me.

VP: What does it say?

OS: It says that Pakistan's ISI—their intelligence agency—made the raid possible by opening its airspace and letting the US in to basically take the man or kill him, as long, of course, as the Americans didn't divulge this. As you know it was staged as a big heroic action, but it was essentially a mercy kill. There was no resistance in Pakistani airspace—none at all. Whereas they are in a state of alert for war against India. And he presents numerous other pieces of evidence of what really happened on that night.

VP: Where can we sit?

OP: Over there—it's pretty. Back to what I was saying about the bin Laden raid, what do you think?

VP: I don't know anything about that.

OS: Is it possible?

VP: Yes, I think it's possible. Well, if they're partners, why wouldn't the Pakistani intelligence and the American intelligence agree on that? That was quite possible. But I cannot comment on that because I don't know anything about that.

OS: And that he was there since 2006 and then he was basically a pariah and he was no longer really running anything. He was a guest of Pakistan.

VP: Well, that's possible.

OS: And we knew about it for a while. But we didn't really verify it until 2012 and then we took him very easily.

ON POWER

OS: Okay, you said you're a global power—Russia is a global power. You did not say a regional power.

VP: Do you think there is a strict definition? Well there are certain issues which cannot be solved without Russia. And in that sense Russia is a world power. So, international nuclear security cannot be guaranteed without Russia. Nor is it possible to globally solve energy-related issues. And in that regard, Russia is also a world power. Russia is a permanent member of the United Nations Security Council. And just as all the other permanent members, it has veto power, which means that a whole number of the key issues of the international agenda cannot be solved without Russia. But we understand full well that after the collapse of the Soviet Union, we lost 40 percent of our production capacities[78] and the Soviet legacy was a semi-ruined and outdated economic management system, as well as technologies which were outdated. But at the same time, it gave us certain chances of making resolute steps to revive our economy and our social sphere. And that's why we are not exaggerating our importance. Nor are we trying to get some status of a superpower. We don't need that. Because the superpower status means a certain burden—primarily a financial and economic burden. And why would we need that? We don't need that at all.

ON DEMOCRACY AND FREEDOM

OS: You've said several times in the last two days that Russia is a democracy. Your critics in America—and there are many—would say that Russia is not a democracy, Russia is a traditional authoritarian state. And the parliament does not make major decisions. It has limited access to television for the opposition parties and that your party dominates the media. The registration process is difficult for these opposition parties. That there's a lack of judicial independence—although that's an old problem in Russia, I gather. That you're opposed to gay rights in Russia. These are the criticisms that are often launched at you. I'd love you to take a chance here and respond to that.

VP: To start with, as to the technocratic character of the Russian state, just have a look—for almost one thousand years our country was being constructed as a monarchy. And then the so-called 1917 Revolution occurred, communists arrived in power, and Stalin found himself at the helm of the state. Certainly, very much a legacy passed down from the Empire to Soviet times even though the plaque on the surface changed. Only at the beginning of the 1990s, events came to pass which laid the foundation for a new stage of Russian development. Certainly, you cannot imagine that we can instantaneously get the same model, the same structures, as in the United States, in Germany, in France. That's impossible to start with, and secondly, that's not required. Society, just as every living organism, has to develop stage-by-stage, gradually. That's the normal development process. When talking about the one party system, I'd like to remind you that the Soviet constitution had a provision saying that the Communist Party had absolute leadership. That was something stipulated in the Constitution. So the only political force was the Communist Party. But, there is nothing like it in the Russia of today. We have a multi-party system. And today, parliament comprises four parties—there are representatives of four parties in the parliament.[79] As to the opposition parties, they are always discontent. And can I ask you how many parties are represented in the US Congress? If my memory serves me correctly, just two. You understand that no one concludes from that there is less democracy in the United States than in Russia—because in Russia there are four parties in the parliament, whereas there are only two in the United States. The American Constitution is fashioned in such a manner that the head of state is elected in two stages. There are electors choosing him or her. And the Constitution is constructed in such a manner that a candidate can arrive in power for whom more electors voted. But those electors might represent the minority of voters. And twice in the history of the United States it occurred.[80] Does this mean that the United States is not a democratic country? I don't think so. But the problem is evident. And we also have problems of our own, but we're developing.

You asked about access to the media. Certainly, the ruling party is trying to create prerogatives for itself. Do you know, or does any of your audience know, that when the head of state is elected where parliamentary elections are held, the ruling party always has an advantage of two to three percent. And why is that? Because all across the world they are using this administrative resource, their power, to secure an advantage. And that's the case all across the world, and it's just like that in Russia. We have hundreds of TV and radio companies and the state doesn't control them in any fashion. Because that's impossible. But the problem with the opposition forces is not just about fighting the power, the government, they're trying to demonstrate to the voters that the program they are putting forward is more advantageous, is better, from the point of view of the interests of the voters. Incidentally, in Russia, the head of state is elected through direct elections—unlike in the United States. Now, regarding the multi-party system and the possibility of registration, just recently we radically liberalized the situation in this domain. And right now the possibility of registering one's organization, one's party is so simple that voters are faced with another difficulty—it's very hard to find what their preferences are. There are so many choices. But I don't see any problems here from the point of view of democratic institutions. But all that is a living organism and the country is moving forward.

Now concerning the rights of sexual minorities. During the Soviet times, there was a criminal responsibility for homosexuals, and right now there is none. We eliminated that part of the criminal code back in the 1990s.[81] Whereas the United States has four states, I believe, that have criminal responsibility, and those laws say that homosexuals are criminals. In Texas and in three other states probably. And recently the Supreme Court of the United States adopted the decision saying that LGBTs should not be prosecuted criminally.[82] But I don't know yet what it's going to lead to, because this area of regulation, as far as I understand, is within the purview of each and every state. So I don't know how these judicial procedures are going to play out in the end. Why did such a surge of criticism against Russia arise? It was because the parliament adopted a law which prohibited the propaganda of homosexuals among minors.[83] But there is no discrimination against people—either on the basis of their religion, or sex. And the LGBT community here have grand careers, they are awarded state awards for their merits. There is no discrimination against them whatsoever. The purpose of this law is the following. This law seeks to protect children who have to grow up, to mature, and only afterwards make a decision of their own on their sexual orientation. We are just telling them to leave children alone. Let children grow up, become grown up persons—there is no discrimination on this basis. So I was very much surprised to hear criticism from the United States, because some legislation in the United States provides criminal responsibility for homosexuals.[84] I think this is just one of the instruments for attacking Russia, trying to showcase Russia as being different from the others, which would mean that some other instruments and pressure would have to be applied against it. And the question is why. And the answer is simple and I already told you the answer. That is done so that on other issues which have no relation whatsoever, either to democracy or to the rights of the LGBT community, or to the media, so that in other issues related to geopolitics and politics, they want Russia to be more malleable. But that is an encroachment and they are not using the right means. There is only one way to achieve balanced decisions, and that's dialogue on equal footing with due regard for mutual interests. And these are not just hollow words—not just hollow phrases. Behind these words are the interests of the government, the state and of the people. Behind them lies the solution to economic issues, to security issues, and personal issues. The citizens of the Russian Federation are interested in that.

OS: You mentioned the parliament passed a law, but has parliament ever passed anything of major consequence against you in recent memory, against your administration.

VP: If I am against this or that law I can just not sign it and then it is regarded as rejected. But as to this law, I have to tell you this was not an initiative of mine, it was an initiative of—

OS: Can you point to an issue where the parliament disagreed with you on a major issue?

VP: You know, we sometimes, quite often have situations when we are required to have very thorough negotiations with different factions of the parliament. And these consultations often prove difficult. And these difficult consultations are certainly those related to social and economic matters. Right now we are at the stage where we're working actively on next year's budget. And there are many options, many forks.

ON THE ARCTIC

OS: Okay, they're pushing us for time so quick answers if possible. The Arctic—I'm hearing rumors that this is the next race between the US and Russia.

VP: There are three major issues related to the Arctic. I'm no military specialist, but I don't think that I'm going to divulge some secret if I say that this territory, the North Pole, has the trajectories of ballistic missiles going over—both the US missiles and Russian missiles. Let me remind you that the so-called flight assignments of both American missiles and Russian missiles are aimed at each others sites, which is regrettable. And these trajectories are right over the Arctic. And considering the deployment of the ABM system by Americans, including the Aegis systems and their military vessels, and in the North Sea, we're certainly contemplating ways to protect our territory. The Arctic is of great strategic importance because it helps us to secure our defense capabilities, which secure the country.

OS: It's not about oil or anything like that?

VP: No, absolutely not. Secondly, mineral resources. And we've started to extract hydrocarbons in the Arctic seas—a couple of years ago we started it. And there might be many discussions, but I think that all these arguments, controversies can and should be resolved within the framework of the existing international law. The international law of the seas. We had long discussions with Norway on certain parts of the border. And we managed to arrive at an agreement on all the controversial issues. And there is the third element—the transport element. Given the fact of global warming, the period of time each year when this part of the planet can be used for navigation purposes is becoming longer. In the past, we can only use two or three weeks for vessels to go through the North Sea. Right now, these routes can be used for several months. And it decreases significantly the costs of supplies from Europe to Asia, from Asia to Europe, and even to the United States. And that's another reason why this region is becoming so important. Very interesting. There are certainly other considerations, but these are the three main elements I believe. That's why many countries of the world—not just the Artic countries—are showing interest in this region. We have the Artic council, we've fostered a toolkit for cooperation. I believe all these instruments are going to be employed, and we're going to seek mutual understanding on all of these most important issues.

ON MUSLIMS

OS: Your Muslim population in Moscow—I was shocked to read that you have the largest Muslim population in Europe—larger than any other city.

VP: Not entirely true. Muslims make up 10 to 12 percent of the whole population of Russia. In France I think the percentage is the same.[85]

OS: Okay, well France is fairly thickly-populated, but you've mentioned in the past the Russian ethnic population is diminishing.

VP: You know, fortunately we've managed to reverse this trend. And it's the third consecutive year that we are witnessing a natural increase in the population, including in the regions which are traditionally populated by ethnic Russians.[86] As to the inter-ethnic relations, this has always been a delicate issue—whenever, wherever. But Russia has certain advantages in this regard. Take Europe and the United States of today and you'll see that people with other religions are mostly immigrants. Russia is different. Those people with other religions are Russians. And it is their homeland and they have none other. From the very beginning, Russia was emerging as a multi-religious and multi-ethnic country. And over a thousand years, we've nurtured a certain culture of interaction. Even Christianity in Russia is called Eastern Christianity. And it has many elements which might be reminiscent of Islam. We have very good relations, there's been an inter-penetration between religion and culture. And those places where mixed population live—Christians and Muslims—there are many situations when people side-by-side celebrate both Muslim feast days and Christian holidays. And I think that based on these huge positive experiences, we will be able to surmount quite easily all those things, sensitive delicate issues of inter-ethnic and inter-religious interactions. Nevertheless, we should still pay close attention to these issues on a permanent basis.

ON KYOTO PROTOCOL

OS: Are you for the Kyoto Protocol and will you sign it?

VP: We signed the Kyoto Protocol. The United States was against it[87] and it was difficult to reach an agreement with our Chinese friends—with India as well there were some difficulties. But Russia supported the Kyoto Protocol from the very beginning and we signed it. Certainly we are in talks. I mean, our territory covered by forests is the lungs of our planet. And we are not just making emissions, we are absorbing emissions and all that should be taken into account when a final decision on the issue is discussed.

OS: Are you going to the next meeting in Paris in December?

VP: I don't know that. I have not yet made a decision that Russia is going to be represented there at a high level.

OS: Fernando, my producer, thinks you should go and represent Russia at a high level.

ON BEING ANTI-AMERICAN

OS: In closing, I'm just going to say—you've said twice that I'm anti-American and that you don't want to be dragged into it. I want to explain—I love my country. I love America. I grew up there. It's like my mother. You have disagreements with your mother, sometimes, but you love her. Sometimes you love your mother and sometimes you hate her. It's like your homeland. And I have disagreements with my country.

VP: You see, you can allow yourself, you can afford and you have the right to give this or that assessment to the actions of your country's leadership as you deem fit because you're an American. And you can even give harsh assessments. Whereas we are fostering partnership relations, not just with your country, but with your government as well. That's why we have to behave very cautiously. And however great the differences are, we have to stick to certain rules. Otherwise international relations cannot be built.

OS: I understand—that's very clear. Lastly, I am not anti-American, I am not pro-Russian, I am pro-peace. It's very important to me, in my lifetime I would like to see peace and I'm scared right now. I'm worried for the world, because I'm worried about my country's attitude towards peace. And it doesn't seem to understand the stakes that it has raised. That's the point I'm trying to make in my documentary here.

VP: And you're a man of peace. It's easy for you. And I'm pro-Russian. And it's more difficult for me.

OS: And I thank you for illustrating for us in these last days the stakes.

Trip 2—Day 1—February 19, 2016

———

OS: How are you, Mr. President? Nice to see you. I thought maybe you could sit over there and I'll sit here and we'll play it by ear a bit. That's an old American expression—do you know it? "Play it by ear?" Playing an instrument without sheet music—improvising, like jazz.

VP: No, I don't. Well, there's a whole gang of people here—so many.

OS: You had a tough day. It's been a while—nice to see you. I think last June was the last time I saw you.

VP: Yes, it was in June.

OS: Did you miss me? [laughter]

VP: Yes, I cried every now and then, but finally we're here.

OS: I'm sure you've cried about other things. I fell asleep upstairs while we were waiting—caught up on my jet lag.

VP: Well, I envy you.

OS: How was your day?

VP: Well—in work. I met my colleagues, I talked about domestic policies and security. Economic issues—talked on many occasions with the minister for finance. I also talked to my assistant on economic matters. So that's about it. That was my day. I met the speaker of the parliament, defense minister, also minister for the interior.

OS: Holy cow. Well, you didn't have a cabinet meeting then?

VP: No, not today.

ON WORK MANAGEMENT AND NATIONAL SECURITY

OS: I'm told there was a National Security Council-type meeting.

VP: Exactly, many years ago I put into place a small group of people comprising the heads of security services and also other special services and ministries. And we call it the meeting of the Security Council of Russia.

OS: I see. A crisis or anything?

VP: No, it's a regular meeting. It happens once a week.

OS: Well, I would just ask you because we were normally scheduled for 3 p.m. and now it's . . . six hours and 40 minutes later.

VP: Well, I knew that you had to have some rest and have some soup.

OS: [laughter] I'm saying there must be crises that come up—there are things that aren't scheduled.

VP: No, there is no crisis. It's just regular work, routine work. But one thing entails another thing. It's like a chain. And when you plan a meeting for 10 minutes and he asks you one question after another and then 10 minutes turns into an hour. And it's very difficult to put an end to this chain of events.

OS: Well, it seems then that you're a man of details.

VP: Yes, I try to be. I don't even read some summaries of reports of my intelligence services or special services. I don't read summaries.

OS: You read the actual report?

VP: Yes, the reports themselves.

OS: That goes to my bigger question, because my producer who's here, Fernando, we were talking earlier and he said you are an excellent CEO—chief executive officer—of a company. Russia is your company.

VP: Maybe. The process of coordinating. It all starts with finding, detecting some problem areas, questions that need answering. And then we get down to finding ways to address these issues.

OS: You're a great CEO. You kick the tires, you deal with these problems and you're trying to solve them on the spot.

VP: Yes, I think that's the case.

OS: Well, sometimes the argument is—I mean I'm talking about work management because it's an interesting question to everybody. Let's say the problem is this, you go into the details and the details sometimes get smaller. And you look at the micro detail. And each micro detail has another micro detail and before you know it you've lost the forest for the trees, as they say.

VP: No, I try not to get to that point. I try not to stop halfway, if I see that we are moving in the right direction. In other words, I am not trying to go into too many details—I'm not too meticulous. I try to respond to the existing issues, to the existing problems, but I do it on the spot. It's a living process.

OS: That can be very irritating. You can probably go to bed at night not having solved some of these things and it really drives you nuts.

VP: Yes, sometimes that happens.

OS: Terrible.

VP: But that's very interesting.

OS: Interesting in what way? It goes into your subconscious and you sleep on it?

VP: I meant that the process itself is interesting. It's not about having some issues unresolved. It's about the very process of addressing these issues. I try to make it more creative. Just imagine a painter is painting a picture and then he has dinner. And he just quits his picture and goes to dinner. But that's not how it happens. The painter tries to complete something and only after that he's ready to have some rest. I'm not comparing myself to . . . .

OS: Well, for example, just using an old fashioned example, if you have a tractor factory. One problem is you don't make enough tractors. That could be one problem and there's ways to solve that. Do you throw more men at it? Modernize the equipment in a certain way? How do you go about making more tractors? Number two, is the management of the factory wrong? Is there a problem with the manager? Do you have to see the manager for yourself to know, or do you trust the associate of an associate of an associate to tell you. And number three—do we need tractors? Should we rethink this thing? These kinds of questions are not solvable right away.

VP: Yes, certainly. Well, it's especially about the market. If the project is required, that's one matter. If you need modernized products then it's another matter entirely. But anyway we always have to seek modernization to be more efficient.

OS: Right, but sometimes it's hard to identify the problem. It's a messy thing and it doesn't solve right away. It could be a problem of personnel or could be a problem of technique or problem of "am I doing the right thing in the first place?" You know—it's messy.

VP: Yes, I agree. And one always has to give it some thought. And then you have to think a lot about dealing with the issue you are faced with—what are the instruments, what are the tools you need to do that?

OS: Which brings us to the larger problem which is you've been doing this as a president, prime minister, now president again for 15 years. 15 years. I'm sure you know the story of Ronald Reagan—one of the most admired presidents by conservatives in my country. He was famous for sticking to his schedule, which required him on most nights to come home to the White House by 6 o'clock and have an early supper and watch TV with his wife. And he managed to do that for eight years.

VP: Here's a happy man. Very well organized, disciplined, and no doubt that was a great achievement of his—to his advantage.

OS: That is my point. He was a smiling man. He was a great greeter and meeter and he was wonderful—how do you say—he made people feel good and happy about themselves, in general.

And we laugh, but he presented a very good image for eight years and it worked. People didn't see through it—most people did not see through it until after he left the presidency. He was very happy eating jelly beans and telling a good joke.

VP: Well, you've said that I've been dealing with one issue for 15 years but that's not the case.

OS: I didn't say that—I said you've been doing this for 15 years.

VP: Yes, but these are different matters. It's one thing to be president, but it's entirely another thing to be the head of the government. The most difficult work, at least in Russia, has certainly been the Chairman of the Russian government because there I can pinpoint issues that need tackling. Much of this work is very closed to the public simply because it doesn't interest the public. But this work is of great importance to the economy of the country. And this work is routine and there is a great deal of this work.

OS: I understand, but Reagan was a big believer in delegating authority to everyone around him and he did that successfully—not always because he didn't know what was going on—but he was successful. I'm just trying to make that example because it's another way of living. If you have good associates that you trust.

VP: You need to address two issues. First you have to find the right people, and then you have to delegate authority to them. And that's the rule. That is something we have to aspire to.

OS: Well, it seems to me you're doing it the hard way.

VP: Well, probably. And yet I understand that and that is exactly what I'm aspiring to. There is a great deal of difference between us. Ronald Reagan was head of the United States. Be that as it may his difficulties are not compatible to the difficulties Russia was going through at the end of the 1990s and the beginning of the 2000s.

ON THE ECONOMY

OS: Well, Reagan would disagree he would say the country, America, was broke and that it needed to be fixed and it was morning in America again and it was his job to bring enthusiasm and positive energy to America. He did a pretty good job of creating that feeling—it's a feeling, an illusion.

VP: Almost being broke and being broke—these are two different things entirely.

OS: Well actually some people would argue that Reagan made America more broke because the debt grew enormously in America.

VP: Yes, certainly—today it's what, $18 trillion?[88] So there you go.

OS: Yes. And Russia's debt is?

VP: Russia's is 12 percent of the GDP.[89]

OS: So 18 trillion US and about 1 trillion Russia.[90]

VP: It's important to remember the share of the GDP. In the United States, the debt's share as compared to the GDP is 100 percent whereas in Russia it's 12 to 13 percent—around—I don't want to make a mistake but in Russia it's for sure 12 to 13 percent.

OS: There's no question about economics—we can go right there. The Russian economy. How is the Russian economy? It's rough, I know—you want to talk about it a bit?

VP: Certainly, there are difficulties. There are difficulties which consist first and foremost of the fact that you need higher oil prices. It is very difficult to push economic actors towards investing into new industries which are less profitable than the oil and gas industry. And that is what the structure of our economy depended upon—our efforts aimed at changing the structure through administrative and financial means. We're reaping some fruit, but not enough to change the structure itself. Right now the oil/gas price has fallen from more than 100 dollars to less than 30—and that is more than threefold. On the one hand it's difficult to get the budget revenue. But on the other hand it creates stimuli to develop manufacturing and agriculture. And that's what we're doing. In terms of prices, the lower price of oil hurts the purchasing power of the population. And it also reflects on certain industries such as machine-building, car-building, construction and a number of other industries. But at the same time it drives economic players toward investing in other industries and that's what we're trying to support. And that's why the first thing we're doing is trying to secure investment. We support certain industries that are going through difficult times such as construction, car-building. But separately, we're also trying to achieve the so-called import substitution.

OS: Import substitution—what's that?

VP: This strategy doesn't seek to eliminate imports. It seeks to create the manufacturing of high technology products inside the country. In the past we could buy anything using the oil money. But that was undermining the stimulus for internal development. And right now the government is trying to support high technology industries, to help both defense and civilian industries. And I have to say that we are achieving success in that regard. In agriculture, as a response to the actions of our partners, we have introduced certain restrictions and we have freed our internal market for Russian producers. But high technology industries, our partners have introduced restrictions on their exports. And thereby they stimulated us to create similar manufacturing processes within the country. I have to say that we are achieving success in this, despite a certain drop in the GDP. We have managed to achieve some good macro-economic indicators which are grounds for thinking that we are not just emerging from the crisis, but that we actually have good prospects for the future. Just have a look. Our budget deficit is just 2.4 percent. Even though we thought that it would be more than four percent. We have a surplus of trade and also a current account surplus. So we sell more than we purchase and the balance of payments of our budget is also very positive. At the same time, we have a considerably higher level of reserves than we did before. It's $360 billion. These are the reserves of the central bank. The government also has at its disposal two more reserve funds—$80 billion and another $70 billion. We have this to fund the small budget deficit that we have. And that's why we managed to maintain the very high quality of the Russian economy—its fundamentals are very good.[91] And what's more important, we now see some success and progress—the contribution of the agricultural sector of the economy is growing.

OS: You're paying, what is it, 83 percent of the Chechnyan budget?[92]

VP: It's not just about the Chechen Republic. Our financial and economic policy is aimed at evening out the standard of living and the income of all constituent entities of the Russian Federation and all the citizens of the Russian Federation wherever they live. Certainly we are not doing that to the fullest. There are certain regions where standards of living are higher, in other regions standards of living are lower. The level of manufacturing or of income is either higher or lower depending on the region, but from those regions that are capable of making a contribution to the federal budget, we're trying to redistribute incomes to those regions that are lacking their own income. We're trying to help them catch up, as far as their level of production is concerned.

OS: The food prices went up 20 percent in 2015. Inflation was running at 13 percent.

VP: 12.9 percent, to be more precise.

OS: [laughter] You've said that 2016 will be better, but what happened in January was that oil slumped below $30. It's a hard promise to keep that 2016 was going to get better.

VP: That's true, but there are two ways to go about it. One way is to fulfill all of the promises without thinking of the consequences, using the reserves that I've mentioned. But the second way is to seek the expansion of non-raw materials sectors of the economy and fulfill the social obligations we have using the generation capacity of our economy. I believe that we are following a balanced approach. We are trying to fulfil our social promises, our social obligations first and foremost. But in a manner that will not destroy the economy, should not undermine it. Meanwhile, we are trying to provide support to those industries that have been most affected by the crisis.

OS: Well, worker unrest is an issue. People haven't been paid in some regions. A great amount has been written about it in the West. People have not been paid—sometimes for one, two, three months.

VP: Well, there are these technical issues related to the arrears in payment—paying the salary, but it's minimum. There are no real problems with paying the salary. There are only issues related to irresponsibility, to negligence, to making decision too late, but economically and from the point of view of the budget, there are no problems whatsoever.[93] And if someone writes about that, saying that is a serious problem, then they are simply doing what's called wishful thinking.

OS: What is the Russian Central Bank about? What is that doing?

VP: The central bank is adhering to a very balanced monetary policy. And it meets the understanding of international financial organizations including the International Monetary Fund.

OS: How so? I was told there were no debts to the IMF.

VP: No debts—I'm not talking about our debt right now. I'm talking about our monetary policy. We are in contact with Madame Lagarde and our colleagues from the IMF. We inform them about what we're doing. We listen to their recommendations. And I know full well that the leadership of the IMF gives a good assessment to the policy of the Central Bank of Russia. Yes, their assessment is positive.[94] Also, because the central bank is taking balanced decisions on time related to the regulation of the national currency rate. And also related to the transition to a market approach to regulating the national currency exchange rate. As of now, the central bank has transitioned to a floating rate of ruble. It has led to depreciation of the ruble, which makes imports more expensive inside Russia. So that is not very good, not very comfortable for those who want to buy different products from abroad or China.

That's not really good for those companies, for those enterprises that try to modernize thanks to products imported from abroad. So that is the negative side of the ruble depreciation. But there is also a positive side, which creates apparent benefits in the internal market for Russian producers. It also creates a better environment for Russian exports both in agriculture and also in manufacturing.

And if you compare these advantages and disadvantages, you will see there are more advantages than disadvantages. And in this sense, the policy the central bank is pursuing can be viewed as a balanced one and as justified. Furthermore the Central Bank is closely monitoring the situation in the banking sector. It is working coherently to improve the banking system in Russia. That is very important, to make this banking and financial system more viable, more competitive.

OS: Well, you still talk as if the IMF is a partner of Russia's, and in some ways I know your struggles, but you act as if Wall Street wants Russia to succeed and I question that. And I would ask you: is Wall Street actively working to destroy the Russian economy in the interest of the United States?

VP: I'm not talking about Wall Street right now. But if we talk about the administration of the United States, then certainly the US administration has been viewing, especially recently, Russia as a rival. But we do hope nevertheless that such international institutions as the IMF, the World Bank, and a number of others are performing the functions they have been established to perform. And I refer to them having to have a positive influence on the world economy. Besides, we approach with some level of criticism all the recommendations that we receive. We do not have any obligation to these international organizations. And yet it is with respect that we view these recommendations and the ones that we believe are useful to us, we use.

OS: Who's "we?" That's a good question, because sometimes every government in the world, through history, the banks and the government can differ in their interpretation of events and what to do.

VP: When I say "we," I mean the Russian leadership. I personally did have some difficult relations with the IMF when I became Chairman of the Russian government at the end of 1999.

OS: That was a different time.

VP: Yes. The hostilities in the Caucasus started once again back then. And that was because there was an attack from the Chechen Republic against Dagestan by international gangs of terrorists. And I have to draw attention to the fact that we didn't attack anyone, that we suffered an attack.[95] And hostilities started once again. And at that moment there was the question of whether to stop paying interest on our loans with the IMF. Back then I was Chairman of the Russian government and the IMF were very clear—they said: stop the hostilities in the Caucasus and we'll accommodate you.[96] If you don't stop the hostilities, we're not going to compromise. Our response back then was: how can you ask the question in this manner? We've always heard that the IMF was above politics. That was the first argument I made. Secondly, I was telling them that we were defending ourselves, we didn't attack anyone—we suffered an attack. But my counterparts were intransigent because they had their instructions as far as I understand and they were simply formulating this. But it doesn't exclude the fact that after we paid back all our debts to the IMF, we still managed to maintain business-like relations. And we highly value these expert assessments that the IMF provides us with.

Incidentally, Russia not only paid back its debt to the IMF, we also paid back the debts of all the former Soviet republics, including Ukraine's debt, which was 16 billion US dollars.[97] We've always had very good relations with the World Bank. Personally, I have very good business and personal relations with the predecessor of the current head of the World Bank, Mr. Wilson. The World Bank has implemented a great number of very good, very useful projects including in some regions of the Russian Federation. Regrettably, right now these relations have been suspended. I do not see that we are too much interested in that, nor do I see that we cannot live without them. We do hope that these relations are going to be rebuilt and that we will be able to work together as fruitfully as we used to.

OS: Well, that was a different time, in the sense that was way before the Munich speech in 2007. In 2007, you said something to the effect that, "They—the United States—bring us to the abyss of one conflict after another. Political solutions are becoming impossible."[98] Which raises the broader question of: What is the US policy? What is its strategy in the world as a whole?

VP: Certainly, I am going to reply to this question very candidly, in great detail—but only once I retire.

OS: Well, I can state it for you and you can argue with me. I could say I think, or many people think, many learned people think the US strategy right now is to destroy the Russian economy, bring it to its feet, back to 1990's levels, and change the leadership of Russia—make a new ally out of Russia for the United States to basically dominate Russia as they once did. And perhaps they feel they did not go far enough and take your new arsenal away.

VP: This train of thought is quite possible. If that is the case, then I believe this is an erroneous policy. Exactly because such a view of relations with Russia is not oriented towards the future. People who believe like that, they do not see 25 to 50 years to the future. And if they had a look then they would probably go about building relations with Russia differently, in a different frame. And they wouldn't try to make Russia their vassal. They would try to make Russia their ally—or at least a partner—to address common issues and to surmount threats in which everyone is interested. And probably that would be more efficient than fruitless attempts at turning Russia into a satellite of theirs.

OS: Yes, absolutely. That's idealistic. But as you know, the United States needs enemies.

VP: Yes, maybe. I believe they need partners and allies more. Philosophy can be changed entirely. Certainly you can try to live and act in a different paradigm. Once a great compatriot of ours, Leo Tolstoy, said—I do not think I can reproduce the quote entirely—but, "There is the realm of possibility and the limit of what is unacceptable. Within this realm of possibilities, one has to build most secure relations—seek relations that are as little dangerous as possible. But that is the minimum of what is required." I only wish we could act in this paradigm, but certainly it would be far better to search for domains in which combining our capacities, our efforts, would yield the best results for everyone who could participate in this process. Let us take the following example—efforts in fighting poverty, protecting the environment, and in fighting the spread of WMDs, in combating terrorism . . . Regrettably, so far we have failed to secure efficient joint initiatives in these fields—almost all of them.

OS: Which brings us back to the realities, which are much more difficult. We have the US elections this year and none of these issues—the environment, fixing our alliances—has even been discussed one time. Everything in the election . . . Rhetoric has been "get tough and tougher." Build up our military again. And that goes for both sides, including Hillary Clinton, who's most definitely become a neo-conservative—a hawk. Strong policies against Russia. She was against Obama's nuclear deal in Iran, she was certainly for the Syrian intervention, and so forth. So there's very little hope for change in that direction. In addition to that, the Pentagon has announced recently—this new general has announced that Russia is the number one threat to the United States. He's been very forceful in those statements.[99]

VP: Yes, we know about that. And certainly we cannot welcome that. Contrariwise, we're always open to dialogue in almost every field. Just an example—even amid these conditions right now, knowing about this rhetoric in the run up to the elections, I know that our women's organizations have extended an invitation to Hillary Clinton to come to Russia. To pay a visit. I do not know whether she is going to accept this invitation or not. But during an election campaign, unfortunately it has become a fashion in the United States to speculate, to even abuse the Russian issue, so to speak. Afterwards, they tell us: "Please do not pay too much attention to that. You have to understand," they say to us, "this is just election campaign rhetoric. Afterwards we are going to arrive at a deal with you." But sacrificing intergovernmental, interstate relations in the name of current political processes is a great mistake, I believe.

OS: Yes I understand. And the administration of Obama may be reassuring you, but Obama himself, with the Pentagon, has escalated recklessly, recklessly, the NATO involvement on the borders of Russia. By the expenditure, they're spending—four times more has been spent in Eastern Europe in this year than before.[100] Not since Hitler's days has there been such a build-up on the borders of Russia, which is very surprising with Obama in office.

VP: That is true and that is a source of concern to us. But that is what I was talking about in Munich in 2007. Just recently, I have been told about the discussions that were going on before the reunification of Germany, and a German politician Aaron Barr—one of the leaders of the Democratic Party in Germany—expatiated his view of what the future of Europe would look like, in his conversations with the then-Soviet leadership. And I thought his train of thought was very interesting, his ideas fascinating. He was saying that NATO should not be extended eastward. He was talking about the need to establish a new military block in Central and Eastern Europe, a military alliance which comprised both the United States and Russia. A new bloc. And within the framework of this alliance, all countries in Central Europe and Eastern Europe would feel safe. But that alliance would also include the Soviet Union and the United States. And he was saying that if that didn't happen, that in the end Russia would be isolated. And that new dividing lines would appear in Europe. He was absolutely right, as history has demonstrated to us. The Soviet leadership have lost this historic chance, and that German politician once said a very interesting thing. He said, "It's very strange for me that so late and so old, I protect more the interests of the Soviet Union than the Soviet leadership themselves. But I'm doing that consciously so that in the future, a stable environment would appear for the development of Europe—without dividing lines and without conflict. And, moreover, he said, "If you don't listen to what I say, if you go on ceding your positions, then there is going to be no need for me to come to Moscow ever again. And I'm not going to come here ever again."

OS: Well, that sounds idealistic again—that was 1991, 25 years ago, and here we are. We're still in that position where the Pentagon, as I said, is putting something like $3.4 billion into NATO in Eastern Europe this year. Last year it was $789 million, so it's four times as much.[101] Which is going to force Russia to put heavy weapons and nuclear tactical weapons, again closer to the border of Poland and the Baltic states, and Ukraine I would imagine. So it's escalation—whatever you call it, it's escalation.

VP: Further escalation is already happening because the United States is deploying its antiballistic missile system in Eastern Europe and we on many occasions proposed real variants, real scenarios for cooperation.[102] And there was a moment when we thought that our American partners were really thinking about how to put into practice those proposals of ours. Personally, I talked about these proposals when I was visiting, I think it was the forty-first president of the United States. I was talking to George W. Bush in his house outside the city, and I elaborated on our proposals. The response was, "Yes that's very interesting," but afterwards it didn't lead to anything. The United States chose their own path, decided to unilaterally implement this program. Right now there are ABM systems in Romania and we hear they're going to appear in Poland and in the Mediterranean they're also going to be deployed. So it's a separate issue which no doubt is going to require a response from Russia.

OS: Do you think the United States knows—really knows and understands the power that Russia has in nuclear weapons?

VP: I don't think so. I believe our partners thought at one time that Russia would not be capable of responding to these challenges they're putting before us because of our economy, because of certain industries that we have—state industries—and due to the underfunding of scientific research. And due to a number of other considerations. But in my view, today everyone can see for themselves that Russia is not only capable of responding to this challenge, Russia is no doubt going to do that.

OS: Well, the United States is very smart. They have great technical help, great computers . . . How could they not understand the risks that they're taking? Or do they think that they could out-bluff Russia?

VP: I would like to reiterate that they had a perception saying that the defense industry of Russia was on the verge of collapse and some dignitaries in the United States were even saying that all the Russian nuclear missiles would soon turn to rust. That was what they were saying.

OS: That was then, what about now?

VP: Right now the program has already been launched. They say the program is very difficult to stop right now. To work together on such a sensitive matter, our partners, well they're simply not willing to do that—not ready to do that. Let me remind you what that signifies. Working together means that you have to work together to detect potential directions from whence missiles can go, it means to create a Joint Center for making decisions, and it also means developing a mechanism for making such decisions. Certainly if we were to pursue this path then we would no doubt have to exchange some technologies. That is what our proposal consisted of—just the outline of our proposal. This proposal was left unanswered.

OS: This is very strange time. And we talked about this last time. I mentioned the 1960 period when the United States felt that they had a large superiority over the Soviet Union and they thought this is the time now. And I compared that to *Dr. Strangelove*, and you said you had never seen the movie and so forth. But the point is, here we are—the United States has a lot of information on Russia. They can't be that stupid to not realize that since you've been in power, there's been a great improvement in Russian nuclear technology—not only anti-ballistic, but also airplanes, and ICBMs—including the one that's so fast it can hit New York in 24 minutes apparently.

VP: That is not everything we have at our disposal and certainly our partners are aware of all of that. But they believe, as far as it seems, that the current level of science, of technologies, the current level of the defense industry of the United States are so high that it gives them grounds to believe that they will be able to make such a breakthrough that no one is going to be able to catch up with them. Just right now, at this very moment, there are ongoing discussions at the International Committee of Armaments Control. This committee was established within the United Nations back in the 1950s and it's still working, still functional. This international committee is working in Russia and has brought up the issue of preventing the militarization of outer space. Unfortunately, our American partners have blocked this proposal.[103] What does it tell us? Apparently, our partners are intending to use outer space for military purposes directly—not just for intelligence purposes, but also for other purposes. We do understand what direction this string of events is leading towards. There are other dimensions of high technology, which according to our partners, are their monopoly. But they are wrong.

OS: I think you are right. I think there might be some confusion but I do believe that there are many officers in the military who are very smart and I know this, and I think there is a divide between the hardcore, let's call it the old regime Pentagon and I think there's a new regime Pentagon that could be borne out of reality and necessity.

VP: Well, it's up to you to tell because you are American. We act from the assumption of what is going on in reality, in practice . . . just have a look: the need for deploying ABM systems in Europe was based on the argument that there was a need to counteract the nuclear missile threat from Iran. Right now, thanks to President Obama's policies, with our support, the nuclear threat of Iran has been removed from the international agenda.[104] And without any exaggeration, it is a great accomplishment of President Obama's administration and his personal victory as well—whatever his critics say abroad and domestically.

There are very many advantages to this accomplishment. More advantages than disadvantages to this nuclear deal. But now that the nuclear threat from Iran has been moved, why is there a need to continue deploying an ABM system in Europe? But the deployment continues.

OS: Yeah, it's shocking.

VP: The question arises, were our partners sincere at least on this matter with us or not?

OS: It's a strange story—Alice in Wonderland, if you know that story. One could argue that the United States doesn't really worry about the threat to Europe. They worry about Russian existence. The bigger issue is not Europe. The bigger issue is US and Russia. And to take out Russia, requires the United States to keep the European Union going. They need to do everything to make NATO feel as if they have some power and say in this matter. But I think the US has its own force and that's the force that matters.

So I think, I return to—the policy of the United States has been from the beginning—from the 1917 revolution on, has been a policy that was born on Wall Street, to destroy communism, to destroy the power of the idea of the working class having control over society. And remember, in 1917, Wall Street was equally powerful with the government, if not more so. The government got more power with Roosevelt.

VP: Well, you didn't ask a question—you simply stated what you think. I'd like to agree with you on the whole. But I'd like to disagree on one matter if I understood you correctly—with regard to the power of the working class. We have to be candid. The working class was not the ruling class in the Soviet Union.

OS: I was saying in the United States. They were concerned about the United States. And they made the Soviet Union a convenient enemy. As we became a war economy. You realize World War I was the first war, but with the Second World War, we became a military industrial complex. We needed an enemy to build all these weapons.

VP: Yes, I think it's not so much about ideological motives. It's more about geopolitical rivalry. To this day, I believe, the mistake is that our partners in the United States still treat Russia as if it were their main geopolitical rival. We have many fields of activities in which joint work would no doubt yield positive results both for Russia, for the United States, and for the whole world.

OS: Yes, but we talked about the possibility of mistake, error, perception. We've talked about—we don't realize perhaps, the power Russia has in its nuclear arsenal. So we are interested first in destroying this economy. And then I think some people in my country think that once that country can be destroyed, the leadership is changed, which means you, Mr. Putin, are gone and a softer leader is around. They will take over Russia and they will basically destroy the nuclear industry here or else co-opt it in some way.

VP: Maybe someone does think like that. And it's understandable there's probably many who seek exactly that. And yet I believe there is a lack of understanding of our country. And this lack of understanding consists in the fact that probably much depends on certain persons and certain people and on the present. And yet, the most important thing about Russia is the Russian people, and its self-consciousness. The inner state of the Russian people, the inability of the Russian people to exist without sovereignty, to exist outside its own sovereign country. And this understanding, and not the threat of a nuclear war, should make our partners choose to build longstanding relations with Russia. And in that case they won't have to spend so much money on their defense sectors. Just have a look—last year, in dollars, we allocated $40 billion US dollars to defense, whereas the United States allocated more than $460 billion US dollars. So it's more than 10 fold. And this year, in 2016, the US is going to allocate more than $600 billion US dollars to defense. It's just too much—more than the total defense expenditure of all the other countries of the world.[105]

OS: Yes. I wholly agree with you. In *The Untold History of the United States* documentary we did a large part of that story—the soul of the Russian people in World War II. And I understand that Russia will not give up—they will go to the end on this economy and they will . . . Under Stalin, in those times, they gave their jewelry, their personal possessions down to their last dollar to support the government against the Nazis.

VP: It's not about the last dollar, it's about life itself. Our people were fighting until their last breath—for their life.

OS: But times change, and I think what America may think is that you have to recognize that Britain, France, and Germany were powerful countries—they had huge histories, imperial countries. France, my mother's homeland, I grew up there partly. Britain, imperial great, and Germany—what happened?

VP: It's the result of the First World War and the second one, so it's quite understandable.

OS: Yes, but my point is materialism works because after World War II, these countries basically became American satellites. And they do what America wants now in the world. I'm shocked at this—this is what I've seen in my lifetime. If you remember, in 1960, Charles de Gaulle said "no" to the American expansion in Europe. He took France out of NATO.[106] He wanted to get rid of the United States in France. Very strong position. When have we seen anything like that in Europe since then? Mrs. Merkel seems to do what the Americans want, as did Mr. Adenauer, back when, and England basically takes our commands. I don't see any independence in any of these countries—that worries me.

So what I fear is that the same thing continues. As the times change, you will see this creeping materialism. In Ukraine, it was amazing to see how effective these NGOs were in selling this approach "join Europe/become rich, materialism works, we want the American way of life."[107] This is the come-on. And I worry that it would creep into this country as well, with their campaigns and media, social media, all these calls to the good life.

VP: I think there are other things we have to fear. I think that however dependent these countries that you've named are on their patron, on the United States, however dependent they are economically, from the point of view of information, politically, from the point of view of security . . . however great this dependence, however solid it is—still, inside these countries, there is a constant movement towards strengthening their sovereignty. There is this tendency.

Right now a certain strengthening of American influence is being witnessed in Europe, partly due to the Eastern European countries, because they are still living in a different paradigm, in a paradigm of fighting civilization. They are trying to resist a former dominating power of the Soviet Union. Right now it's mirrored in Russia, but sooner or later this is going to stop. And even within the Western bloc there's going to be a need to build new relations, relations founded on greater respect for one another, for one's partners, for the interests of your partners, and for their sovereignty.

And I refer to those countries which housed large-scale American military bases. I'm not saying these are occupation forces, but still, the presence of large-scale military units of another country on the soil of a country is telling on the domestic policy of these countries. And it would be right if they started thinking about how events are going to develop in the near future, when they are building relations right now. But instead, as far as I see, American partners are trying to pull their allies toward them, closer. But not through changing the nature of relations within the Western bloc. They are trying to create an image of a common threat. An outside threat. And such a threat is such that they can only protect themselves by pulling themselves around the United States.

In my view, we can say that American partners have achieved certain tactical success following this path. Through initiating the crisis in the Ukraine, they've managed to stimulate such an attitude towards Russia, stimulate viewing Russia as an enemy, a possible potential aggressor. They have prevailed on us to take steps in response to what they did. But very soon everyone is going to understand that there is no threat whatsoever emanating from Russia—either to the Baltic countries, or to East Europe, or to Western Europe. And the stronger this misunderstanding is, the greater the desire is going to be to protect their sovereignty and to fend for their national interests. Right now I'm talking about Europe. But you know, in the East, say the Japanese—they are very sensitive to all outer signs of either respect or disrespect with regard to them. It's a nation with great dignity, with great self-esteem. So this constant feeling of pressure is, let me assure you, something no one is happy about. Sooner or later this is going to have consequences. This is going to happen. And it's better if this happens through dialogue. Certainly you can try to use North Korea or some other countries to paint a darker picture, to elevate tensions there. But I think what's needed right now is the transition to a new paradigm, a new philosophy for building relations among countries.

OS: Good luck, but I don't—

VP: And this paradigm should be based on respect for the interests of other countries, for the sovereignty of other people, not just trying to intimidate them using some outer threat which can only be resisted with the help of the United States. This paradigm will have to shift sooner or later.

OS: One side question, just quickly, is why did Iran give up its—what was their motivation in making the US happy on this nuclear deal?

VP: Well, you have to ask them. They have always maintained that they didn't seek to create nuclear weapons. But to be honest, if we do not pay enough attention to strengthening the fundamentals of international law which would serve as a guarantee of security, not just for the largest states but also for small countries—if we don't do that, there are always going to be those who decide to protect themselves at any cost, including through acquiring WMDs. But as to Iran, they have never said that they were trying to get a nuclear bomb. All suspicions on that account were never justified—there was no evidence. And yet there were suspicions. And to alleviate those suspicions, Iran agreed to this nuclear deal, signed an accord, I believe in order to normalize its relations with the United States, with other countries of the world, which were expressing their concerns on that matter.[108]

OS: What are you going to do with the uranium you got from them?

VP: We're going to re-process it. It's going to be re-processed and converted into nuclear fuel to be used for peaceful purposes.

OS: I know you're tired, so I'd just like to ask one final question—

VP: I'm not tired, but if it's the last question it's got to be a good one.

OS: Just a fun one—what do you think of these candidates in the US election?

VP: I believe that the people of the United States are going to choose the one who deserves it best.

OS: Nah, we want to hear what you think—just as a personal thing—they're characters. People are fascinated by it.

VP: Well, I don't know them very well, or some of them I don't know at all. We see them only on the TV screen. And when a person is embroiled in some combat, especially in the run up to the election during an electoral campaign, they tend to show some of their qualities but not all of those qualities are manifest. Because routine work—both on the domestic, international, and economic fronts—requires some other qualities from the person than participating in debates, meetings, or rallies. We are going to be ready to work with whoever gets elected by the people of the United States. I said that on several occasions and that's the truth. I believe nothing is going to change, whoever gets elected.

OS: How about Bernie Sanders—would you like that?

VP: Well, it's not up to us to say. It's not whether we are going to like it or not. All I can say is as follows—I have some experience of communicating—the force of the United States bureaucracy is very great. It's immense. And there are many facts that are not visible about the candidates until they become president. And the moment one gets to the real work, he or she feels the burden.

OS: But you didn't answer my question about Sanders.

VP: You can take what I've just said as an answer to your question.

OS: [laughter]

VP: My colleague, Obama promised to close Guantanamo. He's failed to do that.

OS: Good point.

VP: But I'm convinced that he sincerely wanted to do that. He still wants to, but he's failed to.
   So what's said in all those pre-election promises has to be remembered. But it doesn't mean that we'll have to deal with that.

OS: But you do realize how powerful your answer could be—if you said suddenly that you didn't prefer X candidate, you would go like that tomorrow. And if you said you loved Y candidate, they would go the other way—it would create a stir. Anyone you liked would go down, and anyone you didn't like . . . Let's say you hated Donald Trump or something because he's a madman, right? What would happen? He'd win. You have that amount of power in the US.

VP: Unlike many partners of ours, we never interfere within the domestic affairs of other countries. That is one of the principles we stick to in our work.

OS: So why are you so hated in the US?

VP: You answered this question at the beginning of our conversation. The ruling class believe that they have to fight Russia, that they have to restrain Russia, to contain our development. Certainly, brainwashing is one of the tools to create the necessary political environment to achieve these goals. These goals are the false ones and this policy is erroneous. I do hope that once the new president is elected, we will be able to build relations which will change the paradigm for the relations between Russia and the United States for the better.

OS: Okay thank you, sir. We'll see you tomorrow.

Trip 2—Day 2—February 20, 2016

———

OS: Hello, Mr. President—how are you today?

VP: How are you?

OS: I'm a little tired—I was sleeping back there, but you look better today.

VP: You were like a bear in hibernation during wintertime. [laughter]

OS: Well, in Russia things are backward. I stay awake later, and I wake up later. So my body doesn't know if it's day or night.

VP: It's very difficult, I understand.

OS: But you look happier tonight than you did last night.

VP: Yes, yesterday evening I had a lot of things to do.

OS: I could tell—it was in your face.

VP: And today I was dealing with economic matters and I like it more.

ON ECONOMICS

OS: You like economics?

VP: Well, addressing concrete issues is always more interesting.

OS: But economics is never concrete.

VP: These economics related to finance, to funding concrete programs, social issues. So these are concrete matters.

OS: Well, economics, they're always projections. They call themselves a social science, but the projections are generally fucked up. [laughter]

VP: Well, at least there are some benchmarks we can use as orientation marks. But you're right—certainly, there is very much uncertainty, many unknown factors, and yet decisions have to be made. And I think it's very close to being an art in itself.

OS: More art than science?

VP: Well, it's also a science—there's no doubt about that. But it's a very complicated science.

OS: The Chinese emperors, every year, used to cut off the heads of the economics minister when it didn't come in exactly like he projected.

VP: Yes. [laughter]

OS: Sergey Glazyev? Is that his name—your deputy?[109]

VP: Right now he's my advisor.

OS: Yes, he's said some very interesting things. How close is he? He's economics, right?

VP: Yes, economics. He's a very talented person, but he has a view of his own on the development of the Russian economy and the global economy. He's always arguing with what the economic part of the government says.

OS: Yes, the Central Bank people—I heard he said some shocking stuff like Russia should establish currency controls.

VP: Yes, controls, some restrictions—restricting the capital flow, the export of capital.

OS: But you haven't done most of that yet?

VP: We have not adopted these measures and we're not intending to. And yet it's always useful to listen to opinions which contradict those that dominate right now.

OS: Well, he must've pissed off the Central Bankers.

VP: The Central Bank is not very happy with him and he's not very happy with the Central Bank. It's normal.

OS: I gather. We were talking about that last night. I was thinking—I forgot to raise the point, but in Brazil for example, because I know Ms. Rousseff, I don't feel she has any cooperation in her administration from the Central Bankers of Brazil.

VP: Well, you should probably ask her about that. She's a very prominent woman. And a good politician.

OS: Can we just walk around so we see the room?

VP: That is the throne room. At the center, that is the throne for the czar and also for the Dowager Empress. And this hall is called St. Andrew Hall—you can see the emblem of St. Andrew—it's the first court, one of the orders of the Russian empire.[110]

OS: You know, they say you want to be czar. They do magazine covers on it.

VP: Probably they like that . . . and that's why I say that. [laughter] They cannot get rid of these old stereotypes.

OS: But you allowed Charlie Rose to make a point, which I think you should have stopped him at one point, because I think he went too far. He said in his interview with you, I was paying attention. In a way that was very leading, he implied, 'You have all the power, you can do what you want.' He made it very clear and that's the way many Americans think—that there's no system here. And you didn't correct him.[111]

VP: The question is not about having much power, it's about using the power that you have in the right way. And those people who say that they lack power in something are those people who cannot use any power whatsoever. And they think that they need more and more power. And they always look at those people who have more power than they do—think they have less power—but they cannot use it efficiently.

OS: Well, then you should shoot the interpreter too. [to Sergei] Was it you? Because I don't think you understood the question that Rose was leading you to. In other words, in English it sounded like you were the czar and you took it for granted. You took it for granted. That's what I meant.

VP: He was trying to argue, probably, to incite a discussion. But I didn't want to have a discussion with him, to debate this, because I have very much work to do.

OS: But I thought it was a good interview for you. I thought you were excellent, by the way. There were a couple of things you missed. But he's a chess player and he's trying to trap you and reinforce what the American public would like to believe. That's my observation.

VP: I'm not trying to make you believe me. I try to express my point of view as clearly as possible on certain concrete issues. And besides, people have to understand for themselves whether what I'm doing is right or not, whether they believe me or not.

OS: As it should be. But you have to understand the American media landscape. Especially in this election year. The surface and some of the most shallow impressions dominate.

VP: I'm afraid, regrettably, that is the case everywhere.

OS: Yeah. Well, you're a man of much thought and you're very articulate. You make your points. My producer, Fernando, said I should ask you a question: do you ever lose it? He says you're so rational every time you're asked a question—do you ever have a bad day?

VP: Well, I'm not a woman so I don't have bad days.

OS: [laughter] There you go. Now you're going to insult about 50 percent of the American public—the way they're going to take it.

VP: I'm not trying to insult anyone. That's just nature.

OS: So, a woman to you tends to be more emotional and you don't want to have your emotions ever cut in and control your reason?

VP: Well there are certain natural cycles and men probably have those too but they are less manifest. And I believe every person has days that are more difficult, other days when we are more efficient. We're all human beings, so that's just normal.

OS: How about you—do you ever have bad day?

VP: Yes, certainly. There are days that are overloaded with work. Sometimes I fail to achieve something. Sometimes I have doubts before I arrive at the best solution. But on the whole, it is a working process, the process for making decisions. And it is a positive one.

OS: Well, who do you like to scream at? Dmitry? You use Dmitry as a sounding board somehow? Sometimes you get pissed . . .

VP: Well, I share my concerns with my workers in those spheres which concern them directly. So I meet the president of the Central Bank and my adviser on economic issues. I meet the heads of the economic block of the government. After meeting with you, I'm going to have a meeting with the defense minister, with the head of the intelligence service.

OS: Later?

VP: Yes, today after we meet.

OS: Why don't you cancel the meeting and have it Monday—take a day off?

VP: Well, that is out of respect for our American partners.

OS: Why?

VP: Because right now we're engaged in an active dialogue with our American friends on a number of international issues on which we have to make a decision.

ON SYRIA

OS: So you're talking about Syria right now, I guess?

VP: Yes. Including Syria.

OS: That's today's news. And we should talk about Syria because we didn't get to it last night. So where do you see this thing going with Syria? How is Russia doing in this?

VP: I'd like to think that we are on our way. I think we are moving towards finding an acceptable solution. It's one of those situations when no country can arrive at a solution unilaterally.

OS: [to Dmitry] Dmitry, does he scream at you?

DP: No, never.

VP: I never scream at all. Because when you scream you cannot hear well. You have to have people hear everything. And if you scream, if you raise the tone of your voice, then people are not very good at understanding the sense of what is being said to them.

OS: So all your energy, your aggressive energy, comes out in Judo in the morning or in exercise.

VP: Yes, I try to do that. It also requires some adrenaline.

OS: Yeah, and a good opponent.

VP: Yes.

OS: You have a trainer or a Judo master?

VP: No, well I used to have one. And I think I'm the master. Of course, the trainer is required for those people who want to perform in competitions and who want to get better. And I'm doing it just for exercise. And besides, I've been doing it since I was 13 or 14—on a permanent basis. There were no interruptions.

OS: So back to Syria—can you describe why you sent troops to Syria and what your objective was? Give us a little history of that and where you are now?

VP: Well, it's very easy to explain. We see what has happened in certain countries of the region. I refer in particular to Iraq and to Libya. As to President el-Sisi of Egypt, the same thing did not happen in Egypt. Other countries are also in a difficult situation. But in Libya and in Iraq, a tragedy has transpired . And that has happened due to the forceful ousting of the current regimes. These regimes were destroyed—they were not simply ousted from power—the leadership was eliminated.

And we don't want the same thing to happen in Syria, otherwise the whole region is going to be plunged into chaos. Moreover, if the same thing that happened in Libya happens in Syria, the position of radical organizations, terrorist organizations, are going to be solidified in a great manner. Right now they're very strong because they control a vast part of the oil that is being extracted in that region.

OS: Who's "they?" Terrorists?

VP: Terrorists, yes. So they sell museum artifacts, cultural artifacts, and they also receive aid from abroad and they have grown very powerful. And we should prevent them from getting even stronger. Because they are trying to create a Caliphate from southern Europe extending to Central Asia.

OS: Right. And this is the biggest concern here.

VP: Yes, it's our biggest concern. But we also have some practical objectives. There are thousands of militants originating from former Soviet republics and from Russia who are fighting there. And they can get back to Russia. And we should prevent that from happening. All that combined has motivated us to take the measures that you're aware of. At the same time we understand full well that the current leadership of Syria has made certain mistakes in building relations within their own country. And that's why before making this decision, we have had a dialogue with President Assad. And we were told that he understands well the many problems that the country is facing, and he is not just willing to engage in a dialogue with the opposition groups—even the armed opposition—but he's also willing to work together with them to elaborate a new constitution.[112] He is ready to agree that early presidential elections be put under very tight international supervision.

OS: Really?

VP: First they have to agree on the new constitution. And this constitution has to be adopted. That is a very difficult task and a very complicated process, but should they succeed in that, then afterwards after a certain period of time, they will be able to have early elections. I think that is the best solution—a democratic way of resolving any contentious issues and also building authority.

OS: Can we go back and discuss briefly the mistakes that Assad made?

VP: I don't think it is my place to discuss mistakes committed by heads of state and governments—my colleagues, my counterparts. But despite these mistakes that he made, the situation in Syria wouldn't be like it is today if there had been no interference from outside. And we hear that President Assad is in conflict with his own people, this is not the whole truth. We know what ISIS says—there are so many mercenaries in it. And those are not citizens of Syria. More probably so, we might have to think about how the leadership should be built in Syria in a manner that will ensure that all ethnic and religious groups feel that they participate in this state—that they participate in the leaders. And these groups should also feel independent—free from any possible pressure, from outside. And they should also feel safe—that is very important.

OS: Well, when you're talking about interfering parties, we're talking about countries like Turkey? Are we're talking about people like Saudi Arabia? We're talking about people like Israel? And ultimately, the United States, France, Britain?

VP: Well, Israel to a lesser degree. Judging from what we see and from what we know, Israel is primarily concerned about the possibility of the spread of radical groups that might damage Israel. But when I was talking about interference from outside, I was talking about those who were sponsoring and arming, buying oil from terrorists and thereby funding them. And who does that? I think it's very simple to determine, even not being a specialist or an intelligence officer.

ON RUSSIAN RELATONS WITH TURKEY

OS: Are you talking about Turkey?

VP: I'm talking about those countries that I call the sponsors.

OS: And Russia's relations with Turkey have been extreme—they've been up and down. I thought that Turkey was a great partner of Russia, up until this event. Then I thought you were united in trying to bring the silk road west.

VP: Yes, that used to be the case. And I think, and there were grounds to think that, that I've done a lot to build relations between Russia and Turkey. To us, Turkey is a great partner, important in general and also in the Black Sea. We have quite a large trade with Turkey. Certainly it has decreased right now. We view Turkey, not just as a partner, but a friendly country. More than 4 million Russian citizens used to spend their vacation in Turkey every year.[113]

OS: Much of modern Moscow it seems was built by Turkish construction companies.

VP: Yes, certainly. In Moscow and Sochi in the run-up to the Olympic games and in other parts of the country—all across Russia.[114]

OS: So what happened? Did all of a sudden Erdogan decide that the Kurds were a more important issue for him than his relations with Russia? What do you think happened?

VP: Well it's not about the Kurds. It is a problem, it is a Turkish problem but we have no relation to it whatsoever. And I simply do not have the answer myself to the question that you've asked. I've met the President of Turkey at Antalya during the G20 summit in November last year.[115] And he and I talked in great detail about our bilateral relations and also about Syria. And he set forth a number of very sensitive issues—issues that are very sensitive to him. And I told him that I was willing to help him and to cooperate with him. And when out of the blue a Russian plane was downed, at that approach of the Syrian-Turkish border, it didn't even come up during our discussions.[116] When we heard talk about some Turkmen and this issue wasn't raised during our discussions either. He didn't talk about that in Antalya at all. I was simply shocked. We demonstrated that we were willing to cooperate with Turkey on issues that were sensitive to them. So why didn't he mention other issues that apparently are very important to him. That's the first thing. But the most important thing consists of the following. From the very beginning, from the first days when we commenced our operation, military operation in Syria, we proposed to our Turkish partners that we should coordinate our work. And at least put in place a mechanism for such coordination. And the Turkish leadership responded, "Yes," and they promised that in two days the defense minister and foreign minister of Turkey would come to Moscow. But they didn't come. On many occasions we made attempts to coordinate our work on a bilateral basis, but to no avail.

OS: Let me clarify one thing. What month of last year did the Russians go in militarily to protect their base and bolster their force there?

VP: I'm afraid I might make a mistake and we have to consult the facts. But I think it was in summer.[117]

OS: Okay, so it was before you met? You met in November?

VP: Yes, certainly.

OS: Did he talk to you about the Russian military in Syria?

VP: We heard that allegedly we were hitting the wrong targets. And we heard that that was what was preventing the solution to all issues. But the answer was very simple. Let's work together to determine the areas which shouldn't be hit and where there are areas which have to be hit. We could have created a coordinating mechanism, but this mechanism has never been created. And there is no coordination or information exchange going on.

OS: You were saying that you were hitting Turkmen in North Syria, near the border. I don't know if they are nomadic, but they've been there a long time. Turkmen.

VP: The thing is, he never raised this issue. He never said a single word about that.

OS: And the roads that ISIS were using to drive the trucks to Turkey—the oil trucks?

VP: One of these routes was going straight through the territory where the so-called Turkmen live. And that is the best route for supplying oil to Turkey, because it's the shortest one and it provides access to a Mediterranean port in Turkish territory. I have to say that from the air—up there our drones, the American drones—our pilots see very well. And besides, you know, I think it was Israel's defense minister and Greece's defense minister who said publicly that they were seeing that radical groups were supplying oil to the Turkish territory.[118] I assure you everyone knows that. And I was disenchanted by the US statement that they didn't know anything about that.

OS: And you confronted Erdogan with this information, correct?

VP: No, I didn't tell him that.

OS: You didn't tell him why?

VP: Do you think I had to do that? Why on earth? This is not his country. We were cooperating with the legitimate Syrian authorities, with the Syrian armed forces, combating radical groups. But if that was important to Erdogan, then he should have at least mentioned that. But he didn't.

OS: Could you have said, in a diplomatic way, Mr. President, we have information, good information, that the oil is coming into certain places in Turkey. And we believe that there are elements in Turkey on the border—smugglers who are cooperating with ISIS and bringing the oil in, and we are very concerned about that.

VP: Well, it's so pleasant to talk to you. You just listen—during the G20 summit, when the journalists left the room, I took out photos just like that—of this size—and from my place where I was sitting, I showed those photos to everyone. I showed it to my counterparts. I showed them the route that I mentioned earlier. And we have shown those photos to our American counterparts. And the United States leads the coalition fighting ISIS. And we simply showed our counterparts these photographs. Everyone knew about everything. So trying to open a door which is already open is simply senseless. It's something that is absolutely evident. So it's not about one single truck—there are thousands of trucks going through that route. It looks as if it were a living pipeline.

OS: Who from the United States was in that room?

VP: Well, you're asking things which probably shouldn't be made public. We showed those photographs to our partners. They saw those photos. And to be honest they didn't have any doubts about that, I assure you. American pilots and everything.

OS: So when John Kerry was saying the other day you were "targeting legitimate opposition groups," what did he mean?[119]

VP: Apparently he is not talking about those oil tracks. Well he is not flying over Syria himself now is he? But he's certain to have information from his pilots. But probably he was not talking about those cavalcades carrying oil. He must have been talking about something else—some other facilities. But our partners do not tell us what exactly they are talking about. On many occasions we have asked them to provide us with information where we should hit and where we shouldn't and they don't give that information to us. And that's why, and I'm deeply convinced, we have to foster a very good mechanism for cooperation. What we're trying to do is to avoid using such things for propaganda purposes. We understand that when hostilities are ongoing, tragedies do occur. As in Kunduz where American planes hit a hospital run by Doctors Without Borders.[120] Certainly our media have talked about that to their audiences. When you can actually see it and watch it as you say it. But we didn't speculate on this tragedy. Right now we know that the American Air Force has hit Libya, Serbian diplomats have been taken captive or killed—certainly a tragedy.

OS: The Chinese embassy in Belgrade.[121]

VP: But that was a long time ago. This tragedy is certainly a tragedy, but it's an accident and we're not going to use it for propaganda purposes. When we're talking about fighting radical Islamic extremists, we have to search for something that brings us together. And we should abstain from using this or that thing.

OS: Do Russian pilots make mistakes in their bombing raids?

VP: I do not have this information. I've never heard or seen that in the reports that I have. We are not simply hitting anywhere recklessly. We're not doing these strikes recklessly. We are coordinating our actions with the Syrian armed forces and with their intelligence services. At the preliminary stage, we did a very comprehensive study of the facilities that were hit. It doesn't take five minutes. It takes several days if not weeks. And we see for sure what's going on there. Anything's possible, but I do not have any good information that our pilots have made a mistake, or that some tragedy has occurred. I do not have any information that would support this claim.

OS: So what happened—out of the blue one day, your Russian SU40 was hit, was shot down by a Turkish F-16? How did that go down?

VP: It was an SU24—a bomber of the previous generation. And some defense systems could have been installed in this bomber, but it didn't carry any at that moment. And we didn't protect it using our jet fighters. The only thing that did—it was flying at a certain altitude so as to prevent it from being hit by a stinger. And no one could imagine that a Turkish jet fighter would strike our bomber. But the most terrible thing that happened was that when those pilots were going down using their parachutes, they were shot at.[122] In accordance with international law, it qualifies as a war crime. And those who were shooting at our pilots we know are at large in Turkey, because they gave interviews. Those are not Turkmen, those are Turkish citizens and they talked about the crimes they have perpetrated.

OS: Well, the shoot-down—I gather that there's NATO oversight over this whole area, so many people have said the Americans knew about it, or NATO knew about it before.

VP: We have an agreement with our American counterparts. As with a country which is leading an antiterrorist coalition, twice a day we exchange information. And before our planes took to the air, we had informed the American military.[123] And they knew where our pilots were going to work. And they knew the area and the projected route those airplanes were going to take.

OS: Any conclusions on your part?

VP: What are the conclusions? The conclusions are very simple—you can use formal logic.

We informed and our airplane was shot down. Then two scenarios are possible. Either this information was transferred to the Turkish side and they performed a strike, or this information was not transferred to the Turkish side. Or the Americans transferred this information to the Turkish side, but they didn't know that the Turks were going to go that far. So I think these are the main three scenarios.

OS: Did you discuss it later either with Erdogan or Obama?

VP: I don't remember how our dialogue was developing on that matter with the United States, but as for the Turkish leadership we didn't discuss anything. Because instead of making a formal apology, instead of stating that they were willing to compensate us, instead of providing support to the families of those pilots who were killed, the Turkish leadership has publicly said that they were going to continue to act in that manner. And then they dashed to Brussels, to the NATO headquarters asking for protection, which in my view, is humiliating to Turkey. They were the ones who made this mess and then they run to find protection somewhere else. No other statement, apart from those that are just mentioned, ever came from the Turkish leadership. Once Turkey's prime minister said that it was not the president who gave the order, but he. And afterwards, we heard that apparently the Turkish side had not known that it was a Russian airplane. Incidentally, if American partners have to receive information from us about the area in which our air force is going to operate and did not transfer this information to the other side, then question arises, how good are they at heading this coalition and who rules whom in that coalition?

OS: So, two times a day you give information to NATO about your missions in Syria.

VP: Not to NATO—to the US military, and they do the same to us.

OS: And you get the same information?

VP: Yes, information from the United States about where their forces are working.

OS: To prevent a major catastrophe?

VP: To prevent incidents in the airspace.

OS: This is a dangerous situation.

VP: Yes, certainly, in one airspace there are airplanes of a number of countries at once. It can always have some consequences. By the way, we are operating there at the invitation of the Syrian government—so, legitimately.[124] And that signifies that we're acting in accordance with international law in the United Nations Charter, whereas all the other military forces can only fly there in accordance with the existing national law—either based on a decision of the United Nations Security Council or at the invitation of the government of the country.

OS: So they're illegal?

VP: Yes, because it's evident. But understanding that, we still say that we have a joint objective in fighting international terrorism and we're willing to cooperate with you.

OS: So we have French airplanes, we have British fighters, we have Turkish fighters. And now we have Saudi Arabian, correct?

VP: So far, Saudi Arabia is not operating there. But there are so many air-planes there, including Australia. And Canada.

OS: Really? What about Iran?

VP: No, the Iranians are not flying there.

OS: So it's a pretty hot airspace, I'd say.

VP: I don't think so. Because you know, on average, our pilots make 70 to 120 strikes, whereas the international coalition—headed by the United States—makes two to three to five airstrikes per day.[125]

OS: You're making 70 to 120 airstrikes per day? Seven days a week?

VP: Yes. Every day.

OS: Wow. So there must be some progress I would think. We're not going to have a Vietnam-type situation here, are we?

VP: There is progress. Everyone is seeing this progress. And I think every-one sees that right now. Certainly, still vast territories are controlled by ISIS, but at lot of territory has already been liberated from ISIS. And this is not just some territory, some desert—these are vital territories for Syria. But it's not just about that. The thing is, many groups, many tribes in Syria, includ-ing the Sunni tribes, have told us that they are willing to cooperate with us and to fight ISIS. And we have established contacts with them. We have in-formed President Assad about that and the Syrian military leadership. We've told them that we're going to support those Sunni groups that are willing to fight ISIS and the al-Nusra Front. In principle, the military of Syria and the Syrian President agree with that. These Sunni groups, supported by our planes, are fighting ISIS and the Al-Nusra Front on their own.

OS: Well, how big are these groups? I mean, it seems to me if you're striking 70 times 7 or 120 times per day at least two months—at 60 days we're down to about 2,000 strikes.[126] I mean, how big is ISIS? How big is this thing? What are they doing for their oil?

VP: The projected number of terrorists participating in ISIS is estimated at 80,000 people. 30,000 of them are foreign mercenaries from 80 countries of the world.[127]

OS: Even Chechens?

VP: They are originating from 80 countries of the world. Including from Russia.

OS: So is it like Vietnam? Is it going to end, or is there a possibility to damage the group, or do they get more support from abroad because they are regarded as martyrs?

VP: In Vietnam, the United States was fighting the government, whereas in this region, terrorist organizations are trying to fight the government. Someone tries to use these terrorist groups to their ends in order to oust the government of Syria. But to resolve this issue, I am deeply convinced that we have to pull our efforts together with those of the United States. And we also have to combine our efforts with those who entered into a coalition by the United States. Your reaction to what I am saying is so skeptical? But I don't think there is any other way to solve this problem.

OS: There's no military solution through bombing—it's like Robert McNamara's problem in Vietnam—you cannot achieve this with bombing.[128]

VP: Yes, that's correct. But to transition to a new stage of the process, I'd like to reiterate, we have to combine the efforts of Russia and the United States. We have to take the initiative. We, for one, have to convince the Syrian government, the United States has to persuade their partners from the coalition. And then together we should arrive at a political settlement.

OS: Can I ask, I imagine you're surveilling these roads 24/7—these roads north to Turkey, the oil supply. Is this a situation where ISIS drives the trucks at different times, at night—like the Vietnamese responded to the bombings? I mean how do you know if you're succeeding on the oil issue or whether they are selling the oil through other means?

VP: We are confident in our actions and we see that. We see that both during the night and during the day. We are going to stop now and I'll show you how we can see that, how evident that is. As to the alternate routes, probably these routes do exist which we do not see. But when we're talking about commercial-level oil supply, let me assure you we see everything.

OS: So that means you're damaging ISIS, unless something else is going on. If the oil routes are cut, that means the money is being cut. That means somebody else is helping them if they're going to go on. Which means Saudi Arabian money.

VP: Let's not try to indicate any country if we do not have evidence to support our claims. Besides, it might not be about a country, but about some sponsors—rich sponsors with deep pockets who are acting based on some ideological motivations. We don't know for sure. And let me assure you, our partners in Europe and in the US, it's also known that we've dealt a very strong blow against oil exploitation by ISIS.

OS: Which brings me to the next area—I really would like to discuss Saudi Arabian/Russian relations because it's been a strange journey.

ON SAUDIA ARABIA

VP: We've done a great deal of work in our relations. In recent days we celebrated the anniversary of the establishment of diplomatic ties between Russia and Saudi Arabia. It was during the 1930s, and the founder of Saudi Arabia—the father of the current king of Saudi Arabia—and back then he came to the Soviet Union.[129] We've had different periods in the development of our intergovernmental ties but as far as I can see today, despite our controversies with regard to the Syrian settlement, on the whole, we have very good relations which have a chance for further development.

OS: Yes, but can you describe—for example, I know China has made a huge deal with Saudi Arabia involving billions of dollars which is a new development. This is new area for them. You said you wanted to show me something?

[looking at drone attack on cell phone]

VP: Have a look—that's how our air force operates.

OS: Who's on the ground?

VP: These are militants. These militants are running with arms—some carry not just machine guns, but they have some serious weaponry at their disposal, which they used to destroy army vehicles. You see, here's the one carrying it.

OS: These people have fought you before in Afghanistan.

VP: God knows where they fought—these are international terrorists.

OS: So they were surprised you found them?

VP: Yes. By the way, they were coming from the Turkish side of the border.

OS: It's an anti-recruitment poster for ISIS. You wouldn't want to join ISIS if you saw this.

VP: You can find this thing on the internet.

OS: Yeah. So, I don't understand—you've always kept good relations with Saudi Arabia. But Saudi Arabia has been mostly involved with the United States and increasingly with Israel.

VP: The world is a difficult place.

OS: But you're competitive with them, and they are perhaps worried about Russian oil too when they raised their production levels.

VP: You know, there is a certain amount of competition. It cannot but exist. But if we're talking about such large oil countries like Saudi Arabia and Russia working on the market, there is a need for coordination as well.

OS: Yes, and there was talk of that recently—what happened?

VP: I think that everyone concurs, if production is not raised then at least it can be kept at the same level. Iran has more difficulty joining in this policy because in recent years it has decreased its oil extraction rate. And they tried to get back the traditional markets they were strong in. And that is a legitimate claim they have. And that's why we have to arrive at a solution here as well.

OS: It's complicated, but it seems that no one has a better relationship with Iran in recent years than Russia. Just to make my point here, it's not that you have a great relationship with Iran—you have a good one, no one has a great relationship in this world, but let's say a good one. You have a relationship with Saudi Arabia. China has a new relationship with Saudi Arabia. Is there a way that these four countries could somehow iron out the Iran/Saudi Arabia issue, the religious issue, as well as the oil issue between them?

VP: As to the oil issue, it's quite complicated, but I think we can agree on that. And Russia has a role to play. Now, as to the regional controversies that exist, as to the relationship among different religious groups, our role can consist only in creating conditions for contacts between the countries of the region. We prefer to abstain from interfering within these difficult issues that exist between countries. I believe it's only up to these countries themselves to sort out such issues. But we're interested in all these controversies being surmounted, because in this region which is so close to us, we want to see stability and sustainable development. They are our partners and we'd like to have stable partners, so that we can work comfortably with one country, with another country, with all countries. And if we work with one country, we don't want any problems with our relationship with another country. But we are at liberty to make our own choices. Traditionally we have had good relations with all of these countries and we highly appreciate these relations. In practice, we take into account the controversies that exist between these countries and we'll try to keep away from those controversies.

OS: Well, how deep is this Saudi-Russian relationship? I always wondered, just looking at the chess board with the United States and Saudi Arabia being so tight, and I don't know who runs who. Sometimes Americans say the Saudi Arabians tell the Americans what to do in the Middle East. I would wonder if Saudi Arabia's well aware of the economic sanctions against Russia and the problems in Russia. They also have their own problems, true, economically, but they might be inspired or motivated by the United States to keep going and to make it harder and harder for the Russian economy, because they know that Russia helps Iran.

VP: We try to stay away from relations between other countries. The United States tries to democratize everyone else. And I don't think that the monarchies of the Persian Gulf like that very much. To be honest, if I were in their place, I would think about what the United States is going to do next. And I think they are thinking about that already. Indeed, if you are consistent about your course towards democratization, so you understand what your next step is going to be after Syria, after Libya, after Egypt . . . I think it would be best to take into account the traditions, the history, the religious particularities of these countries. It's very difficult to put into place structures of government that work in one place and transfer them to another region. I think it's best to treat with great respect what is existing. And even if you want to try to support some processes you have to do it very gently, not try to force something from outside on another country.

OS: Well, you know, some people say that the solution to the Syrian problem is a division of Syria into four or five parts. The question is: who are the parts?

VP: There are many variants and scenarios, but we have always assumed there is a need to preserve the territorial integrity of Syria. Because we have to think not just about pacifying the region at this very moment, we have to take the next step and look further into the future. What happens if we divide Syria? Wouldn't it lead to a permanent confrontation between these parts that have been divided. So we have to be very cautious and we have to do our best so that all warring parties—terrorist organizations excluded—might arrive at a platform to work together.

OS: Did the United States sanctions on Iran contribute to their decision to make a deal on nuclear arms with Kerry?

VP: You often ask me questions which are not within my purview.

OS: Well that's true.

VP: Our American friends think that these sanctions have played a certain role. The Iranians say that they never planned a nuclear military program. The question was about alleviating the concerns of the international community with regard to this matter. And so step by step it was done. All the while, the Iranians did get what they wanted, the right to conduct nuclear research. And second, they've got the right to pursue a peaceful nuclear program, including a certain volume of enriched uranium. Everyone seems to be happy with the results.

OS: So your answer is more ambivalent. You're saying you're not sure that they worked—that sanctions don't work.

VP: Well, the Iranians themselves say that these sanctions have stimulated them to take a number of measures to develop certain industries. Some elements related to these restrictions were probably quite a burden to them. And certainly they wanted the sanctions to end.

OS: How close were we to war in Syria when you negotiated with Assad and the Americans to take chemical weapons out of Syria?

VP: I think we were quite close. There was a great danger of a war erupting and I believe that back then President Obama made the right decision. And he and I managed to agree on coordinated actions.[130] As a matter of fact, he distinguished himself as a leader—as the Americans like to say—and thanks to these concerted actions we've managed to avoid an escalation of the conflict.

OS: A lot of American congressmen were leaning towards enforcing the red line, but it seemed like many people think that they would have said no, they would have voted "no." They would have voted "no" to Obama's desire to enter this Syrian conflict. And they say that if you had not intervened, it would have been an interesting test of the American will to fight a war or not in Syria.

VP: That's quite natural. Because there are so many people and so many opinions. But only one person has the responsibility to make the decision. The most terrible thing is to talk, to discuss ad infinitum without making the final decision.

OS: It seems that many congressmen thought that at that point, when you re-entered the world scene and saved his bacon that that their eyes fell on you and you were a target for them after that—the neoconservatives.

VP: Probably. Well, let them have their fun.

OS: Well, you came close, and now you're close again, so it seems to be a very tense presidency you have.

VP: And when was it simple? Times are always difficult. We simply have to thank God for giving us an opportunity to serve our country.

OS: Well you've had a lot of opportunities and you've done an incredible job of maintaining your cool under this enormous pressure. And I think many—maybe millions of people—owe their lives, without knowing it, to your intervention.

VP: Probably.

OS: And now because you're pissed off at Turkey you have sanctions on Turkey.[131] So you have doubles sanctions—you have sanctions against Turkey and the US has sanctions against you.[132] I thought you didn't believe in sanctions.

VP: You know, I've already told you, we used to have not just a partner relationship with Turkey, we were friendly countries. We had a visa-free border. But at the same time on many we brought to the attention of our Turkish partners the fact that we were seeing the arrival of many radical elements from Russia into Turkey. We saw those radical elements receive support, receive protection. And afterwards, using visa-free programs, using Turkish passports, radicals entered Russian territory and disappeared. It turned out that the Turkish side is acting like that not just with respect to Russia but also with respect to a number of other countries. And my colleagues, my counterparts, have told me about that—I'm not going to name these countries. Turkey has given us a wonderful reason to add an additional layers of protection to our industries—especially to our agriculture. And we have all the grounds to do that. I refer in particular to ensuring our national security. But at the same time I'd like to tell you that we haven't broken any existing contract with Turkey. These contracts are restricted in volume. But this is not something we are doing. This is something economic players are doing—I mean Russian companies.

OS: I can understand you insisting on visas, but I don't understand why you cut off, in this very tough time, the Turkish trade—the new trade with Turkey. It was one of the times when I thought you were the most emotional in your reaction to the shooting down of the jet.

VP: That's very profitable to Russian producers. It can have an impact on pricing. Only in the short term, but it helps the agricultural producers increase their production volume. It creates new jobs, new salaries, new tech. And it also creates tax revenue.

OS: I'm still saying it's a problem because your principle is that there should be no sanctions—you made that very clear.

VP: Yes, sanctions do not work with regard to another country, but this is a country which is already active in our market. And this country creates certain difficulties for our own agricultural producers. And that's why we can pay more attention to issues related to security.

OS: But you can set price controls, the government can do that. I think Glazyev has suggested stuff like that—temporary price controls.

VP: We are pursuing a liberal economic policy and we try to influence pricing, not through administrative measures but through granting support to vulnerable economic groups.

OS: Last question—last night when we were talking and I said something about the 1917 revolution and the fears of Wall Street and the working class getting control of the United States and the richest ones losing control of the country and I talked about that fear and you said yes, but you said also that there is strong geopolitical interest in this area of the world. My question to you is—this is the most geopolitical area where the resources are in the Middle East and the Near East. This is the richest place in the world. Cheney, years ago—Dick Cheney, vice president—said in a meeting that the Middle East and the Near East are the "keys to the kingdom."[133]

VP: Are you a communist?

OS: No, I'm a capitalist! So when you come to this area we're talking about, the Middle East, oil comes up and I always hear that oil makes wars and oil is the reason we go to Iraq, oil is the reason we are now in Syria and Iran and this and that. And Russia, of course, is a big player in oil. So how does oil figure in this? Is it really true that oil is a determinate motive for all this chaos we see?

VP: It absolutely is true that oil is one of the elements which are very important not just for this region but for the whole world. I believe that as the world transitions to a new technological structure, as alternative sources of energy are expanding, the significance of oil is going to decrease. As far as I can remember, one of the oil ministers of Saudi Arabia once said—a thing I agree with—he said that the Stone Age didn't end because the stones ran out,[134] but because mankind transitioned to a new technological level, to new instruments of production. The same thing is going to happen to oil. Coal used to be one of the most important energy sources, then oil came into the picture and then gas, nuclear energy. Probably then hydrogen-based energy is going to be a driving force. But as of today, oil is no doubt one of the most important elements of world politics in the world economy. And oil will eventually lose the role it now plays. I don't know when that is going to happen, but yes—new sources of energy are appearing. But they are too costly, as of now. And they do not allow certain economies to transition entirely to new sources of energy because, if they do, then their competitive advantage is going to vanish. But technologies do develop.

OS: You said "oil is one of"—but what is the second?

VP: The second factor is the geopolitical position of the region, the controversies in the region which reflect on the whole context of international relations. Let's take the Israeli Palestinian conflict. It reflects on the whole range of international relations and ties.

OS: Did the United States go into Iraq because of the oil, and/or because of geopolitical considerations?

VP: [laughter] You have to ask yourself because you are American, not I.

OS: You have to be a world statesman. This is a statesman issue—you're not just a president, you are an international statesman and you've contributed to peace. You're playing a gigantic role.

VP: Let's have a look at the most expensive, the largest contract in Iraq. Who has those? I believe that American companies do. And I think to a certain degree that answers your question. But whatever the motives of our American partners, I believe this path is still erroneous. To use force to address any issues, be they geopolitical or economic ones, to start with because the economy of the country was destroyed. The very country is collapsing. If we have a look at Iraqi, has the situation improved or not? Let me remind you, Iraq used to have no terrorists at all. And in this sense, that Iraq was more in the interest of the world, and at least Europe, than the Iraq of today. It's evident that Saddam Hussein was a dictator. And probably support should have been granted to those who wanted to create within the country a more democratic regime.

OS: I agree.

VP: But this should have been done very cautiously from inside, not from outside. And finally the economy—do you know that now Iraq lacks money even though it is an oil-producing country?

And I think the United States has to support Iraq, including financially. And are the American taxpayers used to sending their money to Iraq? I don't think so. That is the reason we urge the international community to elevate the status of the United Nations charter, international law. We urge them to coordinate how the most important issues have to be tackled. We urge them to find compromises, however much someone wants to act unilaterally. And as for the region itself, it is a very complicated situation and we all share the burden of resolving it.

OS: And let me throw out a twister for you—just you think on this and we'll talk next time. You know, my accountant who watches Fox News—he's right-wing. He's a typical American and he thinks the Saudi Arabians are going after the American oil producers. He thinks that the whole thing from Saudi Arabia is dictated by the growth of the American oil business through shale fracking. And many of these companies in fact I think are going bankrupt—Texas is completely devastated and so forth. So isn't this a major kind of geopolitical interest in the United States right now? Do they not want to rethink their relationship with Saudi Arabia, realign it and say who is our partner here, who's helping us?

VP: I believe that is the philosophy behind the policy the United States is pursuing. I believe that, for the administrative structures of the United States, it doesn't matter who supplies fuel to the American market. The most important thing is for this fuel to be at the lowest price possible. And if, as of today, the American national producers who produce oil using this shale fracking, if their oil is too expensive, too costly to produce, and if there is another supplier who can get the same product to market but at a lower price, then the latter has all the rights. Because in the end that has a favorable influence upon the American economy as the whole. Because the consumers of oil have an opportunity to get it at a lower price, whereas those who have invested money into a more costly product, they were free to take this risk. And that's why they have to suffer the consequences.

OS: Well, let's be cynical and just assume that if I was the United States leadership, it makes practical sense now to have a coup d'état in Riyadh, in Saudi Arabia, and take over. Because if we're going to go to all these wars, we might as well take over Saudi Arabia because that would solve everything for us.

VP: Why?

OS: Clean solution.

VP: And what would it solve?

OS: Well, we wouldn't need Iraqi oil, we wouldn't need Iranian oil.

VP: It only seems to be a simple solution.

OS: I was joking.

VP: I understand, but if some unpredicted events should happen in Saudi Arabia, the international energy market is going to be so volatile and it's going to hit so hard that we'll be regretting that. I think the producers, the consumers, are interested in a stable price, in a justified price. But no one is interested in volatility in the market. Everyone has to be able to forecast their development and their consumption.

OS: Last question—is there any hope for cold fusion?

VP: I don't know. You have to talk to the specialists, the experts.

OS: I thought Russia might have an idea about it.

VP: Traditionally this field of research has been well developed in Russia. I mean research in this field, in the nuclear field, and without any exaggeration I am confident that our scientists are at the front edge of this field of research.

OS: Is there any hope?

VP: Hope—there is hope always. And I'm convinced that sooner or later solutions will arrive which we cannot even imagine right now. But new problems will arrive too, which we will have to face.

OS: So you're an optimist?

VP: Cautious optimist.

OS: Always. Thank you, Mr. Putin.

VP: As to the situation in the Middle East, and the complexity of the difficulties this region is going through. The prime minister of Israel, Mr. Sharon, once told me when I was paying a visit to Israel, he said, "Mr. President, right now you are in a region where no one can ever be trusted on any matter." I think by that time he had already gone through so much, through so many tragedies, that he had ceased to believe in there being any positive shift, any positive change in the region. But I for one believe that sooner or later this region is going to become tranquil again. People will find a balance in which the region is going to be able to exist in a relatively safe mode, however difficult the solution of these problems might seem right now.

OS: Or Moscow will be a Caliphate.

VP: We're going to prevent that. You should watch out so that Washington doesn't turn into a Caliphate.

Trip 3—Day 1—May 9, 2016

———

OS: Well, first of all, I want to say it was exciting to be at the parade. It was a beautiful, wonderful day.

VP: Was that the first time you've seen the parade?

OS: Yes. I wish I could have come last year, but, anyway . . . The marching, the precision, the pride—it was very powerful.

VP: They've been preparing for six weeks.

OS: I liked the women troops too.

VP: This is the first time the women's battalion has participated.

OS: It's a shame the US ambassador was not there. I'd like to ask you, overall, can you reflect on the last year from when you had the 70th anniversary—your feelings on the security of Russia. Has it changed since last year?

VP: Are you referring to the internal or external security?

OS: Both.

ON THE SECURITY OF RUSSIA

VP: I think that Russia is thoroughly protected. We have implemented a program to re-arm our fleet and military forces so that 70% of our weaponry and armed forces should live up to the highest international standards. We are restructuring our armed forces. The number of those working on the basis of a military contract is increasing. That is compared to the structure currently where most of our military are conscripts. Because we need military professionals—those with a very high level of education to operate the new military systems.

OS: So it sounds like you are following the Pentagon example of using contractors.

VP: Yes, to a certain extent, but not entirely. We're still keeping a great number of conscripts.

OS: But in Russia you must serve, right?

VP: Yes.

OS: So that's important to the concept of this day, May 9th.

VP: Yes, absolutely. In our country, serving in the army has always been received as a responsibility and duty, but also as a sacred right. As the authority of the Russian armed forces is growing, the number of those who want to serve in the army, who want to be trained in military institutions and universities has grown as well.

OS: What is the state of the Pacific forces?

VP: To a large extent, we have increased the number of our forces stationed there.

OS: Increased? Why?

VP: We have increased the number of our military as a whole. Our target is 1 million new who will serve. Right now we have 1.2 million people serving.

But we have reduced to a large extent the numbers stationed in the Russian Far East. Given the size of Russia—Russia is still the largest country in the world—we need an armed force that is able to guarantee our security at any point all across Russia, and we are trying to do that, to achieve that. That is why we're going to develop a network of our airports and our airbases—to increase the ability of our armed forces to deploy rapidly when necessary. We're also going to develop transport, aviation—that's what we're doing right now—and also our naval fleet.

OS: What do NATO and the US think of these exercises today?

VP: I think you'll have to ask them. I can say what I think about what they are doing. What are they doing? Last year they carried out at least 70 exercises within the close proximity of Russian borders, and that certainly draws our attention. And that means that we have to respond in some way. Last year we adopted a new national security strategy. There are no revolutionary themes. This is a document which is designed to help us build a security system. But our main task is not about confrontation or intimidation. This is about building conditions for co-operation on security in the areas which we believe are the most challenging, the most menacing to us and to our neighbors.

You asked about NATO and unfortunately it was not our initiative that back in 2014, NATO cut off all contact with us in the framework of the Russia-NATO council.[135] And within the previous months, we've heard it said often that Russia was responsible for that, but we are not. We didn't want to cut this contact and we're not the initiators of that. And just recently, at NATO's initiative, we had first contacts—I think it was at the level of ambassadors—and we have to follow up on that. We have to seek common ground, there are many conflicts, many challenges that we can rise up to together.

OS: Someone told me that two days ago there was some US training going on in Georgia—the US were training troops, I'm not sure what kind—were they NATO troops?

VP: Yes, that's possible. Because on our borders, either there or in some other place, we're always witnessing some intensification of military activity. I spoke in public about these matters and I also talked about that directly to my counterparts, and that is why I can tell you exactly what my attitude is to what NATO is doing. I think that NATO is a rudimentary organism left to us from the Cold War period. NATO was set up when there was a confrontation between the Eastern Bloc and the Western Bloc. And right now the Warsaw Treaty has faded into oblivion--there is no Soviet Union, no Eastern Bloc.[136] And the question begs itself—why does NATO exist? And right now I have the impression that in order to justify their existence, NATO is in constant search of an external foe. And that is why there are some provocations to name someone as an adversary. [As I've told you before,] I remember in one of my last meetings with President Clinton. I told him that I didn't rule out the possibility of Russia joining NATO and Clinton said, "Why not!" But the delegation of the United States was very nervous. Why? Because they need an external foe, and if Russia were to join NATO, then there would be no external foe and no reason for NATO to exist.

OS: Have you applied?

VP: Let me explain to you why the American delegation was so nervous about the possibility of Russia joining NATO. First, if that happened, then Russia would have a vote, and have to be taken into account when a decision was made. Apart from that, the very point of the existence of NATO would simply disappear.

OS: Can you join NATO and keep an independent force?

VP: Certainly. Right now the armed forces of NATO countries are not entirely integrated.

OS: It would be a good public relations coup for Russia to announce that it has applied for NATO membership.

VP: Our American friends would not even consider that. I think that in the current world, the current status quo, we have to follow a different path. We have to leave behind the Bloc versus Bloc mentality. We shouldn't go about building up new blocs—the Eastern Bloc, the Western Bloc, NATO, the Warsaw Treaty organization. Security should be based on an international basis and also on equal footing

OS: So tell me—I mean, all these incidents like in Georgia where the US troops were there training advisors . . . Do you hear about them?

VP: Certainly we're aware of what's going on. So a certain country is demonstrating that they're supporting a neighboring country of ours. But in order to build conditions favorable to establishing security, we need something else—not what's going on right now. We do not need military exercises, we need to build up an atmosphere of trust. Just an example—Mr. Saakashvili, who incidentally has shamelessly renounced his nationality—right now he's governor of Odessa[137]—which in my view is absolutely absurd. But he decided to take a chance and act opportunely and he attacked. He should've been dissuaded from taking this step. On many occasions, on the whole, we had a normal relationship back when he was president. On many occasions I told him that I understood how difficult it was to rebuild relations, but I told him that he had to have patience and that he should never take this terrible step of escalating the situation into a military conflict. And he responded, "yes"—he understood that, and said he would never take this step, and yet he did. When the United States talked about that a hundred times and I told them that we had to prevent a military conflict, and that we also had to rectify the situation and also rebuild relations. But they didn't listen to us and what happened, happened. And we had to respond, because one of the first actions they took was to kill our peacekeepers from our peacekeeping battalion,[138] and that's why we had to react. If this had not happened, then we wouldn't need any provocations or military exercises at all.

OS: Where is most of the activity? Are most of Russia's defense/security forces in the north or the south?

VP: We have more or less equal distribution of armed forces all across Russia.

OS: Except in the Russian Far East.

VP: Yes, a little bit less in the Russian Far East, but right now it's not really that important where they are stationed, because the modern weaponry doesn't need military on the front lines. It's not really important where, during peacetime, military forces are located and stationed. What's important is the means of waging war—how defensive and offensive capabilities are employed, how the military responds. We're even going to implement a new reform of stationing our armed forces so as to create more favorable conditions—not just for the military, but also the members of their families—so that their children could go to school on a normal basis, so that they live in civilized conditions.

ON SYRIA AND UKRAINE

OS: Quick updates on Syria and Ukraine—I'm talking about security on the borders of Russia. I was very impressed with the classical music symphony in Palmyra,[139] but can you give me a quick update on Syria as it concerns Russian security and Ukraine?

VP: As far as Ukraine is concerned, I think you know what is going on. They have this crisis which, in a slackened form, is still going on. I think that the most important component of the Minsk Agreement[140] is the political settlement, but regrettably it is up to the Kiev authorities to implement this part of the agreement, and so far they are not doing that. They should have amended the Constitution in accordance with the Minsk Agreement, and that should have been done before the end of 2015. But they didn't do that. They were supposed to pass a bill, a law on amnesty. This law was adopted by the parliament, but it was not signed by the president, nor has it entered into force yet. There is another law that should be adopted and that should enter into force—that is the law on the special status of these unrecognized republics. The current Ukrainian leadership says the following: they say that since, at the line of conflict, there are still clashes, there is still violence, then they say the conditions are not yet in place to implement this political settlement. But in my view, this is only a hollow pretext because you can easily create a clash somewhere at the line of contact and then this is going to go on ad infinitum. The most important thing right now is to achieve a political settlement. Then there is a second course which explains why this is being done according to the Ukrainian counterparts. The Ukrainian leadership insisting that the Russian-Ukrainian border where the unrecognized republics are located, should be closed. And indeed the Minsk Agreements presuppose the closing of the Russian border by the Ukrainian frontier offices, but only after the key political decisions have been taken.

But until these political decisions have been taken and implemented, until people are safe in those unrecognized republics, the closing of the border will only mean one thing—that they are going to be encircled and later eliminated. We talked about that during the long night when we hammered out the Minsk agreements. We talked about that in great detail. And our

Ukrainian counterparts first agreed to that, but right now they seem as if they do not understand what is going on. Right now we support a proposal set forth by President Poroshenko to reinforce the observer contingent on the line of contact. He is the one who initiated this proposal and I have supported it. Moreover, he suggested that the OSC observers should be equipped with arms and we support that as well. The problem is further aggravated by the fact that the economic and internal political situation in Ukraine has deteriorated dramatically. And right now, some of our partners—I'm not going to name them—are saying that the Ukrainian president is not capable of making these political decisions due to the difficult internal political situation in Ukraine. And a year ago, I suggested that President Poroshenko should hold early elections and thereby reinforce his position, so that, even though we had differences, he would be able to push through all the required political decisions. But back then, our American friends, our European friends told us that the prime minister—back then it was Mr. Yatsenyuk and President Poroshenko had to pull their efforts together, they had to work together and we know how it ended[141]—by a split up in the government and a very difficult political situation. And right now when I remind our partners of that, they simply shrug their shoulders. The question is, how does Russia fit into all this. And the United States and Europe keep coming up with new accusations, trying to accuse Russia of something new because they cannot publicly admit that they've made mistakes. That's why they choose to blame Russia. We have quite a famous poet who wrote fables—his name was Krylov—and one of these fables features a dialogue between a wolf and a lamb. In this dialogue with the wolf, the lamb is trying to justify himself, saying that he is not to blame for anything. And once the wolf has run out of arguments, he decides to put an end to this discussion. And he says, "Dear lamb, you are only to blame because I am hungry." [laughter]

OS: If this happens—you used the word "eliminated" I believe—what's the worst-case? I mean, how many Russian-Ukrainians would be at risk?

VP: It's not about the leadership of those unrecognized republics. You see, it's that everyone who lives in those unrecognized republics—there are about three million citizens there—they participated in the election campaign, they took to the polls, and that's why—in the absence of a law on amnesty— they can all be persecuted as separatists.

OS: Three million people at the great risk. So it could turn into another situation like in Serbia, Bosnia?

VP: Certainly, that's what it looks like. We remember the tragedy of what took place in Odessa. More than 40 people—innocent, unarmed—were encircled and burned to death. And those who tried to get away were beaten to death with iron rods. And who was responsible? People adhering to extreme, radical views and such people can enter the territory of these republics and do the same thing there. When I talk about this issue with some of my Western partners, when I'm telling them that mass infringements of human rights can be transpiring there, do you know what they tell me? They tell me that these people have to go to human rights organizations to seek protection. They have to ask for help—different international organizations. Think of what took place at the trade union building in Odessa and ask yourself who is going to apply to an international organization after the massacre that took place there?

OS: I can't imagine Russia standing by and watching that happen.

VP: Not in the least—certainly not. We are going to help, but we cannot do so unilaterally. Because the key decisions are to be taken by the Kiev authorities.

You asked about Syria—despite all of the military achievements we are witnessing there, the most important thing that has to be done in Syria is a political settlement. We have made a contribution. Through our actions we have reinforced the government institutions. And we have dealt a great deal of damage to the international terrorists, but let us bear in mind, [as I've said before], that ISIS comprises militants from 80 different countries. And let me tell you that ISIS is not just laying claim to Syria or to Iran, they are also laying their claim to Libya and other territories up to Medea, Mecca, and Israel. Certainly we've done a great deal of damage to these organizations [ISIS]. But Syria's problems do not simply stem from international terrorism, they also suffer from internal political difficulties and they have to be settled politically by engagement with the opposition. In our view President Assad is willing to engage in such a dialogue. But what is necessary is that the other side is also willing to do that. We often hear it said that President Assad has to go, but when we ask, "What comes next?" no one is able to respond. There is no answer to that. So I believe that the best, most natural and democratic way forward is to adopt a new constitution to which President Assad has agreed. [As I've said], this new constitution would be used as a basis for early elections.

OS: It's sad when you hear . . . I'm not sure who speaks for America. Obama says one thing and then Kerry says one thing and then Obama says, "Assad must go." It's confusing.

VP: Well, now you understand what's going on in the United States. But the partners are also very difficult to deal with—there are many differences in the region itself. Certainly attempts have to be made to take into consideration the interests of all those who have participated in this process. The most important thing is to ensure the sovereignty and territorial integrity of Syria, of the Syrian people, and create conditions for refugees to be able to get back to their homes.

OS: It was a nice thing about Palmyra—what the Russians did in Palmyra.

VP: That was the initiative of Mr. Gergiev, the conductor.

OS: But clearing the landmines by the Russian troops—that was hard work.

VP: Certainly, but other things also had to be done such as securing safe passage to the airport in Palmyra. We also had to create conditions for them to be able to stay there overnight. And also we had to push back as far as possible the terrorists from the city. In certain places, the terrorists were only 25 km from the place where the concert took place. And the musicians could hear the artillery firing. In the sun, the temperature was plus 50-degrees Celsius and their instruments were not playing very well. It took courage and also a great deal of effort.

OS: Can we talk about Sochi for a few minutes? What is your feeling about Sochi personally? Your relationship to the city?

VP: You know, when we were preparing the Olympic project in Sochi, we had in mind turning Sochi into a sort of all-season resort. A resort at the international level. And when we first announced that, there were many who were skeptical, who were saying that this wasn't possible. The transport infrastructure was not ready, they said, the energy infrastructure neither. The environmental considerations were also cited, the sewage system, there were not enough hotels. I'm not even talking about the sport infrastructure that back then didn't exist there at all. And right now it is an all-season resort. In the winter you can go skiing and you can stay in a hotel on the coast at the seaside because there is a high-speed railroad connecting the mountain cluster and the seaside. There are two automobile routes and it takes around 20-30 minutes. And indeed Sochi has either turned or is now turning into a very good all-season resort at the international level.

OS: Would you live there, if you get to retire in peace?

VP: No, too hot.

OS: They say Russia spent $51 billion—is that right?

VP: I don't want to give you the wrong number right now—I'll tell you later. The question is about where the money went. We have built two gas pipelines—one under the sea and the other one through the mountainside. We have built a power plant and a sub-power plant. We've built bridges and tunnels, highways through the mountainside and a railroad circling Sochi, and 40,000 new hotel rooms.

OS: Your critics say that a lot of that money went to your friends—oligarch friends.

VP: [laughter] That's absurd—it's nonsense. Everything was decided on the basis of merit. And much of this money went to foreign companies which were contractors and they earned more than 1 billion US dollars. In some places we had international teams building tunnels, we had specialists working with us from Canada.

OS: Your defenders say that $44 billion of the $51 billion went to infrastructure.[142]

VP: I don't remember the exact number or the exact figure, but probably that's the case.

OS: Okay, we're landing, but in Sochi you must have some kind of movie theater or screening room. I would like to show you at least 20 minutes of the film *Dr. Strangelove*.

VP: We will find one.

OS: It's important for my film because you have talked about this idea of a nuclear hot war. And I'd love to see your reactions to the war room scenes, which are funny. I know you say you don't have time for movies, but please.

VP: Let me give some thought to a place and time. How long are you going to stay in Sochi?

OS: Well, it depends—until Friday at least.

VP: Do you play hockey?

OS: I don't play, but we're filming you. My wife is here too.

[The plane lands.]

OS: Are you okay, Dmitry? [laughter] This is a very funny scene—the press secretary holding the boom.

VP: Yes, from time to time he has to work too.

OS: I saw Mr. Gorbachev was there today. You didn't stop and say hello. [laughter]

VP: Yes, protocol invites him to official ceremonies.

OS: I know, but I'm saying you did not stop on your way out to say hello.

VP: I didn't notice he was there. I didn't see him. Where did he sit?

OS: In the stands—he was right there. You didn't know he was there? You never see him?

VP: I received him in the Kremlin in my working cabinet.

OS: Many years ago . . .

VP: Several years ago.

OS: Well, I just think if you liked him you would have stopped to say hi—"Hello Gorby!"

VP: I saw him at a recent event organized by our media.

OS: Did you say hello?

VP: Certainly.

OS: First?

VP: No.

OS: [laughter]

VP: I do not have any prejudices. Gorbachev had very bad relations with the first president of Russia, Boris Yeltsin.

OS: Yes, I know.

VP: But our history is not overshadowed by that. And I met him and I have no problem with him.

OS: But he certainly supports you on the NATO issue.

VP: Yes, NATO, and also on the Crimean issue as far as I understand it. There was a time when he supported the opposition, but he has an opinion of his own and in some things we see eye to eye, in others we don't. As former president he enjoys the protection of the Federal Protection Service.

OS: That's nice. I would imagine you protected Yeltsin too.

VP: Yes, certainly. We have a law and certainly we stick to that law.

OS: Maybe next time succession.

VP: Good.

OS: [laughter] Okay, thank you very much.

Trip 3 — Day 2 — May 10, 2016

OS: Well, that was a nice game.

VP: We could have done better, but it's okay. For me, without a warm-up, that wasn't very good.

OS: You fell down one time—you were tired?

VP: I just stumbled.

OS: You started playing hockey at 40?

VP: No, two, three years ago.

OS: Three years ago? Really? At age 50?

VP: 60.

OS: [laughs] I keep thinking you're 53 instead of 63. That's cool. Wow.

VP: I couldn't skate before that.

OS: I know, I heard that. Skiing too.

VP: And that's very interesting—it's always interesting to learn something new.

OS: What's next at the age of 70?

VP: I don't know. Bush Sr. went skydiving.

OS: Have you done deep-sea diving?

VP: I've done that already. I can't say that I liked it all, but it was very interesting.

OS: Well, they didn't hit you too hard—I didn't expect them to. I mean, you get checked and you could easily break a bone, right?

VP: Well, sometimes that happens, but that's sport. I played Judo all my life and didn't have any injuries.

OS: But these are hard hits, these are like football. What if one of the men on the team, on either side, admitted in Russia that he was gay? Would you keep it quiet?

VP: [laughs] I'm fed up with all of that talk about homosexuals and lesbians. There's one thing I'd like to tell you. We don't have any restrictions, any persecutions based on gender. We simply don't have these restrictions in Russia. Moreover, there are many people who have proclaimed their nontraditional sexual orientation and we've maintained relationships with them—many of them have achieved prominent results in their fields of activities. They've even been awarded state awards for the success they've achieved. There are no restrictions whatsoever. This is just a myth that has been devised, saying that in Russia there are persecutions against sexual minorities.

OS: Well, you have the "propaganda" law.

VP: There is a law that prohibits propaganda about homosexuality among minors. And the reason behind this law is to provide children with an opportunity to grow up without impacting their consciousness. A child, or juvenile adolescent cannot make a decision of their own, and unless you're not trying to exert any pressure over him or her, and once he or she grows up, they can make any decision as to how they are going to organize their life, including their sexual lives. And once they become adults at 18, there are no restrictions whatsoever.

OS: I believe you. But there is a tradition, a macho tradition in Russia—a strong one. I mean, I don't know if any of these guys would say if he had been gay all this time, in-the-closet so to speak, would come out and reveal it openly to his teammates? I don't think so.

VP: Well, to a certain extent you might be right. But in Russia we still don't have a situation like they have in certain Islamic states where there is the death penalty threatening homosexuals. In Russia, our society is liberal-minded to a great extent, and if someone were to declare that they are homosexual, that wouldn't be a tragedy. Sometimes I visit events where people who publicly declare that they're homosexuals, these events are attended by such people and we communicate and have good relations.

OS: Is that true in the military as well?

VP: There's no restriction.

OS: No restriction in the military? I mean, if you're taking a shower in a submarine and you know he's gay, do they have a problem with that?

VP: [laughs] Well, I prefer not to go to the shower with him. Why provoke him?

OS: Well, it's a traditional thing about it. You know, it's hard for some men to accept that the guy in the shower with his dick hanging out may have designs on me and all that stuff.

VP: But you know, I'm a Judo master so . . .

[laughter]

OS: Also, I noticed that lesbians are not—the Russians don't care about female/female sex because the tradition again is that babies have to be vital and babies have to be born and man/woman is a natural, Biblical relationship and that gives the child the strength and the vigor to be a citizen of society. So there is no interest in the female who is not interested in being fertilized.

VP: That's true indeed. We have this tradition. I'm not trying to offend anyone but we highly appreciate that these traditions exist, we hold them dear. And I can tell you this that, as head of state, today I believe it's my duty to uphold traditional values and family values. And why? That is because same sex marriages will not produce any children. God has decided so and we have to care about birth rates, in our country we have care for the health of our citizens, for families. We have to reinforce families. This is a natural stance any authorities should take if they want to strengthen the country. But that doesn't mean that there should be any persecutions against anyone and in Russia there are no persecutions.

OS: May I just point out that even in a society where there's some malfunction there will be many orphans and some of those orphans could be adopted by same sex couples.

VP: Yes, that's possible. I cannot say our society welcomes that, and I'm quite frank about that. Incidentally I'd like to draw attention to the fact that many who are homosexuals are themselves against the right to adopt children by same sex couples. Do you understand why that is happening? There is not the same position in all of the gay community that same sex couples should have to have the right to adopt children. A child, I believe, will have more freedom once they grow up if they are brought up in a traditional family. Then they have greater choice.

OS: Good point. As we draw to a close, I mean our time is limited. We are coming to a close this trip. I have one more day with you on Thursday. I've looked at all the footage and I have to ask you some questions again just to clarify. Because sometimes I was not so sure about the answer and I had to ask again. And I also had to raise some concerns that are raised by Foreign Affairs magazine which I consider—not mainstream, but more like the official government viewpoint. This is the Council on Foreign Relations, which is very powerful. They publish this and they have all these experts who come in and they write on their fields in Russia. So some of these questions are raised by them.

VP: Someone, you know, dreams and someone wants to think this about me. These are only dreams, something they want. But that is not the reality and those who write about that know about that.

OS: I understand. This is an official point of view and therefore it is listened to in Washington and this is what you have to deal with.

VP: You know, there are different people in Europe and the United States—different people with different opinions. There are people who look 25, 30 years forward, they think about challenges that will emerge in the future. And they have a different attitude towards Russia.

OS: I'm not going to argue that.

VP: And there are some who would live from election to election and they only think about their own self-serving political interests.

ON RUSSIAN SURVEILLANCE

OS: You have to understand my next question—most Americans think that Russia is certainly as bad as the US when it comes to surveillance—as bad. That's just an assumption. Because of the old KGB.

VP: We are not better than the United States because we do not have the capabilities the United States has at its disposal. If we had, we would probably be as good as you. [laughs]

OS: You're serious about that? You don't think you're as good technically? I'm not talking about money, I'm talking about technically.

VP: The US has great funding for special services—we cannot afford that. And their technical equipment that's been developed. You know, after the Soviet era, after complete authoritarianism in our country, we have certain dislike for special services if they have too much power. We don't like that. And we have this internal repulsion and the authorities have to take that into account.

OS: Is Russia collecting any bulk communication in any form?

VP: No, and I can assure you of that.

OS: Everything is sort of targeted?

VP: Absolutely. Special services are working with a targeted approach, but we do not collect bulk communications with the subsequent selection. That's not what's happening.

OS: I'm just talking about collection. Not reading it, just collecting it. Just using all the phone systems and all the Internet.

VP: No, we're not doing that on a mass basis. We don't have this network.

OS: It'd be nice if you said to me, if you made the point and said to me: "Not only are we not doing it, but we have found a way to do selective targeting without picking up a mass like the US." In other words technically we have solved that problem.

VP: No, this is not about the technical side of the issue. This is about operational maintenance. Our special services work based on who they consider a suspect, based on their connections. We are not trying to take bulk information to search for suspects.

OS: 15 percent of the population is Islamic in Russia.[143] That's what I'm told. And many of them are in Moscow, so you're telling me that there is no bulk collection on Muslims.

VP: No, I can assure you of that 100 percent. Certainly there was violence at the end of the 1990s and beginning of 2000s due to the Chechen events. But on the whole, Russia was built as a multi-religious country. We have a certain culture of maintaining relationships between different religions. And this has been built for many centuries. The Chechen peoples, just as many other peoples of the former Soviet Union, suffered greatly during the Stalin persecutions. But they didn't suffer as representatives of the Islamic world. They suffered for political reasons. As for conflicts between Islam, Judaism, and Christianity. We've never had those. And this positive background is a great help to us. And besides, our Islamic community are all citizens of

Russia. They have no other homeland. Russia is their motherland. They're not migrants or migrant's children.

OS: I'd like to go back to that right after this question. Can you tell me how much Russia spends on intelligence? The United States spends, this is published, $75 billion a year on intelligence of that $52 billion is civilian[144]— CIA, FBI, NSA, and the rest is military.

VP: If the United States built good partnership relationships with Russia, especially in the field of fighting terrorism, then they would be able to at least halve the budget on intelligence. And they would make the activities of their special services far more efficient.

OS: They could halve their budget if they did this?

VP: Yes, if we cooperated on an efficient basis they wouldn't have to spend so much. And their activities would be far more efficient than now.

OS: So you're suggesting that Russia would be spending like $30 billion?

VP: It doesn't matter how much Russia would spend—what's important is that if we pooled our efforts together then we would both work more efficiently together.

OS: So you're not going to tell me the amount.

VP: No, it's a secret. [laughs]

OS: All right.

VP: We have some published data, but I don't remember exactly how much. But as I've already told you, we spend, for these ends, much less than the United States. And as we've discussed, the United States spends more than all other countries in the world combined.[145]

OS: And Russia spends 10 percent of that.

VP: 10 percent of the United States expenditure.

ON CHECHNYA

OS: It's amazing because of what you've achieved. Now, back to Chechnya for a moment. A lot of people don't agree with you about Chechnya which has been really a hornet's nest for 20 years now. Okay there's a radical element in Chechnya—we know about the terrorists—and there is a very authoritarian element in Chechnya run by the leader Kadyrov, who is very loyal to you. Many Russians have been critical of that. Many that I've seen have written about it—not necessarily dissidents, but people who are not comfortable having this relationship with him. He's considered a war criminal and so forth. Other people ask, you know, "Why does the Russian Federation have to include countries that are so crazy like this? Why don't you go and unify the Russian Federation with Russian people?" I know you've argued that Chechnya is part of the motherland, 'Rodina,' but talk to me more about it.

VP: As for the developments in the Chechen Republic and in the Caucasus, I'm not going to tell you any breaking news. These developments started right after the collapse of the Soviet Union. Once a great country dissolves, it's natural that these disillusioned processes permeate all of its territory, and Russia was no exception. That's the first point. Secondly, our economy collapsed as well as our social sphere entirely. And people were searching for a way out of the situation. And on the borderlands of Russia, people started to think how they could improve their life and overcome the difficulties they were faced with. And many, not just in the Chechen Republic, they fueled these separatist ideas. Nothing new about that. But as for the Chechen Republic, all of that was aggravated by the legacy of the Stalin repressions. People remembered the grievances that they had suffered after the Second World War. And that's why the conflict erupted. It was developing and it followed a very tragic scenario. Do you know what was the critical turning point? Not just the military successes of the Russian armed forces. You know the conflict escalated and an attack was carried out from the Chechen Republic against the adjacent territories in Russia. There was even an attack against Dagestan, another Republic with an Islamic population, and the people of Dagestan didn't wait for the federal center to respond, they took up arms to defend themselves. But the turning point was the realization by the Chechen authorities themselves, and the Chechen leadership that Chechnya's development as part of Russia would be far more promising and far more beneficial for the Chechen people themselves than the aspirations for so-called independence. Traditional Islam didn't want to submit itself to certain currents in Islam that outsiders were trying to bring to Chechnya from the Near East. There was a conflict among the local religious leaders, one of them was the father of Kadyrov, and the new religious leaders that had come from abroad from certain countries. And back then I had my first conversation with him and he told me that they were thinking about building a relationship with Russia. It was his initiative entirely. And he was not pressured into doing that. As a result, he became the first president of the Chechen Republic. And his son, the current President, fought together with his father against the federal forces. And together with his father he came to understand that the interests of the Chechen people could not be separated from the interests of Russia. Certainly, there were many people and there are still many people here that have a certain mentality—a heroic type of mentality as it were. Besides, we have gone through the tribulation of a civil war—a bloody one. Today, I'm asked to explain why Kadyrov or one of his entourage are so critical the opposition. I talked about that with him on many occasions and he promised that he would change his rhetoric. But his explanation is very simple. He says, "We've gone through blood and tears—we know what a civil war looks like—and we can't afford to have anyone lead us back there." I do not think this reasoning is correct. I do not support that. I am simply trying to tell you what his position is, what his explanation is. I believe that today he is president of the Chechen Republic and that's why he has to show restraint and he has to abide by Russian law. And I do hope that in the end that's going to happen. But we should not forget about his life before—about his life experience.

OS: But still, you're supporting 80 percent of the budget of the Chechen government—it's paid for by Russia. I forget the exact budget number.

VP: Not just the budget of Chechnya. This is a targeted approach the Russian government has taken. It's aimed at redistributing our budget revenues with a view to leveling out the economic development all across Russia in all its constituent entities. We seek a situation in which all of the economies of all Russian regions are going to be self-sufficient, and in that case we will not have to grant them any support forever. Let me reiterate, this is not just about Chechnya. Out of 85 constituent entities across Russia, there are 10 who bring more money than they spend. But we use our federal budget to support many other entities—the Northern Caucasus, the Russian Far East, the Southern Federal District and some other regions. So the Chechen Republic is no exception.

OS: Did Chechnya have some troops or men inside Ukraine in this last conflict?

VP: They were volunteers. I know about that. That's true.

OS: Let's go—shifting subjects now. I mean you've talked about this in part, but I need to get it clear. Why did you, after 2001, acquiesce in the US military encroachment across Central Asia?

VP: We didn't acquiesce. The US president asked me for support, and I also talked to some leaders of the Central Asian Republics and I asked them to respond positively to the request from the United States.[146] Partly to allow the United States to use their territory for stationing their troops and infrastructure and airports. I assumed that we had a common challenge before us—the threat of terrorism emanating from Afghanistan. And I thought that we had to work together to support the United States. Moreover, the US president told me that they're not going to stay there forever. He didn't say that they were going to stay for decades.

OS: He said that they weren't going to stay forever?

VP: Yes, that's exactly what he said. He said please help us—just for a few years. And we said all right we're going to do that. We will support you. That's what we said.

OS: So when was the wool pulled from your eyes? You know that expression? So, I mean, by 2006 right? 2007 in Munich you're casting another eye on this relationship, correct? In 2008 you have the Georgian war? So what happens between 2002-3—there's the Iraqi invasion, then you have the Ukrainian Orange Revolution in 2004. What did you think when the Ukrainian revolution went down?

VP: Nothing happened. Nothing changed and that's what's important. When I was speaking in Munich, I said that after the dissolution of the Soviet Union, when Russia turned full face to the United States to Europe, we were hoping for joint work, we were hoping that our interests would be taken into consideration so we could cooperate. But instead of that we saw the West expanding their political power and influence in those territories which we considered sensitive and important for us to ensure our global strategic security.[147]

OS: Well, if the US was involved in Ukraine at all at that point, what were you thinking? That the US was provoking these independent movements?

VP: The answer is very simple. The philosophy of American foreign policy in this region consists of and I'm absolutely sure about that, the need to prevent, by all means necessary, Ukraine cooperating with Russia. Because this rapprochement is perceived as a threat. Some people think that would lead to an increase in Russia's power and influence and they think they should use all means possible to prevent a rapprochement between Ukraine and Russia. I think it was based on this ideology and not about seeking freedom for the Ukrainian people. That was the basis for the actions of our partners in the United States and Europe. Supporting radical nationalist elements in Ukraine to create a split—a fissure—in relations between Russia and Ukraine. But if Russia starts responding to that, then it's very easy to demonize Russia, to accuse it of all the deadly sins and to draw allies, because a visible adversary emerges. So in this sense those who were behind it have accomplished their goals and they did that impeccably. But we have a broader look at the picture. Not from the point of view of confrontation, of trying to draw satellites to your side on the basis of the external threat. If you look forward 25 years into the future, if you have a look at how the world situation is going to develop, then you need to change the philosophy, the approach you take with regard to international relations, including those with Russia.

OS: But then somewhere between 2004 and 2007 in Munich, the ball moves the other way. Iraq's a disaster, Afghanistan's a disaster. Somewhere in there you change your point of view.

VP: In Munich, I said how do we assess the situation? The Soviet Union collapsed. There is no longer a foe, an adversary to the United States and to the West as a whole. So what's the point in expanding NATO? Against who? And after that there were two waves of NATO expansion following the dissolution of the Soviet Union, sort of this myth that every country can choose how they're going to ensure their security. Well we've heard that on many occasions. But this myth is nonsense. In order to ensure the security of many countries, if they feel threatened, it's not necessary to expand NATO. You can conclude bilateral agreements on mutual assistance and security. There is no need to create a false image of an adversary. There have been two expansion waves. But after that, the United States unilaterally withdrew from the ABM Treaty. That's a very important issue. An essential one. And they are always saying to us that we are not concerned by that, this is not a threat to Russia. Allegedly they did that to counter the threat of Iran. But right now the Iranian issue has gone. A treaty has been signed. Iran has renounced any military nuclear programs. The United States has agreed to that. They have said they have signed the relevant document. But the ABM development program is still underway in Europe—some of its elements are to be stationed there. Against whom are they doing that? And this requires a response from Russia. There was a prominent world leader, Otto Von Bismarck, who said that in similar situations, conversations are not important—potentials are important. And a potential is being built up right next to our borders. What are we to do? But we have to give it some thought, but we can follow up on this conversation later.

OS: Yes, have a good night sir.

VP: Thank you. Did you like the game?

OS: Yes, it was fun, I enjoyed it. You must be tired in the muscles.

VP: No, it's all right—I'll try to catch up with my sleep.

Trip 3—Day 3—May 11, 2016

BEFORE THE SCREENING OF
DR. STRANGELOVE IN SOCHI

OS: Hello, Mr. President, how are you today?

VP: Okay, how are you?

OS: I'm tired today. Didn't sleep well.

VP: I played hockey, but you're the one who's tired!

OS: Yeah, but your muscles hurt. I took a nice walk with my wife in the park.

VP: Oh, that's wonderful.

OS: I was thinking about Sochi in the Fourth Century B.C.—what it must've been like.

VP: You know, Odysseus went to collect the Golden Fleece here.

OS: Yes, that's what I'm saying—the Fourth Century, Fifth Century too. This is legendary.

VP: And when the travelers were approaching the place where the Sea of Azov unites with the Black Sea—that place is called Tanang here in Russia—and they decided that that place caused the descent to Tartarus, that is, to the underworld. Because in that place there were many underground streams, geysers and earthquakes all the time. In the United States there is a valley like that, and we have a similar valley in the Russian Far East.

OS: And also, Jason and the Golden Fleece, the Amazons in Theseus, all the horse-people. And also in Sochi, weren't they like Americans looking for oil?

VP: No, it didn't used to be like that. Right now we have certain plans to extract hydrocarbons here. We have to be cautious, because traditionally this place has been a resort in Russia. Not far from here, on the coast, there was quite a large oil refinery, and Exxon Mobil has shown some interest in using those ports and operating them.

OS: Last night we stopped at the 2007 Munich speech.

VP: I forgot about that.

OS: That's okay.

ON PUTIN'S FIRST PRESIDENCY

OS: So recovering from 2001, when you made this alliance with the US to now—to 2016. But for the readers, I just want to recount quickly—bear with me as I recount the events and then you can correct me when I finish. So, you know, in the '90s you'd been around and you'd certainly been aware of the US actions in Kosovo, and the bombing of Belgrade. And obviously the break-up of Yugoslavia. But in 2001, you offer an alliance and cooperation and friendship with the US administration and it leads of course to the disappointments and failures of the US-NATO coalition in Afghanistan and Iraq. In that period there's a NATO expansion, another wave of NATO expansion, and the ABM Treaty of 1972 is cancelled by the United States. We have, in that same time period in 2004, you have the Orange Revolution in Ukraine. And we talked about it last night but I gather there is no threat to you—to Russia, yet, of a breakaway by Ukraine. It's not considered. The factions in Ukraine start breaking up, start arguing with each other and fighting with each other, and the threat, the fear, of a unified Ukraine leaving Russian is not yet there.

I gather, in this same period, you're a bit enamored of the idea of a partnership with the United States, and being courted by Wall Street, being encouraged by Wall Street. In 2004, for example, you're seen singing with Sharon Stone. I want to remind you of that. Come over here, Fernando, and show him. It's a very funny clip. [wrong clip plays] Well, keep trying because I would love to get his reaction to it.

So, your first term is coming to an end. In the middle of all this, and you told me a fascinating conversation on my first visit, in 2005 you complained to Bush about US support of terrorism in Central Asia. And that was an interesting story. And you said, I think it was the CIA had sent your Special Services a letter saying that they in fact supported the terrorists in Central Asia—something to that effect. Am I wrong?

VP: Yes, we had that conversation, but this was not about Central Asia. This was the following—according to the data we received, employees of the United States in Azerbaijan contacted militants from the Caucasus. And I told the US president about that, and he said that he would sort it out, and that he would look into it. Later, through our partner channels, we received a letter from the CIA which stated that "our colleagues thought they had the right to maintain contact with all the representatives of the opposition and that they were going to continue to do that." It even named the employee of the US Special Services who worked in the US embassy in Baku.

OS: And all this while they're fighting the war against terror in Afghanistan.

VP: I do not remember the exact year, but it seems like that.

OS: That seems like contradictory behavior and strange.

VP: We have gotten used to these contradictions. Back then I also thought this was somewhat contradictory. But this attitude when you want to use someone for your purposes and you don't want to cooperate to achieve the goals your partners are pursuing, this certainly leads to mutual suspicion and this doesn't create favorable conditions for efficient joint work.

OS: I guess the letter is top secret so it's not available for viewing?

VP: I don't think that would be appropriate. Suffice it to say that I already shared this information with you. Somewhere in the archives this letter is being kept. I think George [Bush] remembers our conversation. We met at an event in another country. I think it was the UK, but I don't remember exactly.

OS: So now it's 2008 and two big things happened in that year. The financial crisis hits the West, but it deeply affects Russia. It's almost as if a rug were pulled out from under you.

VP: Yes, that was a troubling time.

OS: And Russia is told by Wall Street it has to change its ways?

VP: No, I wouldn't say that. There was no dictate, we didn't feel that. A lot was incumbent upon us. Back then I was the chairman of the government of the Russian Federation. According to the Russian constitution, the government is the supreme executive authority of the country and it is responsible for managing the economy of the country. And that's why we acted quite swiftly elaborating an anti-crisis plan which provided support to the most vulnerable branches of our economy. We emphasized supporting the banking sector because that is the cardiovascular system of the whole economy. We tried to create conditions that would allow banks to not just get support from the government and from the central bank of Russia. We also wanted our banks to perform the main functions, that is providing lending, loaning money to the real economy. That was a real problem both to us and to the United States, to Europe. We needed to ensure, amidst great risks, that financial sectors flow into the real economy.[148]

We set forth this special plan to fight unemployment, to create new jobs.

And also actual plans to support the most vulnerable, the most damaged sectors of our economy. I refer in particular to the automobile industry, aircraft construction industry, and some of others. So one of the main goals that we were addressing was to ensure that we performed all our social obligations to the population. We had to pay salaries and pensions and social benefits.

OS: It's a tough time.

VP: But on the whole, we did manage to live up to the expectations.

OS: Right. But, I remember in the West it was scary. And obviously they were bringing up the spectre again—because the private banks misbehaved—they were bringing up the spectre of "you've got to diversify your economy."

VP: I cannot agree with you that someone was not satisfied with the behavior of our private banks. There were great concerns that those banks suffered from margin calls, which were due to economic changes. They had an obligation to pay their credits back to Western banks. And so our enterprises were concerned that they would not be able to. Everyone was asking the government to lend a hand to our private banks and our enterprises that had borrowed money from foreign banks. And that's exactly what we did—we lent a hand—through different tools, like direct funding, quasi-state financial institutions. We prevented all mistakes—in hindsight I can say that there were no serious mistakes made. Moreover, we didn't change the structure of the Russian economy for the worse. You need these conditions in Russia, in the United States and others in the developed countries. There is a great temptation to expand the state-run sector of the economy. We didn't do that. In spite of the fact that certain private companies' owners came to me as chairman of the government and they suggested that the government should purchase their companies at a minimum level—one Ruble—that's the price they offered, because they wanted us to assume the responsibility to pay back their debts and to maintain a certain number of jobs.

OS: Were those the auto companies?

VP: These were different companies. But we didn't do that. We didn't take this path. We decided to support the private sector, and to a certain extent we have saved a great number of private enterprises. The fact is that the business community itself showed great maturity in their judgment. And to me, that was quite a surprise to be honest. Indeed, they were willing to risk their private capital, their money, to assume responsibility. They were ready to fight for their enterprises, and in the end, out of this situation we have emerged without new losses. Moreover, this government used all these measures, providing support to the banking sector, and even made money on that. The government not only helped the private sector, it also got money from that. And this gives me grounds to believe that the plans and consequences had turned out to be quite efficient.

OS: Would it be mistaken of me to say that by 2008 your courtship with the West was reaching an end? That's the period when you could be seen with Sharon Stone and seen as pro-American. You had come to a new beginning, and a new phase?[149]

VP: We have never adhered to a pro-American position, per-se. We have always assumed a position aimed at ensuring our national interests. Back then, we thought it was necessary to forge good relations with the United States. And I still think that. I didn't change my position in this regard. Our partners have to change their attitude towards us. We have to understand that there are not just their interests, there are also our interests. And in order to develop these relations harmoniously we have to treat each other with respect. Right now, you recalled the 2008 crisis. Apart from supporting the national business and lending a hand to the banking system, the Government provided this support to everyone without exception. Including to foreign shareholders and financial institutions in Russia with 100 percent capital of foreign origin, despite the fact that in certain countries, when they were fighting the crisis, they accepted from those who weren't entitled to get government support from Russian enterprises. And what's more important, we didn't take the path of restricting the flow of capital even amid financial constraints. We could have restricted the flow of capital—there are many restrictive instruments like that, but we didn't use any of those instruments. And in the end I think that was the right call, because that brings trust from investors in the government actions.

OS: Okay, let me put it another way. Would you say that in a sense you were being courted by Wall Street before 2008. You were, in a sense, a junior partner of the American century—in their view—and then all of a sudden this happens, as many of us in the West began to doubt the foundations of Wall Street, the foundations of the West. We're not thinking about Russia. We're thinking about the whole economic system—global system. Does it make sense? Were you naïve in other words, to believe in that system?

VP: I'm not going to talk about Wall Street, about what they think, and how they act and how they used to act and think. Wall Street is suffering itself from the faulty, erroneous actions the US administration takes in foreign policy. I'm talking about Wall Street in the broader sense of the term, not just about the financial component of the American economy. I can say that many more American enterprises would still be willing, with great pleasure, to work in Russia—and they want to do that. But their activities are restricted. And in my view that is a great mistake the US administration is making. We have an expression which says that if a place is free, then surely someone will come grab it. And indeed, these places are going to be grabbed by rivals. And business people from Wall Street understand that full well. And we have many friends and allies there—that's why I have to defend and protect them from your accusations. [laughter]

OS: Well, I'm looking for a change in your thinking but it doesn't seem like you admit to it now, so let's move on.

VP: You know, there is one thing I have to say where we agree—the certain naiveté with regards to our relations with our partners—it was there. We thought that our country had changed drastically. We had voluntarily taken due political actions of great importance. We had prevented violent actions from happening when the Soviet Union dissolved. We had opened up to our Western partners. Suffice it to say to remind you that the former head of the KGB had opened to the US partners the whole system of surveillance in the American Embassy in Moscow.[150] He told them everything about that thinking that the US was ready to do the same, with the Embassy of Russia in the United States. And that was not the most well-thought-through decision, because there was nothing in response from the United States.

OS: Well, a lot of the neoconservative historians misinterpreted a lot of the files to favor their point of view in history. So there were a lot of arguments about the old Cold War files that came out of the Kremlin, as well as people who were looking for the JFK assassination papers. There was all kinds of stuff going on—it was quite a commotion in the mid-'90s, as I remember.

VP: I know all these speculations about that tragedy—the assassination of

JFK—and attempts at trying to implicate the Soviet Union. As former head of the Russian FSB, I can say that the Soviet Union had nothing to do with the JFK assassination.

OS: [laughter] I believe you. And I think other people believe you.

VP: You know, if you stick to that logic, you can shift all the blame on Russia saying that all assassinations were done with the participation of the Soviet Union.

OS: Yeah, I was never one of those.

ON GEORGIA, UKRAINE, AND CRIMEA

OS: In 2008, from the American point of view, the war in Georgia marks a prominent return of Russia to an independent position showing off military muscle for the first time since 1991—correct me if I'm wrong.

VP: Sure, something like that. I told you, we have reduced significantly our armed forces. Moreover, we still have plans to reduce our armed forces even more. We're going to do that calmly as new military equipment arrives. Right now we do not have any plans for immediate reductions. But on the whole, as we receive new military equipment, the personnel is also going to change.

OS: That's not what I'm asking. I'm asking, from the US point of view, it's seen as a significant departure from the Russian behavior of the previous years. Tell us a little bit about the war and what was at stake and why you committed the troops.

VP: In the first place, I was not the one who made this decision, it was taken by President Medvedev—the then-president of Russia. I'm not going to conceal it. Indeed, I knew about this decision. Moreover, when I had been president for my second term, we had thought about possible actions, these kinds of actions, from Georgia. But certainly we had hoped that this would not come to pass. And let me remind you how this conflict erupted. President Saakashvili ordered his troops to attack the territory of South Ossetia. And during the first strike they performed, they destroyed the peacekeeper space—Russian peacekeepers. During the first strike, 10 or 15 people died. The strike performed by the Georgian troops with multiple rocket launcher systems, and people simply didn't have time to get out of their barracks. And afterward, Georgia performed a large-scale military assault. I'd like to look at other countries' representatives and ask them what they would do if one strike were to destroy all their peacekeepers. So we did lend a hand to South Ossetia, but we were also—and I'd like to emphasize that—performing our duties as peacekeepers. And apart from that, we suffered losses, unprovoked. We could have perceived that as an attack against the Russian Federation. On many occasions, repeatedly, I told the US, the European partners, the Georgian leadership—I asked them to prevent the escalation of this conflict.[151] I'd like to draw attention to the fact that when I was president, I had met the leadership of the then-unrecognized republics of Ossetia or Abkhazia. I met with them because we harbored a thought that this internal conflict that had been going on for many decades, would be resolved by peaceful means. I'm not talking about what they could have achieved, about the territorial integrity, or other form of association that they could have arrived at, but through peaceful means. Instead, President Saakashvili chose to commit this act of provocation. Back then, I talked to a number of my counterparts and they were saying, "What do you expect, he's mad?"[152] I'm talking about my counterparts from the Western countries.

OS: Oh, so you talked to your counterparts in the West and they blamed it on Saakashvili?

VP: Yes, during the first days of the conflict, and I told them, "Yes, probably he is mad, but he's killing our people. Either stop him, or we will have to act ourselves." But no one was going to check him or they simply couldn't, I don't know. And that's why we had to respond. And I'd like to draw attention to the fact that we didn't respond immediately—it took us several days after the beginning of the aggression. We did expect someone to interfere, to make him withdraw troops from South Ossetia, to stop these actions. But nothing like that happened. So in our perspective, nothing had changed. They simply pushed us beyond a certain point and we couldn't let anyone go beyond that line. We were provoked into doing what we did.

OS: Do you think that the US or NATO, in any way, are supporting Saakashvili to do this or told him that it was okay to try?

VP: I do not have 100% surety that someone had provoked him, that some-one had been behind this. I don't know about that. But I think that he would never be bold enough to do that on his own. In any case, no one tried to stop him.

OS: That was where the issue occurred where President Medvedev appar-ently delayed a day or two, and you urged him to get in, per treaty.

VP: Yes, that's true. However, this decision was being taken. Russia showed restraint, patience, even amid an armed attack against our peacekeepers and killings of innocent people. Afterwards, I'd like to repeat that. It turned out that no one was trying to stop that agent provocateur. In the end, President Medvedev made the right decision.

OS: I heard that the Russian government realized they had to modernize their forces after that brief war—call it a war. The performance of the troops was underwhelming.

VP: They performed quite well. They were quite efficient. But it turned out that indeed modernization was required, new adjustments. These develop-ments convinced us that we had to do it. Because no one was dissuaded from taking such actions against us.

OS: So the modernization of the army starts to really increase and the bud-get goes up, the machinery gets better.

VP: You know, this is not just about the Georgian development, because this was simply about the expiration date of our equipment. It had to be changed because the expiration date was approaching.

OS: Right. What about the nuclear force? What was the status of it then?

VP: Since that time, indeed, we have done a great deal of work to modern-ize our nuclear potential.

OS: Starting then?

VP: We had done that before we had plans. And we had been implementing those plans in accordance with the schedule we had set forth. But afterwards, after these developments, we became disciplined carrying out those plans—the financial discipline, technological discipline. And as of now, our nuclear deterrent forces are in very good shape. This is the most modernized component of the Russian armed forces, including the systems that are devised to surmount the ABM system of a potential adversary.

OS: Okay, I'd like to skip forward from 2008 into the Ukraine crisis. We've had this discussion before on my first visit, on the terrace, and I've listened to it and realized there are things I didn't ask. And I want to go over it, just to be really clear, because this will be very important to the people who will be watching the documentary or reading this transcript.

VP: Certainly. Indeed, it requires a great deal of effort to clarify all that. Because your colleagues, your Western journalists are very talented people. They are capable of convincing people that black is white and vice versa. Just as an example—the tragic events, the assault against South Ossetia—Mr. Saakashvili publicly announced that he ordered his troops to commence that action. One of his dignitaries even spoke on television saying the same thing. I didn't believe it when I heard it, when the media was accusing Russia of this attack. And millions of TV viewers believed that all across the world. This is just astounding, this capacity that your American and European journalists can have. You're all very talented. But when our journalists try to protect Russian national interests, when they take a stance, they are declared immediately the mouthpiece of Kremlin propaganda—much to my chagrin.

OS: It's a double standard. I would love to see a debate—a meeting between Mr. Saakashvili and you—it would be great to see the two of you in a room.

VP: We met on many occasions.

OS: Are you convinced he's still mad?

VP: I have never said that.

OS: I thought you said he was mad?

VP: No, I was told by my Western counterparts that he was mad. And I could never afford to say anything like that to my counterpart, either the incumbent or the previous ones.

OS: When's the last time you saw him?

VP: I do not remember. Certainly before the crisis in South Ossetia.

OS: Not after the war, though?

VP: No, but on many occasions I said to him, "Mikheil Nikolaevich, please do everything to prevent bloodshed. If you want to restore relations with these parts of Georgia, you have to be very cautious." These fictions, these divergences, they had a reason a long time ago—not hundreds of years of ago—but back in 1919 when the Russian empire was splitting up. Those parts of Georgia, which incidentally had been part of the Russian Empire as independent states before Georgia became part of the Russian empire. Back then, those parts declared that they were ready, that they wanted to still be part of Russia. And back then very harsh actions, military measures were employed against them. Local populations still view those actions as genocide and mass elimination of people. In order to surmount all these difficulties, patience was required, as well as certain diplomatic art.

OS: Yeah, I understand.

VP: And that was lacking apparently. That's what the Georgian leadership back then was lacking. Moreover, the current Georgian leadership believe that this action Saakashvili performed was a terrible crime against the Georgian people in the first place, because it has led to very grave consequences.

OS: I was shocked when Shevardnadze—hard name to pronounce—I was shocked because I really respected him as a foreign minister with Gorbachev. You may not agree, but I was shocked when he wanted to join NATO and he became corrupt, I heard.[153] He was a very respected figure in the 1980s.

VP: Well, everything passes, everything changes.

OS: That's true. But just quickly—Obama's in office now, take it from 2008 to the Ukraine crisis and how this . . . nothing really major, dramatic happened, as I remember, except for the Snowden affair in 2013.[154] He was offered asylum here in Russia and that upset America. But was there anything else in that period that you remember, between you and the US that was exacerbated, was argued about?

VP: Well, how can you say that nothing major happened? When President Kuchma's term came to an end—I do not remember exactly the year—presidential elections took place in Ukraine.

And Mr. Yanukovych won that presidential election, but the opposition didn't like that. And mass riots erupted. These riots were fueled quiet actively by the United States. And a third round of elections was announced—in violation of the country's constitution. Per se, this can be perceived as a coup d'état. And pro-Western politicians arrived in power after that—Mr. Yushchenko and Timoshenko. I cannot say that I welcomed this way of changing the government. Nowhere is that proper, but in the post-Soviet space, especially, constitutions cannot be broken. Luckily no bloodshed took place there.

OS: Did you have a phone call with Obama about this issue?

VP: That was before Obama came to office, and yet we maintained cooperation with the Ukrainian leadership of Mr. Yushchenko and Timoshenko. I went to Kiev, they came back to Moscow. We met in third party countries. And we implemented all our plans of cooperation, but their policy, it was not well-liked by the Ukrainian people. That is why after the presidential term of President Yushchenko ended, Mr. Yanukovych won the election once again and everyone acknowledged that. It was recognized by everyone. But apparently this was not the best form of government either. Economic difficulties, together with social difficulties, to a great extent had undermined the trust in the new leadership as well. What needed to be done in order to rectify the situation? They should have organized another election. And they should have chosen people with different economic and social views. These people should have made another attempt at arriving back in power. But certainly they should have prevented any escalation to bloodshed, and what's absolutely certain is that no one should have supported these bloody events.

OS: But you're talking about 2014—you're jumping ahead.

VP: Yes, in 2014.

OS: But between '08 and '14, there was this one election you're talking about which is in 2012, I think?

VP: I do not remember

OS: There were so many, I mean, the Ukraine to us—we were not paying attention.

VP; Yes, well you personally might not have been paying attention, but the CIA was paying a great deal of attention.

OS: I know. It was very confusing. There was a guy with a poisoned face earlier in the century.

VP: Yes, you're talking about Yushchenko—he said that he'd been poisoned during the election campaign.[155] And yet he was elected to office. And he worked and I met with him on many occasions. Why did they need to resort to violence? That's something I cannot quite understand. Moreover, I talked about that repeatedly and the 2014 President Yanukovych was in office and he signed an agreement with the opposition. He agreed to all the requirements that they had set forth.

OS: In the crisis, in the final days?

VP: Yes and he even agreed to hold early elections. So why do they need to perform this coup d'état? I do not understand.

OS: Okay. So we all remember, I remember you vividly on television saying—I think it was with Charlie Rose, I forgot—but you said there was much evidence and you smiled as you said it. There was much evidence—implying that a thousand eyes were upon this. You know that expression, a thousand eyes were upon this coup. It was a coup in slow motion. It was pretty evident, transparent to the Russians.

VP: Certainly.

OS: And you said that on television, but I think the American people find it difficult to understand but, by talking about the evidence and showing it, we might be able to convince the American public that they were being fooled by the Western narrative of events and that there indeed was a coup d'état that went down.

VP: That's very easy to achieve—you simply have to look at the developments. After Yanukovych announced that he had to postpone the signing of the association agreement with the European Union, no one listened to the reasons why, to the terms, to the timetables—mass riots erupted right away after the announcement.[156] These riots led to the seizure of his residence, and on the eve of that, he had signed an agreement with the opposition on settling the situation, on the possible organization of early elections, and three foreign ministers of European countries added their signatures to the agreement. Where are these guarantees? Once the president went to the second largest city of the country to attended a political event, armed men seized the residence of the president. Imagine something like that in the US, if the White House was seized—what would it be called? A coup d'état, or would you say that they have come to sweep the floors. The prosecutor general was shot at. There were so many shootings, so much violence.

OS: I had an interview with Mr. Yanukovych, so I know his version, but it was characterized in the US press as if Yanukovych abandoned Kiev, because he felt the crowd would tear him apart.

VP: Yes, that's the version used to justify the support granted to the coup d'état. Mr. Yanukovych didn't leave to go abroad. He was in the country when his residence was taken.[157] Moreover, one day afterwards, he used our support and he relocated to the Crimea. Back then, the Crimea was still part of Ukraine. And Yanukovych stayed there for more than 10 days—at least a week in the Crimea, thinking there was still a chance that those people who had put their signatures under the agreement with the opposition would make some attempt, with a view to settling this conflict by civilized, democratic, legal means. But it never happened. It became evident that if he was taken by these people he would simply be killed by them. And, afterwards, he found himself in Russia. Everything can be perverted or distorted, millions of people can be deceived if you have a monopoly on the media. But in the end, I believe for an objective and impartial spectator it's clear what happened. A coup d'état had taken place. All right, if this coup d'état had made some positive changes . . . but, on the contrary, the situation deteriorated even further. Ukraine lost territory, not due to Russia's actions, but due to the choice made by those who are live in Crimea. These people didn't want to live under the banner of nationalists. A civil war erupted in the southeastern part of Ukraine, in the Donbass. After that, the country witnessed a terrible drop in the GDP. The largest industrial enterprises shut down. Unemployment soared. The real income of the population, their salaries, plunged, inflation hit 45 or 47 percent. And no one knew how to address these issues, or that this would be further exacerbated by an internal political crisis, by a fight between the Prime Minister and the President. In the end, it led to Prime Minister Yatsenyuk resigning. He had actively supported, and had been supported by, the American administration throughout the crises. And what happened next? The European Union opened its borders to Ukraine. It zeroed out the tariff for Ukrainian goods. But Ukraine's trade with the European Union decreased by 23 percent, and with Russia it decreased by 50 percent. Ukrainian industrial output is not in high demand in European markets and now they have no access to the Russian market. The agricultural produce that used to be traded successfully in Western Europe is restricted by quotas. And these quotas were introduced by the Europeans. They were exhausted during the first two months after the signing of the agreement. Right now Ukraine is fighting to get a visa-free arrangement for its citizens. Do you know why they are doing that? So they could ensure free exit from the country to find new jobs outside of the country. But the people are once again being tricked, because even if a visa-free deal were granted to Ukraine, that would not enable them to work abroad.

OS: Visa-free to Russia?

VP: No, visa-free to the European Union. People heard that they would be able to relocate and work in another country in Europe. There's something I'd like to tell you. Ukraine has always been an industrialized country as part of the Soviet Union. And right now, a Ukrainian's dream is to work as a nurse or a gardener or a nanny in a European country amid the complete de-industrialization of the country. Why did they need all that? I simply cannot imagine.

OS: Well, it seems to me what you're saying is that Russia doesn't need Ukraine.

VP: Russia is a self-sufficient country. We do not need anyone, but with Ukraine we are connected by thousands of ties. On many occasions I've said that and I'd like to reiterate. I'm deeply convinced that the Ukrainian people and the Russian people are not simply close relatives. They are almost the same. As for the language, the culture, the history, each certainly has to be treated with respect. And even when we were one single country, we treated them with respect. Suffice it to say that the whole of the Soviet Union for decades, was managed by those who originated from Ukraine. I think that testifies to a lot.

OS: Yes, but economically, as you say, you're self-sufficient. They're gone—let them have their problems. It's not going to destroy your country.

VP: No, certainly—not in the least.

OS: One point you made in our last meeting. I asked, "What about the Russian submarine base in Crimea?" Sebastopol I think it was. And you said it was not important because you have another base across the water—somewhere around here. In other words, you weren't threatened by the loss of the base. That's what you told me at the time.

VP: Losing the base in Sebastopol was a threat, but it was not too sensitive. Because by that time . . . right now we are commissioning a new military base—indeed not far from here in Novorossiysk.[158] What was presenting certain difficulties to us was the severing of ties between the companies of the defense sector. Because the defense sectors of Ukraine and Russia during the Soviet period were one single system. And if these relations were severed, then that certainly would lead to a certain negative impact on our defense industry. But we have devised a whole system for input-substitution as we call it. And right now, we are actively surmounting all of these difficulties. We are establishing new enterprises from scratch, and these enterprises produce a new generation of military equipment. And that defense industry in Ukraine which used to provide support to Russia is now simply dying out—I'm talking about the missile industry, aircraft industry and also engine construction.

OS: I understand. In other words, the US succeeded in starting the coup, and winning as they did many times over the years. And it was a loss, but not a fatal loss.

VP: You could say that. Moreover, when I say that we started establishing new enterprises that help propel us to new technological levels, I often cite this example. All of our helicopters used to be equipped with engines produced in Ukraine—100% of our helicopters. Once the supplies from Ukraine stopped, we built a new plant, right now we are completing another one. All helicopters can fly—fully functional—and we have engines of a new generation. So as you can see, what our air force is doing in Syria testifies to the fact that we are doing quite well.

OS: Even if NATO entered into an agreement with Ukraine, I still don't see too much of a threat, with the new weaponry.

VP: I see a threat. This threat consists of the fact that once NATO comes to this or that country, then as a whole the political leadership of that country, as well as the population there, cannot influence the decisions NATO makes—including the decisions related to stationing the military infrastructure. Even very sensitive weapons systems can be deployed. I'm talking also about the antiballistic missile systems. And that means that we would have to respond somehow to that.

OS: Plus all the weapons we've put into the Baltic States?

VP: I'm talking about this strategic anti-ballistic missile system (ABMs). There are only two facilities like that in Eastern Europe—in Romania and in Poland. And at sea in the Mediterranean, there are plans to deploy these systems on ships. Right now negotiations are under way to do the same in South Korea. All that certainly creates a threat to our nuclear deterrence system. Let me remind you that I myself proposed to our American partners that we should work on these systems together. What would that imply? That would imply that we would designate the missile threats together, and we would create a joint system for ABM management. Then we would exchange technological information. And all of that in my view would spell cardinal drastic changes in the world as far as national security is concerned. I'm not going into details right now. But our proposal was declined by our American counterparts, [as I've said many times].

OS: Of course. Okay. But it seems to me that Russia adapts and you are adapting to these ABMs. Am I wrong?

VP: We have these capabilities, we are improving them, and when we talked with our American counterparts, we told them that we deemed the construction of those systems as a threat, and they always responded that this was not against us. This was against the missile aspirations of Iran. As of now an agreement has been reached, fortunately, with Iran. But the deployment of this system still goes forward. What does it tell us? We were right. But back then when we were discussing that, we were saying we would have to take actions in response, and these actions were to partly consist in improving our offensive capabilities. Their response was as follows. The ABM system they told us was not established against us. And what we were going to do—that is, to improve our own offensive capability—would be considered by the United States as not aimed against the United States. And we agreed on that.

OS: You know, the American Indians made treaties with the US government and they were the first to experience the treachery of the US government. You're not the first.

VP: We wouldn't like to be the last. [laughter]

OS: In that regard, I'd like to show you a piece of film from Stanley Kubrick's "Dr. Strangelove" set in the war rooms of the United States. One scene we can see and then if you like we can see another one. But first, to just finish this Ukraine thing. My ultimate question is, in hindsight, looking back, did you make a mistake by annexing Crimea because it cost you tremendously— the sanctions, the whole EU turns on Russia, the US—it becomes big news because it's regarded as illegal in the international post-war treaty world. Not to say that other people haven't broken their treaties, but ... Anyway, it did cost you big time and you perhaps miscalculated. Perhaps you thought it would be acceptable in some way. Have you ever thought about that decision in retrospect?

VP: We did not force Crimea into Russia. Those who live in Crimea have decided to join Russia. And when following this path we were very cautious, and in full compliance with international law and the United Nations charter. The first thing that was done in Crimea itself was not by us, but by those who inhabit Crimea. The legitimate parliament of Crimea that was elected based on the Ukrainian legislation, announced a referendum. The Crimean parliament, by an overwhelming vote, decided, after the referendum, to join Russia.

I know of no other way that would be more democratic to address issues of this kind than the free will of the people. The expression of this free will, was that an overwhelming majority had voted for independence and for joining Russia.[159] On the whole, during the referendum, it was 90 percent or even more. If there is a better or more democratic way to address this issue, please tell me about that. Today, I hear only the opinion that contains the attempt at justifying that our actions, with regard to Crimea, were not correct. That is, the central authorities of Ukraine did not agree to that. That's what they argue. But let me remind you that when a decision on Kosovo's independence was taken, the United Nations International Court of Justice decided that on issues related to independence and self-determination, no consent from the central authorities of this or that country were required. And please say for those who will see this film [or read this transcript], that the letter from the State Department of the United States addressed to the UN Security Council on this matter says the State Department supports Kosovo's decision on independence wholeheartedly.[160] Other European countries spoke in the same vein. And in this regard I do not quite understand why the Kosovars would have these rights, whereas Russians, Ukrainians, and Crimean Tatars who live in Crimea in a similar situation would not enjoy the same rights. I think that is absolutely unacceptable.

That is what we call having double standards. And we do not regret anything. This is not just about the future of Soviet territories. We're talking about the future of millions of people, and we didn't have a choice, really. Only one decision was possible—to agree with this request from the Crimeans about the reunification with Russia. Just one more thing—our troops were there. But these troops didn't take a single shot. The only thing they did was to create conditions for these elections to take place and for the referendum to take place. And I reiterate, even though I said that on many occasions, in the course of these events there was not a single victim.

OS: Let me put it this way—did you expect to be excommunicated by the European community because of this?

VP: Certainly I did expect this kind of reaction. But before making this decision, we had conducted a very deep social research in Russia, and the overwhelming majority of Russian citizens—around 80 percent or more—when responding to the question whether it was possible to re-unify Crimea with Russia, even though that would mean a deterioration of relations with the West and other countries of the world, they said yes they thought it was possible. So when making this decision, I was guided not by the preferences of my counterparts from other countries. I responded to the sentiment of the Russian people.

OS: And the Crimeans as of this date, are they grateful? Or are they pissed off?

VP; There are many problems in Crimea, but on the whole, people support the decision which was taken. The best estimate of that support was the poll that was recently conducted in Crimea because the Kiev authorities tried to set up an energy blockade of the peninsula. The overwhelming majority—I'm talking about the same figures—the overwhelming majority re-affirmed the decision they had made earlier on joining Russia.

OS: And Donbass? Well, this is a real problem, I guess, in terms of the thorn that doesn't go away. How do you get out of this one?

VP: Certainly, I think the Minsk Agreement has to be implemented.

OS: But it doesn't seem like Kiev has any intention of doing so.

VP: I do have all the plans, and the Russian leadership as a whole, we have these plans. But the key components of the Minsk agreements are the political components, and the main political component is to make amendments to the Ukrainian constitution. It should have been done, not by us, but by the Kiev authorities, by the end of 2015. And a law on amnesty has to be adopted and it has to have force. It has been adopted, but it has not been promulgated by the president. A special status law in these territories has to be enforced. This law has also been adopted. It has been voted on by the Ukrainian parliament but it has not been enforced. We cannot do that for them. But I'm hopeful that in the end this is going to be done. And the conflict is going to end.

OS: So we should maybe look at some film? We'll adjust the lights and darken the room. You can sit there and we can talk about the scenes afterwards.

Trip 3—Day 3—May 11, 2016

———

OS: Thank you for indulging me by watching "Dr. Strangelove." I thought the Russian Premier was very good.

VP: Thank you. There are certain things in this film that indeed make us think. Despite the fact that it's all just imagination—the things that we see onscreen—there are certain serious issues, things that make us think about real challenges, real threats that exist. I think from a technical point of view, he anticipated many things.

OS: The concept of "nuclear winter'—the end of the world—that was the hydrogen bomb. Scientists talked about this after the war and Truman went ahead anyway. This was about communication. The Russians have *The Doomsday Machine*, the US goes ahead with a unilateral attack and all of the planes are recalled except for this one pilot who is very clever and manages to elude the radar system.

VP: The thing is, since that time, little has changed, honestly. The only difference is that modern weapon systems have become more sophisticated, more complex. But this idea of a retaliatory strike and the inability to manage these systems, yes, all of these things are relevant today. It will become even more difficult and more dangerous.

OS: I believe that. Should we finish our conversation? The next question has a few parts to it. It has to do with the economy, it has to do with the oligarchs. No question that under you, Russia has seen a period of great growth in overall living standards. But the US criticisms are essentially that you have created a system of centralization, authoritarianism, and what they call "an oligarchic state capitalism." Which they say is similar to the old styles of Tsarism and communism. On the other hand, they were quite pleased with the 1990s Russia, where the oligarchs thrived, before you came in. And then you knocked out or derailed some of them—you told me that story in our first meeting—that you had a meeting with them in Moscow and you made a point in this meeting that there was a responsibility to the people and the state.

So the Western elite says that you have put your oligarchs into power in the last 15 years, whereas these older oligarchs are sitting in places like London. That's the situation as phrased by the West. I have to say, I have friends in London and when I go there, there's incredible stories and many of the oligarchs in England tell people that they have accumulated great wealth, but they say that you led them to the wealth and that you shared in it. It's clear that these people are trying to deflect the heat from themselves by blaming someone else. But what amazes me is the intelligent people I know in London who truly begin to believe this story over the years—that you are, in fact, the single richest person in the world.[161] Not since Rockefeller, or Morgan, or Onassis—[Putin laughs] you may laugh, and I appreciate it, but as a leader, of your people, like Chavez or Castro or many other people who have been accused of corruption, is there some way you could make your personal wealth clearer.

VP: Well, to be honest, I do not have the wealth they attribute to me. To make it clear, this phenomenon of oligarchy, we have to remember what was going on at the beginning of the 1990s in Russia. After the collapse of the Soviet Union, regrettably, democracy began to be abused by many people who were seeking to gain money through political power. This democracy began to be seen as all-permissiveness. I remember when I moved to Moscow from St. Petersburg, I was astounded and shocked by how many of them had gathered here in Moscow. And their behavior was so astounding I couldn't get used to it for a very long time. Those people didn't have any scruples at all. What is oligarchy? It is the integration of money and power, with a view to influencing the decisions that are being taken, and the final aim to continue to accumulate wealth.

Back in the 1990s we had this notion of seven bankers.[162] Many of them were saying that the Russian economy was too small to allow additional play-ers. They said that seven to ten players were enough. And in order to change the situation that was noted by many in the West to be a corrupt system, and many of those who live in Moscow today or in other parts of the world were forbidden to enter Western countries—they were not granted visas. But once we started fighting against these oligarchs, they started to turn into a sort of internal opposition. And the Western attitude toward them, these ruling classes, started to change drastically. These oligarchs started to get support. When necessary, they got asylum abroad, despite crimes they had committed before—very serious ones. I don't know who manages to say they got money thanks to my help. If they did get money thanks to my help, what are they doing in London? Well, probably it's not as simple as that. When the emblematic figures of the oligarchic community, a person who's no longer with us, as Mr. Berezovsky, at the end of his life wrote a letter to me asking my forgiveness and for a chance to get back to Russia. Certainly one con-versation was not enough with whomever that might have been. We had to stick to a consistent harsh policy so as to dissuade people who had managed to enrich themselves through power from influencing this power. And I did that step by step. But it was a consistent policy. Just to make it clear how it was implemented from the very beginning, let me cite an example. One of the employees of the President's administration back then, once he got into office, he was approached by the head of one of our largest companies. And that person said he would be in charge of whatever that employee was going to do. He would help him with administrative issues as well as with his finan-cial situation. And indeed some of these people are now hiding abroad. My task was to differentiate between power and money. And to prevent people from influencing power through unconstitutional means, either in economy or in politics. On the whole I think I've managed with some success in this regard. As for those who have accumulated their capital over the last decade, indeed there were many people like that. Some of them I had been acquaint-ed with before I became president, some of them I became acquainted with while serving as president or prime minister. But all of them have gotten their money honestly and fairly. And they don't have any connection to the power or any capacity to influence the decisions that are being made. I think that's the key element to fighting this oligarchic system of power. But the most important thing is, starting from 2000, we have increased almost two-fold our national economy, and during this time many enterprises have risen including private companies. Certainly the main emphasis is being made on the people that I know personally, but when this emphasis is made it is only a tool for manipulating public opinion and using it for political purposes, primarily by those who were ex-communicated from that power. But this doesn't mean at all that we have managed to address all of the issues related to abuse of power or corruption, and we are going to continue this work in the future.

Right now I'm concerned not by oligarchs, who we are going to keep in place where they are supposed to be. We do not have the oligarchic system that used to exist in Russia. In 2008, I said that many entrepreneurs with whom I had not been acquainted before, to my surprise they showed great qualities, they assumed great responsibility for the state of our enterprises, for keeping their employees, they were even willing to risk their capital. I'm hopeful that in compliance with the legislation we're going to continue to develop our private businesses. But as of now, the issue of oligarchs and power is not as acute as it used to be in the 1990s. But we have a greater task right now, and that task is about the gap in income between the rich and those people who have a low level of income. This gap, this divide, is where the injustice lies and the legitimate grievances of people against the current state of affairs in this hemisphere. In this regard, ahead of us lies the task of reducing the number of people who live below the poverty line. Unfortunately, amid the crisis in our economy it is difficult for us to accomplish this task. Even though the number of those who lived below the poverty line between 2000 and right now has decreased by almost 50 percent. Back in 2000, we had around 40 million people living in poverty. Right now the figure is still high, but it's almost halved.

So as for the oligarchs, I do not pursue it as a problem anymore. Large businesses know their place, they know the tasks that are ahead of them, and we treat the captains of our industry with respect. Any issues we discuss within the government before taking decisions, are also discussed in a forum with entrepreneurs, but this is done transparently and openly. Not behind closed doors with the view toward making decisions in the interest of this or that industrial or financial group. Even though, yes, I admit there are groups that lobby in their interests—sometimes we witness that and know it's happening—but we fight that and will continue to fight that.

OS: So there is no oligarchic state capitalism. How would you describe it, then—the economy?

VP: I think that we have a market economy. No doubt about that. Otherwise I do not think we would have been able to exceed WTO standards. But there are certain issues related to the large role the state plays in the economy. Indubitably, we will follow the path of gradually decreasing the state share in certain sectors of our economy. But we're going to tread cautiously, bearing in mind that certain economic sectors are very monopolized all across the world, in general. Just as an example—the energy sector, the electricity sector, railroads, space exploration, aviation—certain countries have their own forms of these industries and their development. But these sectors are monopolized everywhere. And everywhere there are direct ties to the government and there is government support. We see that and understand that full well. And we are going to improve the structure of our economy to prevent the destruction and dissolution of large enterprises and large industries.

OS: So, there are no bank accounts in Cypress?

VP: No, and never have been. That's just nonsense. If that were the case, then we would have had to face it a long time ago?

OS: What did you think of the Panama Papers when they came out?[163] They named you in the headlines.

VP: We had known they were going to be published. We knew that in advance. We didn't know the details, so it was with interest that we were expecting their appearance. But the thing is, my name is not in those papers, the names of my friends and acquaintances, yes, but those people are not in the government. And the thing is they had not violated any laws—either Russian laws or the legislation of other countries. Well, I knew that they would make a connection with my name, everything else would remain in the shadows and my name would be in the headlines. This is just an attempt at using this instrument to influence the internal politics of Russia. Russian citizens are quite literate and intelligent enough to sort it all out—I have no doubt about that. People see who is doing what and who is pursuing what interests. And I'm grateful to our citizens because they see the attempts I and my colleagues are making with a view to reinforcing our economy, our social sphere, and also the defense capabilities of our country.

OS: Well, I have to say, from personal observation, I would have a hell of a lot more fun if I was rich.

VP: You know, I don't think that is what brings great happiness. And with this crisis you would be thinking what to do with your assets, how to save them, where to place them. It would only bring you headaches. You are far wealthier than those who have great amounts of money in their accounts. You have an opinion of your own, you have talent, you have the chance to show this talent, and you also have the chance to leave a great legacy afterwards. Money doesn't bring this kind of happiness. Because when you are in a coffin you don't have any pockets to take your money to the grave with you.

OS: If you run again in 2018 and you win, you will be in power for another six years until 2024. You would have been in power as president and prime minister for 24 years—longer than Roosevelt, who was 15 years, less than Castro, who was close to 50 years, and close to Stalin who was give-or-take 30 years . . . Mao, 27 years. Does that not scare you? Do you not get used to power? Does it not distort your point of view? Do you feel that Russia needs you that badly or can there not be a healthy competition for successors inside the system? The Chinese one-party system being an example of competition within the party—the successors are checked out over many years as party members in different provinces.

VP: The Soviet Union also tested those people for many years and yet it collapsed.

OS: That's true.

VP: So the question is not about selection. The question you had formulated about whether Russia needs anyone that bad—it's up to Russia itself to decide. No one from outside can enforce this choice, and influencing this choice is very difficult. People in Russia have felt that they have a chance to make a decision of their own, and no one will take away this right from them. As for this alteration of power, it has to exist. Indubitably there needs to be a healthy competition in these processes. But this competition should be among our people who have in mind the interests of the nation. We have to think about the interests of the Russian people. In the end, let me reiterate, the citizens of Russia are going to make the final decision concerning the 2018 elections. First, I'd like to say that for four years I was not president. I was the chairman of the government, whereas Mr. Medvedev was the president. And what was being said by his political opponents and my political opponents about his not being independent, that's not true. He was the real president of the Russian Federation. It was not difficult for him to stay in power after he came in after me. And yet he lived up to high standards. So counting all of these years as my being in power, that's not the correct thing to do. As to what is going to happen during the 2018 elections, I'd like to say there are things about which there should be some intrigue, some mystery. So I'm not going to answer this part of your question.

OS: I understand that—I said "if".

VP: Well, it's not about the subjunctive mood you know—we shouldn't use it.

OS: Mr. Putin, I don't doubt for one moment your love and pride in serving Russia. It's clear you're a son of Russia and you've done very well by her. I think we all know the price of power, and when we've been in power for long, we feel people need us. At the same time, we've changed and we don't even know it sometimes.

VP: Indeed—this is a very dangerous state. And for persons in power who feel they have lost it, this nerve, this bond connecting this person to the country and to the rank and file citizens of the country, it's time for them to go. But in the end, it's something I've already said, and I'm going to repeat it—the ordinary citizens and voters, they are the ones who decide the future of power. No doubt power is connected to a great burden and it requires sacrifice.

OS: There is also great grace in yielding power. And many great examples of men and women who had succeeded in history and who gave up the desire to rule and let someone else do it.

VP: For everyone, there comes a time when you have to do it.

OS: And of course, democracy itself, whatever we call it, is flawed. And America's system is hardly perfect. We know that money often buys power in America. Certainly Russia has a flawed system, everyone says it from outside. No one could say that it's a system that's wholly responsive to the voters. The voters in Russia are probably split on many lines—a lot of chaos might result and that is always a danger. And given the short history of Russia and its democratic experiment which you said has only existed since 1991-92, it is very unlikely that the next election will convince the world that this is a functioning democracy, unless international monitors are brought in, as Mr. Chavez did in Venezuela, so that it became a really transparent process.

VP: Do you think our goal is to prove anything to anyone? Our goal is to reinforce our country, to make our country better for life, more attractive, to make our country more valuable, to turn our country into something that could respond swiftly to the challenges of time. To strengthen it from the internal political point of view, and to strengthen our external political stance as well. Those are the goals we are pursuing. We're not trying to please anyone.

OS: That is a dangerous argument because it works both ways. Those who abuse power always say it's a question of survival.

VP: We're not talking about survival and we're not trying to justify ourselves. Are we talking about the need to keep this or that authority in emergency conditions? Right now there is no emergency situation. What we have to do is to ensure a stable, sustainable development of the country. So in taking into account all of the negative tendencies you've been talking about, the Soviet legacy, the imperial legacy—that's something of the past. But we also have to think about the positive legacy that's been passed down to us. Russia has been built over a thousand years. It has a tradition of its own. We have our notions of what is just and unjust. We have our own understanding of how an efficient government should work. When I said that the Russia of the future should be very mobile, that it should respond swiftly to the challenges of the times, it should adapt efficiently, this means we should use everything we have as the groundwork, but still we should look into the future. This is not about helping someone cling to power, or cling to power myself, this is about ensuring economic growth, sustain its rate, improve the quality of life, including the defense capabilities, on a regular basis. Not amid crises or political difficulties. There is only one criteria to help us with regard to power. There is the law and there is also the Constitution. If the Constitution is violated or if it's twisted to suit the interests of this or that group or this or that individual, then that is unacceptable. But if a democratically accepted constitution is observed, then this has to be treated with respect.

OS: I don't doubt that the Constitution of Russia is a great constitution, it's always the execution of it that's been problematic. And I have no problem with the Asian economies, the "tiger economies" with Lee Kuan Yew of Singapore, for example, announced he was going to make an authoritarian regime that would work and would make the economy work and the economy would come first in Asia—very practical. South Korea, Japan to some degree, certainly Taiwan, and then ultimately China. China emerged with a very strong party and a major power but definitely not a democracy. So I don't know that it's necessary to dress up the language in democracy.

VP: There's no need to disguise anything or to dress it, but there are some fundamentals like the constitution of Russia which I've been talking about. It has never been questioned as a constitution of a democratic society, a democratic country. Since the constitution was devised it was considered as such. No one said there were flaws that allowed someone to talk about the undemocratic nature of Russian society. If you tried to twist this constitution to suit the interests of an individual or group, then suspicions certainly might emerge. But if this doesn't happen, then we have to treat what is happening with respect.

OS: Okay. So what time is it?

VP; It's time.

[laughter]

OS: Thank you very much.

VP: You've never been beaten before in your life?

OS: Oh yes, many times.

VP: Then it's not going to be anything new, because you're going to suffer for what you are about to do.

OS: No, I know . . . but it's worth it. It's worth it to try to bring some more peace and consciousness to the world.

VP: Thank you so much.

[Stone hands Putin the DVD case.]

OS: You might want to watch this at some point.

[Putin thanks Stone, waves, walks away, opens the DVD case, sees nothing inside. Everyone laughs.]

VP: Typical American gift!

[Rob takes the DVD out of the player and gives it to Putin.]

Trip 4—Day 1—February 10, 2017

————

OS: Hello gentlemen. So, you are going to sit here, Mr. Putin. I'm going to sit here. You remember Anthony from our first shoot—Anthony Dod Mantle—he'll be our cinematographer. The plan is for you to walk in and walk in that door.

[Mr. Putin walks in]

OS: I would prefer you to come from back there. I will meet you halfway.

VP: I can descend from the balcony . . .

OS: I like it better from there. It gives you some depth. In fact, there's a bar back there if you'd like. . . . Further back, further back. Good. All right, ready? [smiling] Now, pretend like we don't know each other—pretend we haven't seen each other in months. Okay. Action! [pause] Action! Where's my A.D.? Tell him "action" in Russian. He went into another meeting! Oh no!

Interpreter: He's bringing you tea.

[Putin comes from the other room carrying two cups of coffee]

VP: Coffee, Mr. Stone?

OS: Thank you.

VP: Black okay?

OS: Fine ...

VP: Sugar?

OS: Thank you Mr. President. How've you been? It's been a long time.

ON THE 2016 ELECTION

OS: There's been quite a lot of activity the last few months. My country, America, has had an election.

VP: I congratulate you on that.

OS: Donald Trump won. This is your fourth president, am I right? Clinton, Mr. Bush, Mr. Obama, and now your fourth one.

VP: Yes, that's true.

OS: What changes?

VP: Well, almost nothing.

OS: Is that your feeling? In between all of the four presidents or do you think ... ?

VP: Well, life makes some changes for you. But on the whole, everywhere, especially in the United States, the bureaucracy is very strong. And bureaucracy is the one that rules the world.

OS: The bureaucracy rules the world. In all countries?

VP: In many countries.

OS: You said this to me last time—there was a system, we call it the military industrial security complex in America.

VP: Yes, we've got a similar system—such systems exist everywhere.

OS: Some people call it the Deep State.

VP: Well, you can call it different names, but this doesn't change the essence.

OS: Is there any possibility, a hope of change with Mr. Trump?

VP: There is always hope. Until they are ready to bring us to the cemetery to bury us.

OS: [smiles] Wow, that's very Russian. Very Dostoyevsky.[164] The election has been heavily criticized and the narrative as written by the West has now become that Russia interfered in this election to the benefit of Mr. Trump.

VP: You know, this is a very silly statement. Certainly, we liked President Trump and we still like him because he publicly said that he was willing, he was ready to restore American-Russian relations. And when journalists from different countries were asking questions about that, they were trying to catch me, so to speak. I was always asking back, "Are you against good relations between the US and Russia?" All journalists were saying, "Yes, we want good relations between these two countries. We support that." Well, that would simply be ludicrous in Russia not to welcome that, certainly we welcome the re-establishment of relations. And in this sense we are glad that Donald Trump has won. Certainly, we've got to wait and see how, in reality, in practice, the relations between our two countries are going to develop. He was talking about a re-establishment of economic ties, of a joint fight against terrorism. Isn't that a good thing?

OS: Yes, so why did you bother to hack the election then?

VP: We were not hacking the election at all. It would be hard to imagine that any other country—even a country such as Russia—would be capable of seriously influencing the electoral campaign or the outcome of the election. And some hackers indeed revealed problems that existed within the Democratic Party, but I don't think that it has influenced in any serious manner either the electoral campaign or its outcome. Yes, these unrecognized hackers, they have brought to light the problems that existed, but they didn't tell any lies, they were not trying to deceive or fool anyone. And the fact that the chairwoman of the executive committee of the Democratic Party has resigned testifies to the fact that she has admitted it's true—everything that has been said. So hackers are not the ones to blame. These are internal problems of the United States. These people who tried to manipulate public opinion shouldn't have tried to create an image of an enemy in the face of Russia. They should have apologized to the electorate, but they didn't do that. But that is not right, that is not the main problem. Judging from everything, the US people have been waiting for some serious change.

I refer in particular to security-related matters, to the fight against unemployment and the need to create new jobs in the country. I refer to the protection of traditional values, because to a great extent, the US is a Puritan nation, to a great extent. Well, at least the hinterland. And Donald Trump and his team have been very wise in running their electoral campaign. They knew, they understood where their voters were located. The states where the concentration of electors was. And they knew what people living in those states required. They knew how to get the majority of electors to win. When I watched his speeches during the electoral campaign, I thought that he went a little bit too far from time to time. But it turned out he was right. He knew the fiber in the souls of the people. He knew how to play to win their hearts. And I think that no one is going to be able to challenge the outcome of this election. Instead, those who've been defeated should have drawn conclusions from what they did, from how they did their jobs, they shouldn't have tried to shift the blame on to something outside. And I think that Obama's outgoing team has created a minefield for the incoming president and for his team. They have created an environment which makes it difficult for the new president to make good on the promises that he gave to the people. But in reality, we're not waiting for anything revolutionary. We are looking forward to the new administration when it's been completed, when they are willing to launch a dialogue with Russia, with China, with Asia, with all the other countries. So that we can finally understand when the new administration addresses the key issues on the international agenda, and our bilateral agenda as well.

OS: But, you know, even Trump has said the Russians hacked the election—that was a quote.[165]

VP: I do not understand what he means when he says, "Russia has hacked the election." I've heard different statements of his saying that any hacking attacks, given the current level of technologies, can be produced by anyone anywhere, by a person who lies in his bed somewhere and has a laptop.[166] And you can even make it seem as if the hacker attacks are coming from another place, so it's very difficult to establish the original source of the attack.

OS: Well, this all seems to me still historically enormous—I've never seen where the two leading political parties, Democrat and Republican, the intelligence agencies, FBI, CIA, NSA, and the political leadership of NATO believe this story that Russia hacked the election. It's enormous.

VP: This is not exactly how it is. Well, I think you've read the documents related to that, the analysis that have been published.

OS: Have you read the 25 page report?

VP: Yes, I have. One intelligence service says that there is a great probability that Russia has interfered. Another intelligence service says that the probability, the certainty is not that great. They make some conclusions based on the analysis that they have conducted. But there is nothing concrete. Nothing clear-cut. You see? I don't know if that is proper. It reminds me of an ideology, kind of a hatred for a certain ethnic group like anti-Semitism. If someone doesn't know how to do something, if someone turns out to be incapable of addressing this or that matter, anti-Semitists always blame the Jews for their own failure. They blame the Jews. Those people have the same attitude towards Russia, they always blame Russia for anything that happens. Because they do not want to recognize their own mistakes and they are trying to find someone to shove the blame on, on our side.

OS: And it seems that Senator McCain, for example, today or yesterday was proposing a veto, a Senate veto against any lifting of sanctions from Trump—in advance.

VP: You know, there are many senators like that in the United States, unfortunately, many senators who think the same. Well, probably not that many but there are still some. Well, honestly, I like him—Senator McCain—to a certain extent.

OS: [laughter] Okay.

VP: And I'm not joking. I like him because of his patriotism, and I can relate to his consistency in fighting for the interests of his own country. You know, in Ancient Rome there was Marcus Porcius Cato, the Elder, who always finished all his speeches with the saying, "One and the same, Carthago delenda est." [Carthage must be destroyed.] The Romans had grounds to hate Hannibal who approached Rome during the Second Punic War and he was very close to Rome—70 miles or so. We and the US have never been involved in a confrontation such as Carthago and Rome. In the end, Rome emerged victorious from that war. And how did that end? Hannibal, as is known, took his own life. And Rome, in 400 years or so, was destroyed when the barbarians came. And certain conclusions, and certain lessons, can be learned from that. If these cities had not fought one another, if they had agreed on fighting a common enemy, if that had happened, then one [Hannibal] wouldn't have taken his own life and the others [Roman Empire] would have survived as well. People with such convictions like the Senator you mentioned, they still live in the Old World. And they're reluctant to look into the future, they are unwilling to recognize how fast the world is changing. They do not see the real threat, and they cannot leave behind the past which is always dragging them back.

We've been supporting the US fight for independence. We were allies during World War I and World War II. Right now there are common threads we are both facing, like international terrorism. We've got to fight poverty across the world, the environmental deterioration which is the real threat to all humanity. After all, we've piled up so many nuclear weapons that it has become a threat to the whole world as well. And it would be good for us to give it some thought. There are many issues to address.

OS: Well, Russia has been accused of enormous treachery now. Now this is a major charge and the media repeats it and repeats it, and it seems to have entered into the lexicon in the United States—it's just taken for granted. You can say Russia hacked the election, and many people say Trump is in the Kremlin's pocket, has a debt to the Kremlin. So, you see where this leads. It makes it impossible to correct relations with Russia. Very difficult for Mr. Trump if indeed he intends to do so, to reset relations.

VP: As I said, and I can say that again—any talk about our influencing the outcome of the election in the United States, all these are lies. But we that see this campaign of manipulating the information has a number of goals. First, they are trying to undermine the legitimacy of President Trump. Second, they are trying to create conditions that preclude us from normalizing our relations with the US. Third, they want to create additional weapons to wage an internal political war. And the Russia-US relations in this context are a mere instrument, a weapon in the internal political fight in the US.

OS: But many people are frustrated—and I can say this from talking to people in America who agree that this hacking charge is nonsense. It's fraudulent. Many people agree with Julian Assange of WikiLeaks who said that the leaks that were given to him from the DNC were from a non-state actor. And he swore to that, and his record has been solid. To my knowledge—he has been extremely forthright in his methods of operation since 2006 when he formed WikiLeaks. That's my prelude, but I'll ask the question now. The question is—many Americans are frustrated that Russia has not really made an effort, a bigger effort, to defend itself, to come out on the public relations front, for example, taking the 25-page report and technically shredding it and dealing with all the inaccuracies in it, as best it can, and making a bigger public response and objection to the accusations thrown at it. Why haven't you done that?

VP: You see, it's internal politicking inside the United States and we do not want to get mired in that. Many in the US think that all these claims about hacker attacks are fraudulent and we are glad that there are people like that. However there are people who promote this idea and express this is an insane notion because they want to use it as an instrument of political attack, and our refutation is not going to stop them from doing that. They are only going to use our refutations in order to continue this war using new instruments. We know all their tricks.

OS: Well it seems to me that if you know their tricks you could make some kind of statement about cyber warfare and give specifics of why this was not possible, why there should have been a trace, I mean there are so many different avenues you can explore. It seems as if Russia doesn't care about defending itself against these accusations. Many accusations fly by but Russia treats it as if it's business as usual.

VP: Well, yes, you are right. We do not particularly care about those accusations because we're not concerned about that. This is an internal issue for the United States. I'd like to say once again—I want to be heard—whoever those hackers are, they couldn't have made any serious difference in the course of that electoral campaign. And if they have revealed something, they have brought to light the real problems of American political life. They have not lied. They have not made up anything. The political forces have to handle these issues themselves, instead of trying to put the blame on the hackers who have only shed light on the problems that exist. It doesn't matter where these hackers come from—from Russia, from Latin America, from Asia, maybe they're from Africa.

OS: Well, is there any evidence in cyber space that Russia can present in its defense?

VP: There is no evidence that we are the ones to blame. And that is the greatest proof, the greatest defense we've got. Those reports that you mentioned from the NSA and the CIA, they've got no concrete facts. All they have are some promptings and also some suppositions, allegations.

OS: Yeah, I just think there is a more effective response that could have been made. And I understand how difficult it is, but it just seems like there's an energy lacking in the Russian response, not to be upset and angry at this. To take the adult position and try to say something that would resonate with people in the American populace so they would understand Russia's point of view, that has not come across to me.

VP: Yes, and that's exactly what I'm doing, I'm saying these things.

OS: Well, I wish there was more of it. So right now you're waiting it out, and at the same time, you know, Mr. Trump has called for, on more than one occasion, for another massive US military build-up, in both nuclear and conventional arms, which makes no sense to me. How can America spend more than it's already spending? But that's what they're talking about—increasing the military budget.

VP: I think we talked about that. The US spends more on defense than all the other countries in the world combined spend on their defense—more than six hundred billion US dollars.[167]

OS: Aren't you worried that Mr. Trump, in calling for more, is infantile in his demands?

VP: We're always concerned about any build-up in military expenditure of other countries, including the United States. We always have to analyze how this is going to impact our own security. But I think the American taxpayers have to think about that as well. How efficient are these expenses going to be? How it's going to correlate with the current economic situation, because apart from military expenditure, there are other things to spend money on, like healthcare, education, pension systems.

There are many other issues—social issues to address, servicing the public debt which is almost 20 trillion US dollars. All those are issues that have to be handled. But the military is always discontent with the money it gets from the state. It always wants more. Trust me, we've got the same disputes between the civilian departments, the defense ministry, the finance ministry. This is the same everywhere.

OS: Do you have any hopes of a meeting sometime in the coming months with Mr. Trump or not?

VP: I think we're going to meet some time. But we're not trying to rush. The American administration is still being built and they are still drafting their position on the key issues. We understand full well that, together with his allies and his partners, President Trump is going to come up with his own position on the most important issues. He'll have to work with the intelligence services, with the State Department, the military. He'll have to work with the Republicans and with the Democrats and will have to consider. There are many elements to consider. So once the administration is ready to get down to some practical work, we're going to respond.

OS: And how is he going to work with the intelligence agencies if the intelligence agencies are telling him that Russia hacked the election? It's a dead end.

VP: No, it's not a dead end. This is a question of human personnel.

OS: If Mr. Trump wanted to declassify or see the files on Ukraine—all the files—all the files on Syria and see the origins of these problems. Is there a possibility of that, that he might change some of his thinking?

VP: I think that is possible. But I'd like to reiterate, he'll have to work in a certain framework. We're adults and we understand what's happening. Well, I do hope that once he has grasped the crux of the matter, he'll come up with a vision of his own of what is happening.

OS: I hope you're right.

VP: So do I. I do hope that we'll find some common ground and reach mutual understanding.

OS: When is the next G20 meeting?

VP: I think in summer—in July.

OS: In July, so that would be the first you see each other, if you did?

VP: Yes, maybe.

OS: I gather you've had two phone calls with him?

VP: Yes. One telephone conversation took place before his inauguration, and the other one afterwards.

OS: And I gather some of the talk may have been about terrorism.

VP: We've talked about the fight against terrorism, we've touched upon North Korea, we've talked about nuclear disarmament. And we've touched upon Ukraine. And we certainly agreed that we've got to open a new page in Russia-US relations.

OS: On terrorism, it seems like again the intelligence agencies of the United States will not agree with the Russian position on terrorism. It seems like, fundamentally, the US intelligence has been politicized.

VP: You know, indeed, with the Obama administration we almost reached an agreement on working jointly in Syria.

OS: Almost?

VP: Yes, almost. We had talked about coordinating the matters related to the security and safety of our aircraft flying over, but unfortunately this is all that we did. We didn't go further. We were willing to agree on joint activity, that would have implied designating on the ground, in accordance with our data and their data, the location of terrorist groups. I believe that we should have designated targets to fight against. And we also would have agreed on the strikes to be performed jointly. And we were very close to achieving this agreement. But at the last moment, I think due to some political reasons, our American partners abandoned this project.

OS: Well, Mr. Trump has talked very tough about Iran. And this is an example, fundamentally, if many Americans believe in the official policy that Iran is the number one terrorist organization in the world, you, Mr. Putin would not agree. And many people would say that the number one terrorist organization is the Saudi Arabian government. Now, that becomes a Shia/Sunni split. So many Americans are fighting pro-Sunni and anti-Shia and many other people feel that the source of the problems is Sunni and the allegiances should change. But Saudi Arabia and Israel have very solid American support and, unless that changes, there is a basic, fundamental contradiction in this and in the Russian and American positions.

VP: You know, there is no world religion that is a source of evil. Islam has many denominations, many streams, and the main movements are the Shia and the Sunni. Indeed we see there are some deep divides between these two factions, but I think this divide will sooner or later have to be bridged. We've got very good friendly relations with all Islamic states. Moreover, we are an observer at the Organization of the Islamic Conference since 2003. Because around 15 percent of Russian citizens profess Islam—they're Muslim. And I once attended the summit of the Organization of the Islamic Conference. We know that our attempts at helping Syria, supporting its legitimate government, some hope will lead to a contradiction, to disputes with the Sunni. But this is not what is happening. I can go in greater detail. As far as the difference of approach to the Iranian nuclear issue is concerned, I can say that, in order to understand if there is any difference in our approaches, we need to talk substance with the US at the State Department level, or at the intelligence services level, and also at the National Security Council level. Because public statements are not sufficient either from our side, or from the American side. We want to hear the arguments that the American side can produce for us, not the arguments that can be voiced publicly. We want to have a constructive professional dialogue with them. We want our position to be heard as well. We managed to arrive at many agreements on these matters with the previous administration. And I do not rule out that with the new administration, we are also going to be able to find common ground. To that end, we need a concrete dialogue on the substance of the matter.

OS: Right, I understand. Was there US interference in the 2012 election in Russia?

VP: In 2000 and in 2012, there has always been some interference. But in 2012 this interference was particularly aggressive.[168]

OS: Can you describe some of that?

VP: I'm not going to go into detail, but just to site an example, our American partners know that and we said that. I told that to Obama and John Kerry. We could hardly imagine diplomatic workers who were in a country, well in that particular case in Russia, would be so aggressive in interfering in the electoral campaign that was going on in Russia. They rallied the opposition forces. They funded rallies and the opposition. Diplomats have to do different things. The diplomatic service is supposed to foster good relations between countries. NGOs can pursue different avenues regardless of their nationality or origin. But very often NGOs are funded through a number of structures set up either by the State Department or controlled indirectly.

OS: Like the Ukraine situation?

VP: Not just in Ukraine, all across the post-Soviet space in Eastern Europe and in many other countries in Africa in Latin America as well, we see the same thing.

OS: Yes.

ON CYBER WARFARE

OS: Was there cyber interference in the 2012 election?

VP: To be honest, I don't pay particular attention to that matter. We've got an agenda of our own which we have to address. I think many partners of ours live in a world of their own, and very often they're out of touch with what is happening in other countries in reality, including Russia.

OS: Well, let's clarify, because cyber warfare is here with us. We started down that road a few years ago. The United States will not admit it, but it's known that in 2010 we succeeded in planting the Stuxnet virus in Iran.[169]

VP: We know that, we know how the NSA is working. We know that after Snowden's confessions. And I'd like to say that what we know from Mr. Snowden, we know from the media as well. Because what he thinks necessary, he passes to the media. He uses the Internet to deliver that information. So we are witnessing that all across the world. We know about surveillance of private lives and the private lives of political leaders, which I believe is a very bad practice.

OS: But cyber warfare is not surveillance. But it's with us, as pervasively as surveillance. In my film *Snowden*[170] he told me this story, he was in Japan stationed in 2007/2008 and the NSA asked the Japanese to spy on their population. The Japanese said "no" and we spied anyway.

Not only that but we went on once we knew their communication systems to plant malware in their civilian infrastructure in the event that Japan would no longer be an ally.

Snowden also described similar situations in Brazil, Mexico, and many countries in Europe. It's quite surprising that we would do this to our allies.

VP: Well, you see, Americans have much to attend to—there are many things they've got to look after. And they've got to work everywhere. Six hundred billion US dollars spent by the Pentagon is not all the money that is spent on security and defense.

OS: No, I mean come on, this is a serious . . . You're acting innocent, but Russia must be aware of the power of cyber warfare and what the Americans can do. If I'm saying that they're planting malware in Japanese infrastructure to destroy power stations, railroads, close the country down, black it out, the Russians are miles ahead of me, they must realize the dangers here and they must have been working on them for some time to prevent such a situation from happening to Russia. Because they are one of the obvious enemies of the United States.

VP: Well, you will probably not believe me, but I'm going to say something strange. Since the early 1990s, we have assumed that the Cold War is over. Russia has become a democratic state. Of its own accord, Russia has decided to help build the statehood of former Soviet republics. Russia has been the one that initiated this process. We proposed that sovereignty should be granted to former Soviet republics. We thought there was no need to take any additional protective measures because we viewed ourselves as an integral part of the world community. Our companies, our state institutions and administrative departments, they were buying everything—hardware and software. And we've got much equipment from the US, from Europe, and we use that equipment, it's used by the intelligence services and by the defense ministry. But recently we certainly have become aware of the threat that all of that poses. Only during recent years, have we started to think about how we can ensure technological independence, as well as security. Certainly we give it much thought and we take appropriate measures.

OS: Well, if Snowden is saying the US is doing this to an ally in 2007 in Japan, 2008—if they're planting malware in allies, do you understand what I'm saying? What are they doing in places like China, Russia, Iran, and so forth? I mean, you understand my point is that Russia had to be aware as early as 2007 that the US was planting malware. Were there attacks on Russia as early as 2007, '06, '05?

VP: You know, we didn't pay attention to it back then. Our nuclear plants, the plants that produce nuclear weapons, they had American observers stationed at those factories and plants.

OS: As late as what year?

VP: I think it was as late as 2006. But I don't remember exactly. So the trust and openness of Russia, they were unprecedented.

OS: Yes. And then what happens?

VP: Unfortunately, they didn't recognize that. They didn't want to take note of that and appreciate it.

OS: When did Russia build up its cyber capabilities?

VP: This process has been a long one. We had to catch up. We've got a very good foundation. We have a very high education level and very good school of mathematics. Many Russian scientists work in the United States achieving illustrious results. Some of our companies, three or four years ago, they started from scratch. And right now they get seven billion dollars or so yearly. They've become competitive in the software market. And they're also quite active in pursuing hardware. We see supercomputers being built. So this field is undergoing rapid development, not just for the sake of defense and security. This is also for the sake of science and economy.

OS: But Snowden is describing a situation where they're basically doing cyber attacks on China. This is in 2009/'08, in that era. I would imagine he never knew about the Russian side of the cyber equation, but I would imagine Russia is having an ongoing battle with the United States. An ongoing battle, secret battle, with cyber warfare. I would just imagine that. I would imagine the United States is trying to do things to Russia. And Russia was trying to defend itself and do things to the United States. I would just imagine that as practical—I'm not making it up. That seems to me obvious.

VP: Maybe when there is an action there is always a counter action.

OS: You're acting funny about this story, like a fox that just got out of the hen house. [laughter]

VP: There were no hens in the hen house, unfortunately.

OS: A few weeks ago on RT, I saw a report—it was not followed up on, it disappeared after a day or two, but in that report, 20-plus countries were reported as being part of a Botnet attack on the banking system in Russia—six major banks.[171] I saw the RT report. This seems to be of such a magnitude that it points to a possible US attack—this was after the election. It points to a possible US attack on Russia's banking system, which would make sense to me. But because the story disappeared, I'm sure that you're aware of it, but what happened to that story, if it was true?

VP: No, the story didn't disappear. Indeed, there were reports that such an attack was being prepared. We were not 100 percent sure that this was going to happen, but just to be on the safe side, the banking community, they addressed the media. And they informed their clients, the citizens, that such attacks were possible, they were imminent. And they called on the citizens not to get nervous, not to get confused, not to rush to the banks to get their money, from their deposits. They said they had everything under control. There were no grounds to be anxious and they wanted people to know that if this were to happen, then they should know that it was a hacking attack in order to destabilize the financial system of Russia. We are not claiming that the US is to blame for that. We do not have evidence to support that claim.

OS: Right. It's a gigantic piece of business. I mean, you have Mr. Biden, first of all, saying, "We will attack Russia in the same manner as they attacked us in this election."[172] We will attack Russia in the same manner, at the time of our choosing"—something of that nature. And Mr. Obama seconded that and said that we will respond to the election hack or whatever he called it—the attack. This is an outrageous conversation. But those are big words from the vice president and then from the president. They're serious people. So something happened before Inauguration Day.

VP: Certainly there is nothing good about that when such claims come from such a high level. Indeed you're right, it was said that it would happen "at a time of their choosing." There were two reasons. First, they wanted to challenge the outcome of the elections. They said a time of their choosing, but certainly the administration back then didn't have any time left. To be honest, I do not want to offend or insult anyone, but what we've seen happen in recent days, it reminds me of what the Politburo of the Communist Party of the Soviet Union was doing at the beginning, especially when they awarded orders to each other. That was very funny.

OS: I don't understand the analogy.

VP: We've seen President Obama give an award to his vice president. Yes he gave him some kind of a medal, and it reminded me of the members of the Politburo of the Communist Party of the Soviet Union. They gave orders and stars and medals to one another. So back then I understood that the administration had run out of time for any serious decisions.

OS: Well, you're making light of it but in view of how much money we have invested in cyber warfare and our cyber command, it seems like a serious threat to me. I have the feeling that you're playing it down because something did happen and you don't want to reveal it because of sensitive relations.

VP: You are disappointed because the US failed to do something? Or do you just regret the money of the American taxpayers that has been spent on that cyber warfare?

OS: No, I believe that cyber warfare can lead to a hot war. I really believe that because of the past. You know, the Stuxnet virus came very close to creating chaos in the world. I think this is very dangerous, very dangerous, and I think we're playing with fire.

VP: That is very dangerous.

OS: I know. Well, you're obviously sitting on some information and you may not want to make it public.

VP: Yes. That's a great secret. Top secret.

OS: [laughter] I know. But are we going to be able to handle the capabilities of this? It seems to me that what happened in Iran could be as serious in its way as what happened in 1945 at Nagasaki and Hiroshima. That was the beginning of a new age.

VP: The weapons used at Hiroshima and Nagasaki, it opened a tragic page in the history of humanity, because they released a terrible genie from the bottle. Our military specialists believe that there was no military sense behind using nuclear, atomic weapons against Japan which had already been put to rout. But I think this comparison between Stuxnet and the nuclear weapons is too overreaching. But should we fail to agree on a certain code of conduct in this field, and I agree with you on that one, the consequences of this spiral of action, they can be very grave and even tragic.

OS: It seems to me a secret war, but no one knows who started it. No one knows if it was a proxy country, if it was North Korea that hacked Sony—you know, these rumors go around. But if all the lights go out in Russia, and let's say some of the grid in Russia were to close down overnight, there would be tremendous fear in Russia, as there would be the United States and people wouldn't know who did it. Secret War.

VP: It is almost impossible to sow fear among the Russian citizens.

OS: [laughter] Ohhh!

VP: That is the first thing I wanted to say. And secondly, the economies that are more sophisticated, in technological terms, they are more vulnerable to this types of attacks. But in any case, this is a very dangerous trend. A very dangerous avenue to pursue for competition in and we need some rules to be guide us all.

OS: A treaty.

VP: I don't want to say that, but you are simply drawing this information from me. You make me say that. One and a half years ago, in autumn 2015, we came up with a proposal that was submitted to our American counterparts. We suggested that we should work these issues through and arrive at a treaty, an agreement on the rules to be followed in this field. We came up with a similar proposal at the United Nations. The Americans didn't respond, they kept silent, they didn't give us any reply. Only at the very end of the Obama administration, the State Department, we called and they said they were willing to get back to talking about this matter. Our Foreign Ministry said that we would have to talk to the new administration because there was no time left. And this is one of the very important topics that we're going to have to explore in the near future.

OS: Perhaps this is something that Mr. Trump and Mr. Putin can really open up and it could become a gigantic success.

VP: This is just one of the issues that we've got to address together. It is very important and I agree with you on that one. But I'd like to reiterate, the proposal is on the table but so far our American partners have not said anything about it. This proposal was submitted to them before the active phase of the electoral campaign.

[After a break, at 11 p.m., Mr. Putin and Mr. Stone walk the corridors of the Kremlin with the interpreter.]

OS: You know this is a pretty big place you've got here. How do you heat it? . . . Don't tell me.

VP: Yes, you should have asked something simpler. Somehow it just happens. But I can assure you that we do not use firewood to heat it.

OS: To close out the cyber warfare thing—just a few weeks ago here, in Moscow, they arrested the chief of detectives. They escorted him out of the office with a bag over his head.

VP: It was one of the hacker groups.

OS: But he was an official. An official of the government.

VP: No, no, no. He is a private person. A hacker.

OS: Three people were accused, and the rumor that I heard was that they were colluding possibly with the Americans.

VP: I don't know about that. I know that there was a hacker group. They were perpetrating attacks against financial accounts of private persons and companies, they were taking money from people.

OS: So you think it's a private affair. It's not involved with this American-Russian situation?

. . . You ever walk down these long corridors to get exercise?

VP: No, I've got a small gym here.

OS: You're never lonely at night when you walk the corridors?

VP: During the night, I don't walk through these corridors.

OS: When I last saw you, we talked about mass surveillance. And you agreed that it didn't make sense. It was ineffective. And since then, a new law has been passed. And I think you've signed it. In Russia, it's called the Big Brother Law.[173] And it provides exactly the kind of surveillance that you deplored about the United States method.

VP: Well, it's not exactly like that—I'm going to tell you about it. It's no secret, to be honest.

OS: Well, last time we talked about surveillance, mass surveillance—I had the impression you were against it and that you deplored the American technique. It was ineffective against terrorism, and as our "Snowden" movie pointed out, it was selective targeting that would work best on terrorists. And since that conversation there is a new law in Russia and you signed it. And I'm surprised. And Snowden has condemned it here in Russia. So I'm surprised. I mean, what is your feeling about this?

VP: Well, as for the law that you've just mentioned, this law doesn't authorize surveillance all across the world—surveillance of people no matter who they are. It doesn't authorize that at all. This law is about something entirely different. You mentioned Mr. Snowden. He revealed that there was surveillance performed by the NSA and the CIA of citizens all across the world, of political leaders and their allies. Whereas the law that we have adopted says that data, information has to be preserved for a longer period of time. The information should be preserved by the companies that provide internet services and telecom services. But private information, essential information, can only be obtained by special services, or by law enforcement agencies, but only if the court so decides. If there are grounds provided to the court, if the judge decides whether personal information should be provided to the law enforcement agencies or to the special services, or not. This information cannot be obtained by special services automatically from private companies. And such a law is in place in the United States, in Canada, in Australia, and in a great number of other countries. And I think that is justified and that is necessary in the fight against terrorism. Because if this data is simply deleted, then all opportunities vanish to pursue the suspects, the criminal suspects.

OS: But why? Why are you doing this? I didn't see that there was any great terrorist threat in Russia. It seems like a dragnet on all Russian citizens.

VP: Let me say once again—the law enforcement agencies and special services can only get information if there is a decision taken by the court. This law introduces a responsibility for private companies—telecom and internet providers—to preserve data for longer. But this law doesn't give an automatic authorization to our special services to get this kind of information. Nor should private companies provide this information to special services. Why is this law so important? Just have a look—we talked about Syria, you and I. Right now, regrettably, in Syria there are 4,500 Russian citizens aligned with Daesh, with other terrorist organizations fighting there. And another 5,000 citizens from Central Asian countries, former Soviet republics. And they've got connections of their own in Russia. And they prepare terrorist attacks.[174] Last year, our special services thwarted 45 terrorist attacks. So luckily we are not seeing any serious terrorist activities, but this is not because terrorists are not fighting against us, but simply because, luckily, so far our special services have been successful in thwarting the terrorist's activities. But Russia has been attacked by terrorists on many occasions, and people know that full well. And we have suffered very great losses and we've got to protect our population, our citizens.

OS: Does this have anything to do with the way Google operates, or fear or paranoia about Google, let's say its omnipresence in Europe?

VP: I'm not sure about this paranoia. But I know that terrorists do use these channels for communication. Sometimes they use closed channels of communication.

OS: Well, I heard it was also very financially punitive for the companies that have to store the information because it costs quite a bit.

VP: This is an over-exaggeration. It's going to be worth several trillion rubles. But to be honest, experts say that if the government thinks it all through—all the actions that need to be taken—then these costs can be reduced to one hundred billion rubles.

OS: Phew!

VP: As far as this law is concerned, when I signed it, I instructed the government to come up with a set of measures with a view to reducing the financial consequences for the companies.

OS: Yeah, that'd be good.

ON INTERNATIONAL RELATIONS

OS: The US and China have had some serious issues in the South China Seas, maritime issues. This must be of concern to Russia. Have you had any conversations with the Chinese premier?

VP: No, maybe we've touched upon it but only in general terms. Our position on that matter is well-known and it consists of the following. All regional disputes, problems, have to be addressed in the course of consultations by the countries of the region. Any interference from outside is always counterproductive. As far as I know, China is engaged in this kind of dialogue with the regional powers.

OS: Except the regional powers feel like they're small, and they go to the United States for their nuclear umbrella.

VP: I'm not so sure about that. I think that the Philippines no longer thinks that.

OS: Yes. You have a different point of view.

VP: But you know that this dispute has even been elevated to the level of the Permanent Court of Arbitration. And it was started from the Philippines.

OS: Okay. So is that a solution?

VP: I don't think so. I'm going to tell you why. The thing is, for such a decision to be recognized, several conditions have to be met. First, all the parties to a dispute have to apply to this court. And China has not applied to this court. And the second condition is that the court has to listen to all the parties to the dispute. But China has not been called to that court and its position has not been heard. So I think this court ruling can hardly be recognized as valid. But let me reiterate, the current leadership of the Philippines didn't insist on this court ruling. We see right now the Philippines champion a dialogue with China on this matter, and I think this is the best avenue to pursue.

OS: Japan and South Korea are two gigantic countries—very Western, very capitalist in a sense . . . . Very capitalistic economies and Japan has the second most US bases in the world, and South Korea has many bases. Some of these are US bases, and obviously because of the US bases it becomes a US issue.

VP: If they think so. Let me say once again that the best way is not to add fuel to these disputes, to these contradictions. These disputes should not be tried, shouldn't be used to secure someone's position in the region. On the contrary they have to push forward in normal, positive, constructive dialogue with a view to finding solutions to the outstanding issues.

OS: In Russia, in every country there are reactionaries and hardliners. America, Russia, all the countries of the world. In Russia, would you say that you were getting pressure from nationalists, hardliners, for Russia to take a harder position on all these matters?

VP: I wouldn't go so far as to say that I feel any pressure, but we've got people of different points of view. Some of them quite influential—they are influential with regard to public opinion. And I certainly have to take their position into consideration. Just as I should take into account the position of more liberally-minded people. That is my job. I've got to consider different positions and arrive at an acceptable solution.

OS: What's this?

VP: This is one of the working offices where my colleagues and I organize video conferences. We can organize video conferences with different regions of Russia, with different agencies, government ministries. We can hold conferences here without making people come here in person. To save time.

OS: 10 or 11 time zones?

VP: I think 11.

OS: Can we talk? I think I'll sit on this side, it might look nicer. I love this map. So, this is a situation-type room?

VP: Yes, indeed so.

OS: This is commando raids and stuff?

VP: No, are you talking about my functions as Commander in Chief and from where I perform those functions? Well, we can do that from here, we've got the necessary means of communications, we've got a direct link to the Ministry of Defense. Incidentally, have a look at those time zones—you can see them. The westernmost point, Kaliningrad—on the left. And the easternmost point. Everyone calls Japan the country of the Rising Sun. But New Zealand is to the east from Japan. And eastwards from New Zealand is Chukotka. It's one of the Russian regions. And before Chukotka, between Chukotka and Alaska, the Bering Strait, is just 60 miles. So once again Chukotka is the easternmost part of Eurasia. I would call Chukotka the country of the rising sun.

OS: Okay, so in conventional military terms your budget, as you said the American budget is six hundred billion and your annual budget is 66 according to Russian statistics—66. That's about a tenth of American spending. The Chinese are 215 billion. Saudi Arabia is at 87. Saudi Arabia, again . . . which leaves Russia in fourth place at 66. Is this an accurate figure?

VP: Yes, it's roughly just as you said.

OS: So Saudi Arabia's spending more money than you are.

VP: Well, it turns out they do spend more than we do.

OS: How do you do it? I mean, you have quite an army, quite an intelligence service. But what's the trick? I mean, you don't have lobbies that cost a lot of money? There's no graft, no corruption in this thing?

VP: Well, certainly just as in any other country we've got all of that. But we've got this understanding that the most important thing is that the country is a well-functioning, well-performing economy. So we've got to coordinate our ambitions and our needs and our opportunities in the military field. In defense, we've got certain traditions—traditions that have been established by our predecessors. One of our prominent commanders, Suvorov, used to say, "It is not with numbers that you've got to fight, it is with your skills." The armed forces have to be compact, but very modern and efficient. We spend enough. What I mean is that the ratio to our GDP—our military expenditure amounts to more than three percent of our GDP. And for Russia, that is quite a lot. This year, we have managed to economize when drafting our budget thanks to bringing down our military expenditure. So step by step we're going to bring our military expenditure to 2.7/2.8 percent of our GDP in the coming three years.

OS: The US makes a lot out of building up—they keep talking about its anti-missile systems. Is there any reason to believe there's been some kind of breakthrough in their technology? Some kind of first strike superiority. . . . They have a plan, they're doing something. I feel like they are really working, that they can get an advantage. . . . In which case, your missile silos would be knocked out on a US first strike, and we'd be able to absorb whatever you had left to throw at us.

VP: So far there has been no breakthrough. But this is possible. And we certainly have to take that into account. And we're working to ensure our security in the mid-term and in the long term.

OS: But they have a plan, they're doing something to gain first strike capability. I feel that they are really working. They feel they can get an advantage, if they can break through that ABM missile system.

VP: Certainly that is exactly the case.

I think pulling out of the ABM treaty was a mistake. They're trying to build an umbrella to protect themselves. But in reality, this sparks an arms race. New suspicions pop up. To cite an example, deploying this ABM system in Romania,[175] let's do the following—they deploy a ground system which can be used to station cruise missiles of intermediate range that are sea-launched. And the US has such missiles and they are not prohibited by the existing treaties. And these missiles can be stationed there and deployed there. We're not going to see that. It is only going to take several hours to re-configure the computer program. And that's that. Yeah. And apart from that, should this system become fully operational, we'll have to think about how we can penetrate the system. We can overcome it and we can relocate our ground-based nuclear weapons. We're lucky, you see, because we would have to re-equip to change and modernize our ground systems anyways. Because the time has come that from the technological point of view they have to be modernized. And we're going to do exactly that given the situation that we see. And given the ABM system deployed by the Americans.

OS: Any more news developments that you can reveal on the US/NATO exercises on the Russian borders in their war games? Has there been any change of strategy, for example, in Poland?

VP: Well, I would say no. This has more of a psychological effect than a military effect per se. Militarily this is of no concern to us. But it undermines trust in the political process that would allow us to work together, certainly that is not a good thing that we're seeing—this is doing damage to our relations.

OS: Interesting.

ON SYRIA AND DEFENSE

OS: Can we quickly get back—in the matter of Syria, it seems to have quieted down. The showing of Aleppo was much-played-up in the Western media as barbaric. And I've seen the RT reports from a different perspective about what was happening there in West Aleppo—a different sense of, where the US media was not reporting some of the atrocities that were happening in Aleppo.

VP: You know, this is all part of an information confrontation. Certainly the media are used. If they present lopsided information, they discredit themselves in the end. In any case, when a question arises inevitably, if people are taken hostage by terrorists does it mean that we have to stop fighting terrorists? Should we just give them a blank check to do whatever they please? The question always arises—is the source of this evil the ones who fight terrorists or the terrorists themselves? Just have a look—there has been much talk about the need to provide immediate humanitarian aid to Aleppo. Right now, Aleppo has been liberated of terrorists. And no one talks right now about the need to provide humanitarian aid to Aleppo, even though security and safety have been ensured there. Many partners of mine, my colleagues were telling me that they were willing, they were ready to provide that kind of humanitarian aid, but so far nothing has happened. There were always those who said that we would be in conflict with the Sunni world sooner or later. I think this is, to me, a provocation. Many in the Arab world, and in Turkey, they do understand what our intentions are. There are those who disagree with that. But our position is clear. Our goal is to support the legitimate authorities, to prevent a disintegration of the Syrian statehood, otherwise this territory is going to be yet another Libya or worse. Or another Somalia. Secondly, our goal is to fight terrorism. And this is no less important to us. Just as I said, according to our data, 4,500 people from Russia and around 5,000 citizens from Central Asian countries—the former Soviet republics—are fighting there. And our task is to prevent them from coming home. Nonetheless, it is with respect that we treat the concerns of our partners from Turkey and from the Arab countries. What did it result in? First, at the final stage of the fight for liberating Aleppo, this stage didn't end with hostilities. No, it ended with separating the forces. And we helped part of the armed opposition to evacuate from Aleppo. And we were the ones to facilitate this process. We were the ones to organize all of that. But everyone just made it look like they didn't see what was happening. Secondly there were talks that once Aleppo was liberated, ethnic or religious cleansings would take place there. Do you know what decision I took? I decided to dispatch a battalion of Russia military police to Aleppo, from the Northern Caucasus, mostly from the Chechen Republic[176] and a number of other republics in the Northern Caucasus. Incidentally, all of them are Sunni.

OS: [laughter] I see.

VP: And the local population gave them a very warm welcome. They see them as their protectors. Certainly we did that with the concern and with the support of President Assad. He said he was interested in fostering a dialogue between different religious groups. Do you know what it led to? I'm going to tell you something that no one is aware of so far, but probably they are going to learn that before your film appears. The representatives of the armed opposition in one of the suburbs of Aleppo asked us to increase the number of our military policemen. They want us to bring this number to a great number in the regions they control.

A week ago I decided to dispatch another battalion of military police there. But this is not all there is to it. Together with our military police, a Mufti from the Chechen Republic has appeared there.

He is also a Sunni. He talks to our military, to the local population. We're not interested in adding fuel to this conflict. Quite the contrary, we are interested in fostering dialogue, so as to preserve the territorial integrity of this country which is a very complicated matter. I'm particularly concerned about what we are witnessing. We see some sort of a divide of different religious groups. People are moving from one part of Syria to another.

These religious groups are isolating themselves and separating, and this is very dangerous because it might result in a split. But I've got to tell you that we are successful because we've got the direct support of the Turkish leadership, as well as the leadership of Iran. This is a very difficult matter and it's not always easy to find consensus. But direct contacts are being upheld with the Iranian partners and the Turkish partners, and this is what gives us hope and that is why we achieve success. What you've said about Syria quieting down, that is true. Indeed, hostilities have all but ceased between the armed opposition and the armed forces of the government. But hostilities are still ongoing against Daesh, the Islamic State.

OS: What would you say is the result of the Russian military intervention— in a few words?

VP: I can sum that up very easily. First, we've stabilized the legitimate authorities. Secondly, we have achieved a reconciliation and we've managed to bring to one negotiating table both the Armed opposition and the government. And we've managed to foster a dialogue in a trilateral format which engages both Turkey and Iran. We need the support of the United States as well as the support of Saudi Arabia, Jordan, Egypt. We're going to tread very cautiously. So that each step secures what has been achieved at the previous step instead of undermining it.

OS: Again, what was the distance between Damascus and Moscow. You told me once it was kilometers . . .

VP: Well I never counted. I think 3,000. 2,000 to Sochi, another thousand to Istanbul. 3,500 or 4,000 kilometers.[177]

OS: Okay. And one quick question. I mean, I definitely get the feeling from what you said that Mr. Erdogan in Turkey feels that the US CIA was involved in the coup d'état against him recently.

VP: Did he tell you that?

OS: No. He said things that hinted at it—in that direction.

VP: I don't know anything about that. But I can see the rationale behind what he said. Mr. Gülen, whom he suspects of organizing this coup d'état, is living in Pennsylvania[178] and he's lived there for more than nine years.

OS: And Mr. Erdogan never said anything to you, he never whispered . . . ?

VP: No, he told me that he suspected Gülen and his organization, his movement, of organizing that coup d'état. He has never told me anything about the role of the United States. But I can see his logic—you can guess it. If indeed Mr. Gülen had taken part in this coup d'état attempt—of which I have no idea—it would be very hard to imagine that at least the intelligence services of the US would be unaware of what was happening. That's the first thing. Secondly, the Air Force stationed at the Incirlik Air Base has been active in this coup d'état attempt. And that is exactly the air base where the main part of the American Air Force that is stationed in Turkey is located.

We are a little bit concerned. And why is that? The thing is, tactical nuclear weapons are deployed in Turkey, US nuclear weapons. And when such dramatic events occur, the question arises as to what might happen to the nuclear warheads.

OS: Well, if the army is loyal to Erdogan, then I'm not sure. A lot of them are involved with the United States.

VP: Well, probably you know better than I do.

OS: Well, he rounded up a lot of military people.

VP: You know, Mr. Erdogan was one step from being assassinated. He moved from the hotel where he was staying. Some of his security officers were staying there. And one of the Special Forces, a commando from the armed forces came to him, there was a clash with his security officers and his security officers were killed. I think we can say that if Erdogan had stayed there than he would have been assassinated. These are just bare facts from which I infer no conclusions whatsoever. But this is what happened. I do not want either to analyze or give an assessment to what he did afterwards. But we know the historical role that the armed forces have been playing in Turkey. They've been the grantor of a secular avenue of development in the country. We've got this Golden Rule which we stick to—we never interfere within the domestic affairs of any country.

OS: Not even the US election?

VP: No, never. It's up to the people of the country.

OS: I believe you.

VP: You know, even earlier, sometimes half as a joke, half on a serious note, we were saying that the American Constitution was not perfect.

OS: The Electoral College.

VP: Yes, absolutely right. Because the elections are not that direct. There was this electoral college that you mentioned. But their response was always, "This is none of your business. We're going to sort it out ourselves." So we do not interfere, either within the domestic affairs of the US or any other country. We have not interfered in Turkey.

OS: How close were you to a war—the United States said to Syria you crossed the red line in 2013 and General Shoygu, your Defense Minister said the Syrians were about to launch a massive attack of 624 cruise missiles within 24 hours. And it probably would have ended the sovereignty of the Syrian state at that point, when Obama said they crossed a red line, and you were involved with that, in stopping that and in removing the gases, the chemical weapons from Syria. How close was it? And were you worried about a US strike on Damascus?

VP: Honestly, I don't know—I think you've got to ask the Obama administration about that, about how close they were to the brink of war, to making that decision. Another decision finally was made, luckily.

OS: You were involved in it.

VP: Yes, I was, when the G20 Summit took place in St. Petersburg, President Obama and I, we talked about this topic. And we agreed to try to take steps to eliminate the remains of chemical weapons in Syria.

OS: You sound very casual. It doesn't sound right. I mean, if Shoygu said 24 hours, you guys have to be worried about it. This is your ally.

VP: Well, it's all about the subjunctive mood, so to speak. Be that as it may, both I and President Obama agreed to work together back then, and luckily our joint work resulted in success.

OS: Well, you make it sound casual, but weren't you worried that your ally would disappear and maybe ISIS was going to get all the way to Damascus right then and there? Didn't you see all the implications of this?

VP: Yes, certainly we were concerned. And that's why we talked about how we could address that matter with other means and we were successful in doing that.

OS: You seem very cool about it, but I would imagine in that time period it might have been much tenser.

VP: Look, what happened back then happened back then. And right now we have a very well-organized and well-performing system of air defense deployed there.

OS: Ah!

VP: —We have the S-400, with a range of more than 300 kilometers, S-3000, also with a range of 300. The DEBO system with a range of 60 kilometers. And there are other systems that are more efficient in the shorter range. So we've got a multi-tier plan for air defense. And there are also the ships stationed off the coast that all also have this system of air defense.

OS: So you could have prevented it?

VP: And the most sophisticated air defense systems with a range of 300 kilometers.

OS: Well that's some conversation you're having with Obama—you're saying Russian weapons are going to shoot down US weapons and you'll have an international crisis. It'll be quite a situation. The Pentagon is going to go wild, no? You know, this is close to war.

VP: Back then, we didn't have those missiles in Syria.

OS: Oh, I thought you did.

VP: Our missiles were not active in Syria back then.

OS: Well, you had a long-term alliance with them since the early 1970s?

VP: Yes, but we didn't take any part in what was happening there. We were just providing medical and technical military assistance to them, financial assistance.

OS: So, in other words, if the Assad regime had been, let's say, weakened, would Russia have come to help it against an ISIS move towards Damascus?

VP: This once again depends on the subjunctive mood, and it's difficult to talk about, because it's all about myriads of factors that have to be taken into account.

OS: Let's talk about another war situation since we're in the Situation Room. More recent. In the Crimea, when the referendum was coming up, the US destroyer Donald Cook was moving towards the Black Sea with Tomahawk missiles. Correct me if I'm wrong, but I saw a documentary . . . Well, first of all, NATO announced military drills in the Black Sea and the Russian naval commander was talking about how close—in this documentary—was talking about how close Russia came to using its missile system for coastal defense. The US ship Donald Cook was apparently coming right into the Black Sea when it made a U-turn and didn't carry through its mission.[179] It seems like it was similar to the Cuban Missile Crisis when the same thing happened, where a ship was coming towards the demarcation line and made a U-turn because it had been threatened by the US Navy back in 1962. So where were you at this time when this Donald Cook situation was happening and were you nervous about his?

VP: Remember how the Ukrainian crisis unfolded. [We've discussed it.] The three foreign ministers of European countries were acting as guarantors of an agreement between the opposition and President Yanukovych. Everyone agreed to that. President Yanukovych even agreed to hold early elections. At that time, at the initiative of the United States of America, they told us, 'We ask you to prevent President Yanukovych from using the armed forces.' And they promised in their term they were going to do everything for the opposition to clear the squares and the administrative buildings. We said, 'Very well that is a good proposal. We are going to work on it.' And as you, know President Yanukovych didn't resort to the armed forces. But the very next day the coup d'état took place during the night. We didn't have a telephone conversation, we didn't get a call, we simply saw them [the Americans] actively support those who perpetrated the coup d'état. And we could only shrug our shoulders. Such conduct, the way the Americans acted, even among individuals is absolutely unacceptable. They should have at least told us afterwards that the situation had spun out of control. They should have told us that they would do everything to put them back on a constitutional track. No, they didn't do that. They started to come up with lies saying that Yanukovych had fled. And they supported those who performed that coup d'état. How can we trust such partners?

OS: Question—is this when Victoria Nuland, the Undersecretary of State, had that conversation with the American ambassador and said, "Fuck the EU"?[180]

VP: Well, it doesn't matter, honestly. It was on February 21st. Or maybe the 20th. The coup d'état took place the next day. So now that Crimea has become a full fledged part of the Russian Federation, our attitude towards it changed drastically. If we see a threat to our territory, just as any other country, we will have to protect it by all means at our disposal. I wouldn't draw an analogy with the Cuban Missile Crisis, because back then the world was on the brink of a nuclear apocalypse. Thankfully, the situation didn't go as far this time, even though we did indeed deploy our most sophisticated, our cutting-edge systems, for coastal defense.

OS: But the Bastion is a big missile and the destroyer, the Donald Cook, has Tomahawk missiles.

VP: Yes, certainly—against such missiles as the ones we've deployed in Crimea—such a ship, destroyer as Donald Cook is simply defenseless.

OS: Yes, that's probably why they turned around?

VP: I think this captain was smart and also a responsible person. This doesn't mean he's weak . . .

OS: No, no.

VP: —He simply understood what he was dealing with. He decided not to continue.

OS: But your commander had the authority to fire?

VP: Our commanders always have the authorization to use the necessary means for the defense of the Russian Federation.

OS: Still, it's a big incident potentially.

VP: Yes, certainly. It would have been very bad.

OS: Were you notified?

VP: Yes, certainly. Where is that ship stationed usually—the Donald Cook? Where is the base?[181]

OS: The Mediterranean, I presume.

VP: Yes. But I think that the mother port is somewhere in the United States—the place it's registered. So, thousands and thousands of kilometers from. . . . And even if the port is somewhere in the Mediterranean, somewhere in Spain, it is still thousands of kilometers from the Black Sea. And we are determined to protect our territory.

OS: I understand. But were you available, were you—

VP: Who was trying to provoke whom? What was that destroyer doing so close to our land?

OS: I understand, but were you contacted at the time? In what timeframe did all of this take place, this challenge?

VP: I think it was real time. Once the destroyer was located and detected, they saw that there was a threat, and the ship itself saw that it was the target of the missile systems. I don't know who the captain was. But he showed much restraint. I think he is a responsible man and a courageous officer to

boot. I think it was the right decision that he made. He decided not to escalate the situation. It doesn't at all mean that he would have been attacked
by our missiles. But we had to show them that our coast was protected by the
missile systems.

OS: Was there a warning sent out to him?

VP: The captain sees right away that his ship has become the target of missile systems—there is special equipment. He has special equipment to detect
such situations.

OS: And all of this takes place in two minutes, 30 minutes, 50 minutes?

VP: I don't know—the experts can give you the answer. Seconds, mere seconds, I think.

OS: I mean, does this happen all the time? You sound very cool.

VP: It sometimes happens. And that's why our American counterparts have
suggested we should build a system for exchanging information about the
aircraft that are flying over, so as to avoid any kind of incident. Because when
an aircraft is targeted, is eradiated by another aircraft this is considered a
serious incident.

OS: I'd say.

VP: And this is always a very serious incident.

OS: So there have been others—there have been other incidents we don't
know about?

VP: I don't know. NATO aircraft are flying over the Baltic Sea without
transponders—the systems that are used to identify them—and our aircraft
have started to fly without our transponders as well. And once our aircraft
have started to do that, there's been so much ruckus saying that we do not
use transponders, but when I publicly declared that the number of our flights
is many-fold fewer than the number of NATO flights the ruckus has quieted
down. The president of Finland has proposed that we should make a decision
making it obligatory for everyone to use these transponders, to detect them,

to identify and we suggested right away that this should be done, but our NATO partners have refused. You see we need a dialogue all the time, we do not need new provocations.

OS: I understand, it's very scary. At that time, you made a strong speech, I thought, addressing NATO. You said, "This is our historic territory. These are Russian people. They are in danger now. We can't leave them alone. It wasn't us who staged the coup. It was done by nationalists and people with far-right views. You supported them, but where do you live—5,000 miles away. But we live here and it is our land. What do you want to fight for there? You don't know, do you? But we do know. And we are ready for it."

VP: Yes indeed we were brought to the brink, so to speak.

OS: To the brink—you admit to the brink?

VP: Yes, certainly. We had to respond somehow.

OS: Well, finally you're admitting it.

VP: Yes, we were open to positive dialogue. We did everything to achieve a political settlement. But they had to give their support to this unconstitutional seizure of power. I still wonder why they had to do that. Incidentally, that was a first step to further destabilization of the country. And this happens still. So, first the power is seized and right now these forces that have seized power are trying to make those who disagree with that accept this as a fact. This is what is happening to the south and eastern part of Ukraine. Instead of engaging in a political dialogue, which is quite possible, that is what they're doing.

OS: Well, you have to get your story out there. Your side of the story—not only on RT, but hopefully with some intelligence releases, some shots, some images that would tell the story. You have to tell this story, you have to somehow get your raw intelligence into the system.

VP: You see, that's quite impossible, because this point of view that we present is ignored by the world media. And if it's ignored, not on equal footing with the other perspectives, then almost no one hears it. So a narrative is being constructed of some evil Russia—

OS: —I wouldn't give up on that, I wouldn't give up. You have to fight back.
And you're doing a great job but more, better.

VP: I'll bear that in mind, but I think this critique is justified.

OS: [teasing] No, Dmitry's done a lousy job on that. [Putin's press secretary
and confidant]

VP: Well, this is not up to him. This is not the task he's supposed to do.

OS: I know.

VP: His task is to provide information and support to my everyday functions. . . . It's my job and I'm not doing a very good job of it.

OS: You're doing a great job, but you work too hard—you've got to relax. I
think you should take a vacation. Go to Palm Beach, relax, sit on the beach,
play some golf, talk.

VP: I understand the hint. Well, I envy him.

ON SOVEREIGNTY

OS: In closing, you inherited a Russian state that was collapsing at the end
of the last century. You came to office accidentally and people were in great
misery. There was no sense of a central power and the point is that I think
Russia had to be rebuilt so that it wouldn't collapse again. Mr. Gorbachev's
ideal of restructuring didn't happen. The West, in a sense, supported disor-
der. A vision which, you said, Russia must never again embrace. Then you
said sovereignty is the key. Sovereignty is the key. I believe you said one time
that a state in order to exist and have sovereignty has, amongst its obligations, to pay the pensions of older people. Yes?

VP: Yes, certainly. In general, and especially right now, a country can only
ensure its sovereignty if it secures a good economic growth rate—not just the
economic growth rate, you've got to secure economic development. And in

this sense, despite the good assessment you've given to my job, I think both myself and my colleagues could have done an even better job. Even though that would have been immensely hard, because we were always facing a dilemma. We had to choose between a bad decision and an even worse decision. But that happens all the time everywhere. You are always faced with a choice. And you've got to make it. Liberally-minded people think that we should have taken harsher, tougher measures. I thought that the harshness had to correlate to the standard of living to help people. We had to go step by step in improving the lives of our people.

Back then, in 2000, more than 40 percent of our citizens were living below the poverty line, the system of social security was in ruin, let alone the armed forces which all but ceased to exist. Separatism was holding sway. I'm not going to elaborate on that, but I'm going to say that the Russian constitution didn't apply all throughout our territory and the Caucasus was seeing a war that was raging—a civil war, which was fueled by radical elements from abroad. And in the end that civil war degenerated into terrorism. The situation was very difficult. But the Russian people and all the peoples of Russia, they've got a very important quality and that is love for their own nation, for their country. The sense of danger, the sense of compassion as well as the willingness to make sacrifices for the interests of their country. And thanks to these qualities of the Russian people and other peoples of Russia, we have managed to get through that difficult period. But we cannot exploit these qualities endlessly. We want our people to have better lives. Liberal-minded economists say we should have economized more or we shouldn't have increased the wages, the salaries, the pensions. But you see our people still have a very, very modest standard of living. I want rank and file citizens, families to see that our country is recovering. Anyhow, we are trying to pursue a very restrained, reserved economic policy.

OS: Getting back to sovereignty.

VP: We are trying to use the revenues from oil and gas. We will save this money, but we try to spend what we get from other sectors. For us that is a very difficult task. As you can see we have increased the real income of our population by a magnitude of several times. Last year, because of high inflation, real income was reduced a little bit. But at the end of last year we saw a pickup of that real income. Last year we managed to reduce the inflation rate to a historical record low—it was 5.4 percent or so. Even though our target was 6.2 percent. And we're going to target inflation and I do hope that we'll be able to bring it down to four percent. We've got a relatively low unemployment rate at around 5.4 percent. In spite of all the political restrictions, we've managed to keep our reserves, to stabilize our economy. I'm confident that this year we're going to witness more economic growth, albeit modest.[182] Our monetary policy is very well-balanced. It's being implemented by the Central Bank and by the government.

OS: You should thank Obama—sanctions were good for you.

VP: Our agricultural producers have to thank the Obama administration. Due to the measures we've introduced to counter the sanctions against us. These countermeasures are mostly related to closing our market to agricultural produce. And thanks to these measures, the agricultural producers have managed to increase annually their production by more than three percent. Last year we saw record crops of wheat and other grains. And I know you love Russia, so it gives me great pleasure to tell you that Russia ranks first in the world in terms of wheat export.

OS: I like bread—the black bread is my favorite.

VP: We used to buy grains and wheat.

OS: From Canada, yeah.

VP: Right now we produce less than the US or Canada or China. But these countries have larger consumption rates. And as far as per capita production is concerned, it's very good.

OS: I believe you. Sovereignty is not just economic though. I just want to tell you a quick story—last night . . . I mean the Russian people have guts. And last night there was a TV series on television Channel 1, I think it was. I saw it—prime time, 8 p.m. It was about the Germans and the Russians. And it was a very interesting story. It was in Russian. I didn't understand much. But I got a sense of it. In that story, the Russians again behaved very courageously, very courageous and were very good fighters, and outwitted the Nazis. And you know, TV stuff, but it was damn good. It was well-made. The actors were really terrific.

It was kind of ugly in a way, but in a good way—gritty. Very impressed and I remembered when I was here during the Brezhnev era, when they used to show all the old black and white Soviet films on TV, I saw the same kind of movie where the Soviets were taking on the Nazis again. And I made the connection. This is 34 years later, and I say the Russian people have a certain quality of courage which manifests itself time and again and they never forget. And by watching these old movies and remembering the tradition, remembering history, you go a long way towards keeping that sovereignty.

VP: Yes. That is very important. But no less important than this rigid framework of tradition is to be willing to accept new things, novelties, and to advance.

OS: Like cyber warfare! I'm not going to bug you anymore. I've got my hands full, 25–30 hours to cut. No more questions! Promise. A handshake across the countries. I wish I wish I wish. You did a great job, you did a good job.

VP: [a warm handshake] If they're going to beat you for this, you can come back here to Russia and we'll help heal you.

OS: We'll see. I'm proud of the film. You got to tell your side of the story and that's all I can do.

VP: I don't know if anyone is going to be interested in that.

OS: That's also possible. Goodnight, Mr. Putin.

END

End Notes

1. Background Information:
The Siege of Leningrad (now St. Petersburg) lasted for 872 days from Sept. 8, 1941 to Jan. 27, 1944. During the Siege, the Nazis were able to encircle Leningrad and cut off nearly all of the supplies, including food, to the city. In 1942 alone, 650,000 city residents died as a result. https://www.britannica.com/event/Siege-of-Leningrad

2. Background Information:
The actual number of casualties relative to the number of men mobilised during World War I is appalling. Total number for the Allies was 52%. The total for the Central Powers was 67%. See, "First World War Causalties," Chris Trueman *The History Learning Site* (April 17, 2015). Retrieved at: http://www.historylearningsite.co.uk/world-war-one/world-war-one-and-casualties/first-world-war-casualties/

The numbers on Trueman's site are supported by those found on the *International Encylopedia of the First World War*. See, "War Losses," Antoine Prost (October 8, 2014). Retrieved at: http://encyclopedia.1914-1918-online.net/article/war_losses

3. Background Information:
Perestroika, was, in the words of the Library of Congress, "Mikhail Gorbachev's program [starting 1986] of economic, political, and social restructuring, [which] became the unintended catalyst for dismantling" the Soviet state. "Revelations from the Soviet Archive," Library of Congress, retrieved at: https://www.loc.gov/exhibits/archives/pere.html

4. Background Information:
The August coup of 1991 was a short-lived plot hatched by what the West referred to as "hard-line" Communists who made a last-ditch effort to save the Soviet Union in the face of the chaotic situation brought about by Gorbachev's *Perestroika*. The coup was short, lasting only a few days, and most famously involved the kidnapping of Gorbachev and the attempt to reinstate Communist control over the Soviet Union. The plot backfired miserably, making a hero out of Boris Yeltsin who openly led protests against the coup, hastening the collapse of the USSR. See, "The KGB's Bathhouse Plot," VICTOR SEBESTYEN, the *New York Times* (Aug. 20, 2011). Retrieved at: http://www.nytimes.com/2011/08/21/opinion/sunday/the-soviet-coup-that-failed.html

5. Background Information:
According to the *New York Times*, "Anatoly A. Sobchak, the former mayor of St. Petersburg and democratic reformer . . . gave Acting President Vladimir V. Putin his start in public life." It was Sobchak who, as mayor, renamed Leningrad to St. Petersburg after the August, 1991 coup. "A.A. Sobchak, Dead at 62; Mentor to Putin," Celestine Bohlen, Feb. 21, 2000. Retrieved at: http://www.nytimes.com/2000/02/21/world/aa-sobchak-dead-at-62-mentor-to-putin.html

6. Background Information:
The French Utopian Socialists believed in an egalitarian society which would be established through small, "model communities that set examples of harmonious cooperation to the world." Theirs was a vision of radical democracy on a small scale, gradually leading to a better world. The Marxian socialists, on the other hand, especially as manifested in the creation of

the Soviet Union, believed that socialism would be built through a "clash of social forces," eventually leading to a workers' state which initially would take the form of the dictatorship of the proletariat. In other words, this was a view of socialism brought about, not gradually or gently, but, out of necessity, by the revolutionary struggle of workers (and, the Russian revolutionaries would add peasants) which initially would have to create a strong state to suppress the former ruling class made up of industrial owners and large land owners. See, e.g., "Socialism," Terence Ball, Richard Dagger, *Encyclopedia Britannica*, retrieved at: https://www.britannica.com/topic/socialism

7. Background Information:
For more detail on the economic chaos and social dislocation brought about by the rapid changes of *Perestroika* and the collapse of the USSR which resulted, see, Cohen, Stephen F., *Soviet Fates and Lost Alternatives: From Stalinism to the New Cold War* (Columbia University Press, 2011).

8. Background Information:
The First Chechen War, waged by President Boris Yeltsin, lasted between 1994 and 1996. The war was waged by Moscow to re-assert control of the Republic of Chechnya which was attempting to break away. The Second Chechen War, began on the Russian side by the new President, Vladimir Putin, was carried out in defense of the Chechen Republic leadership against radical Islamic extremists, many who infiltrated from abroad, who were attempting to topple the upstart Chechen government. Thousands died on both sides of these conflicts in what came to be considered "Russia's Vietnam War." Russia did not declare victory in the Second Chechen War until 2009. "Chechnya, Russia and 20 years of Conflict," Mansur Mirovalev, *Al Jaazera* (Dec. 11, 2014). Retrieved at: http://www.aljazeera.com/indepth/features/2014/12/chechnya-russia-20-years-conflict-2014121161310580523.html

For an actual chronology of these conflicts, see, "Chechnya and Russia: timeline," *The Guardian* (April 16, 2009). Retrieved at: https://www.theguardian.com/world/2009/apr/16/chechnya-russia-timeline

9. Background Information:
Boris Berezovsky was a controversial billionaire oligarch who got rich, as many did, by taking over industry during the privatization of the Russian economy shortly before and after the collapse of the USSR. He died under mysterious circumstances in 2013. Forbes Magazine believes that Berezovsky may have killed its editor Paul Klebnikov. "Did Boris Berezovsky Kill Himself? More Compelling, Did He Kill Forbes Editor Paul Klebnikov?" Richard Behar, *Forbes* (March 24, 2013). Retrieved at: https://www.forbes.com/sites/richardbehar/2013/03/24/did-boris-berezovsky-kill-himself-more-compelling-did-he-kill-forbes-editor-paul-klebnikov/#621359176729

10. Claim: "You're credited with doing many fine things in your first term. Privatization was stopped. You built up industries—electronics, engineering, petrochemical, agriculture, and many others. A real son of Russia—you should be proud. You raised the GDP, you raised incomes, you reformed the army, you resolved the Chechen war."

Supporting: According to London's *Guardian* newspaper, Putin is favorably remembered by the Russian people for helping to "usher in an era of unprecedented prosperity . . . with real disposable income doubling between 1999 and 2006," and with the GDP growing by a multiple of 2.7 from 2006 to 2014. "15 years of Vladimir Putin, 15 ways he has changed Russia and the World," Alec Luhn (May 6, 2015). Retrieved at: https://www.theguardian.com/world/2015/may/06/vladimir-putin-15-ways-he-changed-russia-world

11. Claim: "Immensely popular in 2004—you're reelected with 70 percent of the vote."

Supporting: Oliver Stone is correct that Putin won the 2004 Presidential election with about 70% of the popular vote. See, "Russia in 2004," Elizabeth Teague, *Encyclopedia Britannica*. Retrieved at: https://www.britannica.com/place/Russia-Year-In-Review-2004

12. Background Information:
After first taking office in 1933 as America's 32nd president, Franklin Delano Roosevelt, a Democrat, would eventually be elected to a record four terms in office. However, he was unable to fully complete his fourth term. Two years after his death, on March 21, 1947, Congress passed the 22nd Amendment to the US Constitution, stating that no person could be elected to the office of president more than twice. The amendment was ratified in 1951.

See, "FDR nominated for unprecedented third term," *History*, Retrieved at: http://www.history.com/this-day-in-history/fdr-nominated-for-unprecedented-third-term

13. Claim: "I have to tell you that President Medvedev performed independently all his functions. There was this division of functions according to the Constitution. I never interfered within his domain."

A clear division of functions does indeed exist between the president and prime minister positions in Russia. See, "FACTBOX: Russian president and prime minister: who does what?," *Reuters* (May 7, 2008). Retrieved at: http://www.reuters.com/article/us-russia-inauguration-president-duties-idUSL0718325420080507

However, the question remains how independent the Putin-Medvedev relationship actually was from 2008 to 2012, when Dmitry Medvedev served as President and Vladimir Putin served as Prime Minister. Western media consistently portrayed the two as friends, who at times experience tension regarding reforms proposed and implemented by President Medvedev, however, more specifically, western sources concurred that Prime Minister Putin was the one who called the shots in Russia. See, "Vladimir Putin Is Medvedev's Friend - And Boss," Dmitry Sidorov, Forbes (February, 23, 2009). Retrieved at: https://www.forbes.com/2009/02/23/russia-president-prime-minister-opinions-contributors_medvedev_putin.html

14. Background Information:
Dmitry Medvedev served as Russian President from 2008 to 2012, while also serving as Russian Prime Minister during Vladimir Putin's terms as President. "Dmitry Medvedev, Fast Facts," CNN (Aug. 30, 2016). Retrieved at: http://www.cnn.com/2012/12/26/world/europe/dmitry-medvedev—fast-facts/

15. Claim: "Five assassination attempts, I'm told. Not as much as Castro, whom I interviewed—I think he must have had 50—but there's a legitimate 5 that I've heard about."

Assassination attempts on Putin's life are unclear and unverifiable. However, Cuban officials claim that the number of assassination attempts, also unverifiable, on Fidel Castro's life reach upwards of 638. See, "Fidel Castro survived 600 assassination attempts, officials say," Patrick Oppmann, CNN (November 26, 2016). Retrieved at: http://www.cnn.com/2016/08/12/americas/cuba-fidel-castro-at-90-after-assassination-plots/

16. Claim: "Libya, as a territorially integral state has ceased to exist."

Supporting: It is well-recognized that Libya was destroyed as a country by the 2011 NATO intervention. See, "The US-NATO Invasion of Libya Destroyed the Country Beyond All

Recognition," Vijay Prishad, Alternet (March 22, 2017). Retrieved at: http://www.alternet.org/world/us-nato-invasion-libya-destroyed-country-beyond-all-recognition

17. Background Information:
Gaddafi, known as the "Brotherly Leader," was a revolutionary who, at 27 years old led a coup to depose the monarch. For the next 42 years, he ruled Libya and implemented the strict fundamentals of Sunni Islam across his country. He was a staunch defender of his country and leadership, often leading his men into bloody battles, which were viewed by the rest of the world as erratic displays of showmanship. Ghaddafi survived many coup and assassination attempts until he was ultimately killed in 2011. See, http://www.nytimes.com/2011/10/21/world/africa/qaddafi-killed-as-hometown-falls-to-libyan-rebels.html

18. Background Information:
See, "Bush saw Putin's 'Soul.' Obama Wanted to appeal to his Brain," Steven Mufson, *Washington Post* (Dec. 1, 2015). Retrieved at: https://www.washingtonpost.com/business/economy/bush-saw-putins-soul-obama-wants-to-appeal-to-his-brain/2015/12/01/264f0c7c-984b-11e5-8917-653b65c809eb_story.html.

19. Background Information:
See, "911 a 'Turning Point' for Putin," Jill Dougherty, *Washington Post* (Sep. 10, 2002). Retrieved at: http://www.edition.cnn.com/2002/WORLD/europe/09/10/ar911.russia.putin/index.html

20. Background Information:
It is also true, as Stone states, that Putin gave significant, concrete assistance to the US in its post-911 invasion of Afghanistan. Ibid.

21. Claim: "Al Qaeda is not the result of our activities. It's the result of the activities of our American friends."

Supporting: See, "Frankenstein The CIA Created," Jason Burke, *Guardian* (Jan. 17, 1999). Retrieved at: https://www.theguardian.com/world/1999/jan/17/yemen.islam

22. Claim: "Although Bill Casey, Director of the CIA under Ronald Reagan, made it a special effort—this is documented—to excite the Muslims in the Caucasus in Central Asia against the Soviet Union."

Supporting: See, "Ghost Wars: How Reagan Armed the Mujahadeen in Afghanistan," Steve Coll & Amy Goodman, Democracy Now! (June 10, 2004). Retrieved at: https://www.democracynow.org/2004/6/10/ghost_wars_how_reagan_armed_the

23. Claim: "And when those problems in the Caucasus and Chechnya emerged, unfortunately the Americans supported those processes."

Supporting: See, "Chechen Terrorists and the Neocons," former FBI agent Coleen Rowley, Consortium News (April 19, 2013). Retrieved at: https://consortiumnews.com/2013/04/19/chechen-terrorists-and-the-neocons/

24. Background Information:
The letter from the CIA to Putin about the former's possible support for rebels in Chechnya is referenced in the article: "Chechnya, the CIA and Terrorism," Michael S. Rozeff, *Russia Insider* (April 28, 2015). Retrieved at:
http://russia-insider.com/en/chechnya-cia-and-terrorism/6179

25. Background Information:
"In Afghanistan, Taliban surpasses al-Qaeda," Joshua Partlow, *Washington Post* (Nov. 11, 2009). Retrieved at: http://www.washingtonpost.com/wp-dyn/content/article/2009/11/10/AR2009111019644.html

26. Claim: "OS: Do you have any belief that the United States was involved in any way supporting the Chechens in the first or second war?

VP: Yes. We're 100 percent sure that we have objective proof of that."

Supporting: See, "Chechen Terrorists and the Neocons," Ibid.

27. Background Information:
See, "Miscalculations Paved Path to Chechen War," David Hoffman, *Washington Post* (March 20, 2000). Retrieved at: https://www.washingtonpost.com/archive/politics/2000/03/20/miscalculations-paved-path-to-chechen-war/e675f17a-d286-4b5e-b33a-708d819d43f0/?utm_term=.2549af78ab19 Hoffman explains that "[o]n the Chechen side, rebel leaders launched an attack against neighboring Dagestan last August in the mistaken belief that they would encounter weak Russian resistance and spark an Islamic uprising. The uprising didn't materialize, and the incursions were repelled."

28. Claim: "Moreover, we had exact data that there were no WMDs whatsoever in Iraq"

Supporting: It is true, as Putin claims, that the Russia's assessment, which it shared with the US at the time, was that Iraq possessed no Weapons of Mass Destruction to justify the 2003 military invasion. As Newsweek explained, "[p]lenty of the best-informed intelligence sources were certain the WMDs were a fantasy. French intelligence knew it; so did Russia and Germany." "Dick Cheney's Biggest Lie," Kurt Eichenwald, Newsweek (May 19, 2015). Retrieved at: http://www.newsweek.com/2015/05/29/dick-cheneys-biggest-lie-333097.html

29. Claim: "OS: . . . there was a deal with the Soviet Union not to expand NATO eastward.

VP: They were all saying there was one thing that the Soviet Union could be sure of—that the eastern border of NATO would not be extended any further than the eastern border of the German Democratic Republic.

OS: So this was a clear violation."

Supporting: "Russia's Got a Point: The US Broke a NATO Promise," Joshua R. Itzkowitz Shifrinson, *LA Times* (May 30, 2016). Retrieved at: http://www.latimes.com/opinion/op-ed/la-oe-shifrinson-russia-us-nato-deal-20160530-snap-story.html

30. Background Information
See, "US Withdraws From ABM Treaty; Global Response Muted," Wade Boese, Arms Control Association (July/August 2002). Retrieved at: https://www.armscontrol.org/act/2002_07-08/abmjul_aug02

31. Background Information:
"Bush Pulls Out of ABM Treaty; Putin Calls Move a Mistake," Terence Neilen, *New York Times* (Dec. 31, 2001). Retrieved at: http://www.nytimes.com/2001/12/13/international/bush-pulls-out-of-abm-treaty-putin-calls-move-a-mistake.html

32. Background Information:
"Putin Warns Romania, Poland Over Implementing US missile Shield," Fox News (May 28,

2016). Retrieved at: http://www.foxnews.com/world/2016/05/28/putin-warns-romania-po-land-over-implementing-us-missile-shield.html

33. Background Information:
As tension from the Cold War peaked, and paranoia of Communism spread throughout America grew, husband and wife Julius and Ethel Rosenberg, former members of the Communist party, were sentenced to death under the Espionage Act of 1917 for suspicion of sending nuclear information from the United States to Russia. Despite public outcry and demand for their clemency, both Presidents Truman and Eisenhower refused to pardon them. Until their last days at Sing-Sing Prison in New York, the couple maintained their innocence. They were executed by electric chair on June 19, 1953. See, http://www.coldwar.org/articles/50s/TheRosenbergTrial.asp

34. Background Information:
For more on the fascinating story of Klaus Fuchs who shared atomic secrets with the Soviet Union out of his ideological commitment to Communism, see, the description in PBS's "American Experience," at http://www.pbs.org/wgbh//amex/bomb/peopleevents/pandeA-MEX54.html

35. Background Information:
See, "Putin's Prepared Remarks at 43rd Munich Conference on Security Policy," *Washington Post* (Feb. 12, 2007). Retrieved at: http://www.washingtonpost.com/wp-dyn/content/article/2007/02/12/AR2007021200555.html

36. Background Information:
See, generally, Pauwels, Jacques R. *The Myth of the Good War: America in the Second World War* (Lorimer, 2016).

37. Background Information:
See, generally, *Price, David. Base Nation: How US Military Bases Abroad Harm America and the World* (American Empire Project). (Metropolitan Books, 2015).

38. Background Information:
See, "The United States Shares the Blame for the Russia-Georgia Crisis," Paul J. Saunders, *US News & World Reports* (Aug. 12, 2008). Retrieved at: https://www.usnews.com/news/articles/2008/08/12/the-united-states-shares-the-blame-for-the-russia-georgia-crisis

39. Claim: "Not exactly—yes and no. We were surprised when we saw that the aggression by President Saakashvili was not just supported by Bush. They tried to paint the picture saying that Russia was the aggressor, when it was quite evident that it was Saakashvili who decided to launch the aggression."

Supporting: See, "The United States Shares the Blame for the Russia-Georgia Crisis," Paul J. Saunders, *US News & World Reports* (Aug. 12, 2008). Retrieved at: https://www.usnews.com/news/articles/2008/08/12/the-united-states-shares-the-blame-for-the-russia-georgia-crisis

40. Correction:
Edward Snowden's passport was annulled before he left Hong Kong for Russia. See, "AP Source: NSA leaker Snowden's passport revoked," Mathew V. Lee, *US World & News Report* (June 23, 2013). Retrieved at: https://www.usnews.com/news/politics/articles/2013/06/23/ap-source-nsa-leaker-snowdens-passport-revoked

41. Claim: "And that also would have stipulated it for mutual extradition of criminals, but the United States refused to cooperate with us."

Supporting: For a good explanation of why the US and Russia do not have an extradition treaty, see, "3 Extradition Cases That Help Explain US-Russia Relations," Eyder Peralta, NPR (Aug. 7, 2013). Retrieved at: http://www.npr.org/sections/thetwo-way/2013/08/07/209846990/3-extradition-cases-that-help-explain-u-s-russia-relations. In addition to a Russian defector, the article explains that the US had refused to extradite a Chechen terrorist and Nazi War Criminal accused of running a death camp to Russia despite the latter's requests.

42. Background Information:
For more information on the huge amount of information the NSA collects on Americans, see, "FAQ: What you Need to Know about the NSA's Surveillance Programs," Jonathan Stray, *Propublica* (Aug. 5, 2013). Retrieved at: https://www.propublica.org/article/nsa-data-collection-faq

43. "AP Source: NSA leaker Snowden's passport revoked," Ibid.

44. Background Information:
The US infuriated Bolivia by forcing the presidential plane of President Evo Morales to land because it wrongly suspected Morales of carrying Snowden upon the plane. See, "Bolivia: Presidential plane forced to land after false rumors of Snowden aboard," Catherine E. Shoichet, CNN (July 23, 2013). Retrieved at: http://www.cnn.com/2013/07/02/world/americas/bolivia-presidential-plane/

45. Background Information:
See, "Congress Passes NSA surveillance reform in vindication for Snowden, Bulk collection of Americans' phone records to end as US Senate passes USA Freedom Act" Sabrina Siddiqui, *The Guardian* (June 3, 2015). Retrieved at: https://www.theguardian.com/us-news/2015/jun/02/congress-surveillance-reform-edward-snowden

46. Claim: "President Yanukovych said he had to postpone the signing of the association agreement with the European Union. That was the starting point. And our partners in Europe and the United States managed to mount this horse of discontent of the people. And instead of trying to find out what was really happening, they decided to support the coup d'état."

Supporting: For a good explanation of how the US helped stoke violence and chaos in Ukraine and helped to bring about the 2014 *coup d'état*, see, "Chronology of the Ukraine Coup," Renee Parsons, *Counterpunch* (March 5, 2014). Retrieved at: http://www.counterpunch.org/2014/03/05/chronology-of-the-ukrainian-coup/

47. Background Information:
Ibid.

48. Background Information:
In provocative move, Ukraine government banned Russian as a second language. See, *Ukraine Crisis: Timeline*, BBC (Nov. 13, 2014). Retrieved at: http://www.bbc.com/news/world-middle-east-26248275

49. Background Information:
See, "Ukraine's sharp divisions," BBC, (April 2014). Retrieved at: http://www.bbc.com/news/world-europe-26387353

50. Background Information:
For good explanation on how and why the uprising in Donbass against the new, coup government began, see, "It's not Russia that pushed Ukraine to the brink of War," Seumus Milne, *The Guardian* (April 30, 2014). See, https://www.theguardian.com/commentisfree/2014/apr/30/russia-ukraine-war-kiev-conflict

51. Background Information:
The "Odessa tragedy" that Putin refers to was the massacre of 42 individuals, among them 32 pro-Russian protesters, in the Trade Unions House in Odessa in 2014, see, "Ukraine crisis: death by fire in Odessa as country suffers bloodiest day since the revolution," Roland Oliphant, *The Telegraph* (May 3, 2014). Retrieved at: http://www.telegraph.co.uk/news/worldnews/europe/ukraine/10806656/Ukraine-crisis-death-by-fire-in-Odessa-as-country-suffers-bloodiest-day-since-the-revolution.html

52. Background Information:
Putin is correct that thousands have died as a result of hostilities in the Donbass. According to the United Nations, as of December of 2016, approximately 2,000 civilians have been killed in the conflict in the Donbass region of Ukraine, with another 6,000 to 7,0000 injured, while the total dead, including soldiers reached nearly 10,000. See, http://www.un.org/apps/news/story.asp?NewsID=55750#.WRxo1JIrLcs

53. Background Information:
For more on the contours of the Minsk Agreements that Putin references, see, "What are the Minsk Agreements," N.S., *The Economist* (Sept. 14, 2016). Retrieved at: http://www.economist.com/blogs/economist-explains/2016/09/economist-explains-7

54. Claim: "…the economy and the social sphere of Donbass have to be restored. But instead the authorities are strengthening the blockade of these territories."

Supporting: Putin is correct about the blockade of the Donbass by the central government and the resulting suffering. Indeed, UNICEF reports that, due to the blockade of the Donbass region of Ukraine, one million children are at risk of starvation. UNICEF's position is that the Minsk Agreements must be complied with to stop the war and this humanitarian disaster. See, https://www.unicef.org/media/media_94886.html

55. Background Information:
See, https://www.unicef.org/media/media_94886.html

56. Background Information:
Putin is exactly correct when he says that 2.5 million Ukrainians have fled to Russia since the 2014 coup. See, "Obama's Ukrainian Coup Triggered the Influx of 2.5 Million Ukrainian Refugees into Russia," Eric Zuesse, *Global Research* (Mar. 12, 2017). Retrieved at: http://www.globalresearch.ca/obamas-ukrainian-coup-triggered-the-influx-of-2-5-million-ukrainian-refugees-into-russia/5579719

57. Background Information:
The numbers here are not fully clear in terms of relationship among areas defined and: 1. Ukrainian citizens in Russia; 2. number of citizens who used to live in the territories, and; 3. number of people remaining. As cited earlier, two and a half million Ukrainian refugees did indeed go to Russia. And as noted by a OHCHR report, three million people live in the areas directly affected by the conflict."

See, "Report on the human rights situation in Ukraine 16 November 2015 to 15 February 2016," Office of the United Nations High Commissioner for Human Rights (March 3, 2016). http://www.ohchr.org/Documents/Countries/UA/Ukraine_13th_HRMMU_Report_3March2016.pdf

58. Claim: "People came, the turnout was more than 90 percent. And more than 90 percent voted in favor of re-unifying with Russia."

Supporting: Putin is correct that well over 90% of the Crimeans who went to the polls voted to leave Ukraine and join Russia. See, "Crimeans vote over 90 percent to quit Ukraine and join Russia," Mike Collett-White and Ronald Popeski, *Reuters* (Mar. 16, 2014). Retrieved at: http://www.reuters.com/article/us-ukraine-crisis-idUSBREA1Q1E820140316

59. Background Information:
Putin here is referring to Article 1, Section 2 of the UN Charter which reads, "To develop friendly relations among nations based on respect for the principle of equal rights and self-determination of peoples, and to take other appropriate measures to strengthen universal peace." Similarly, Article I, Section 1 of the International Covenant on Civil and Political Rights, a binding human rights instrument, provides: "All peoples have the right of self-determination. By virtue of that right they freely determine their political status and freely pursue their economic, social and cultural development." As Putin indicates, this right to self-determination is not dependent on the will of the central government of any state.

60. Claim: "I was always wondering if Kosovars were allowed to do it, why is that not allowed to Russians, Ukrainians, Tatars, and Crimeans? There is no difference whatsoever."

Supporting: Others have, as Putin, made the comparison of the Crimean referendum to join Russia, which the US opposed, to the Kosovar referendum to secede from Serbia, which the US pushed for the point of war. See, "From Kosovo to Crimea: Obama's Strange Position on Referendums," Brian Cloughley, *Counterpunch* (July 17, 2015). Retrieved at: http://www.counterpunch.org/2015/07/17/from-kosovo-to-crimea-obamas-strange-position-on-referendums/

61. Claim: OS: Was there any UN condemnation of the annexation of Crimea?
VP: No, I don't know anything of that."

Contradicting: In truth, contrary to Putin's stated recollection, the UN General Assembly did declare the Crimean referendum on secession invalid, and the UN General Assembly Human Rights Committee went so far as to condemn the annexation of Crimea by Russia. See, http://www.un.org/apps/news/story.asp?NewsID=47443#.WRyU3JIrLcs; http://newsinfo.inquirer.net/844707/un-committee-votes-to-condemn-russian-occupation-of-crimea

62. Claim: "There are two principal versions. The first version is that this plane was shot down by the Buk air defense system of the Ukrainian armed forces. And the second version is that the same system, the same system of arms—the Buk systems are produced in Russia—was employed by the militia, the separatists."

For a discussion of the different theories as to who (whether the Ukrainian government by another plane or Russian separatists by ground-to-air projectile) may have shot down Malaysian Air Lines, Flight 17 over the Russia/Ukraine border, see, "MH17 prosecutor open to theory another plane shot down airliner," *Chicago Tribune* (2017). Retrieved at: http://www.chicagotribune.com/news/nationworld/81796669-157.html

63. Claim: "Now as to the aircraft, the planes which were in the air—as far as I know, right away after this terrible catastrophe, one of the Ukrainian air controllers, I think he was a specialist originating from Spain, announced that he had seen a military aircraft in the corridor assigned for civil aircraft."

Supporting: For more on the downing on the MH17 flight, and in particular about the Spanish air traffic controller in Kiev mentioned by Putin, see, "MH17 Verdict: Real Evidence Points to US-Kiev Cover-up of Failed False Flag," *21st Century Wire* (July 25, 2014). Retrieved at: http://21stcenturywire.com/2014/07/25/mh17-verdict-real-evidence-points-to-us-kiev-cover-up-of-failed-false-flag-attack/

64. Background Information:
While many conspiracy theories abound in regard to George Soros' role in Ukraine, even the well-respected *Financial Times* acknowledges his significant investment in Ukraine since 1990 and his open partisanship in favor of the current government in Kiev during the current crisis between Ukraine and Russia. See, "Save Ukraine to Counter Russia, Says Soros," Christian Oliver (Jan. 7, 2015). Retrieved at: https://www.ft.com/content/4ddfb410-9664-11e4-a40b-00144feabdc0

65. Background Information:
Former Georgian President, Mikheil Sakashvili, who studied law in the United States, served as the Governor of Odessa from May of 2015 until his resignation in November of 2016. See, "Georgian Saakashvili quits as Ukraine Odessa governor," BBC (Nov. 7, 2016). Retrieved at: http://www.bbc.com/news/world-europe-37895588

66. Claim: "Yanukovych didn't give an order to use weapons against civilians"

Supporting: Then Ukrainian President, Victor Yanukovych, later claimed that he regretted the bloodshed during the 2014 uprising, but that, as Putin claims, he never ordered weapons to be fired on demonstrators. See, "Ukraine crisis: Yanukovych regrets bloodshed in Kiev," Gabriel Gatehouse, BBC (June 22, 2015). Retrieved at: http://www.bbc.com/news/world-europe-33224138

67. Claim: "But I have to say that the so-called protestors were very aggressive."

Supporting: For detail on the violence perpetrated particularly by far-right anti-government protesters in Ukraine in 2014, see, "The Ukrainian Nationalism at the Heart of 'Euromaidan' Coverage focused on the call for European integration has largely glossed over the rise in nationalist rhetoric that has led to violence," Alec Luhn, *The Nation* (Jan. 21, 2014). Retrieved at: https://www.thenation.com/article/ukrainian-nationalism-heart-euromaidan/

68. Background Information
See, "Profile: Ukraine's ultra-nationalist Right Sector," BBC (April 28, 2014). Retrieved at: http://www.bbc.com/news/world-europe-27173857

69. Claim: "OS: I see. Have you heard of the Azov battalion?
VP: Yes, certainly. There are certain armed formations which are not accountable to anyone, nor are they accountable to the central authorities in Kiev. I believe that is one of the reasons why the current leadership right now cannot put an end to these hostilities. That is simply because they are frightened that these uncontrollable armed forces will return to the capital."

Supporting: There is no dispute about the nature of the Azov battalion as a violent, neo-Nazi military organization. Indeed, Congress was so alarmed by this battalion, and the US support for it, that it passed legislation banning the US from funding and training this battalion. Incredibly, this ban was later repealed. See, "US Lifts Ban on Funding 'Neo-Nazi' Ukrainian Militia," Sam Sokol, *Jerusalem Post* (Jan. 18, 2016). Retrieved at: http://www.jpost.com/Diaspora/US-lifts-ban-on-funding-neo-Nazi-Ukrainian-militia-441884

70. Background Information:
Putin is indeed correct that John Kerry, as Senator, was highly critical of Reagan's proposed "Star Wars" missile defense program, calling it a "cancer on our nation." See, "Kerry Says Star Wars 'Based on Illusion,'" Lawrence L. Knutson, *Associated Press* (June 4, 1985). Retrieved at: http://www.apnewsarchive.com/1985/Kerry-Says-Star-Wars-Based-on-Illusion-/id-959d3c-5dace13d1264c5c18833522d2e

71. Background Information:
It appears that it was the Johnson Administration that first floated the idea with Soviet Premier Nikita Khrushchev to engage in joint talks about limitations on Anti-Ballistic Missile (ABM) systems, though this idea had been in consideration for years by the United States, including in the Kennedy Administration. See, "Cold War International History Conference: Paper by David S. Patterson" (1998). Retrieved at: https://www.archives.gov/research/foreign-policy/cold-war/conference/patterson.html

72. Background Information:
Indeed, there is evidence that Khrushchev's decision to place missiles in Cuba was a predictable result of the US's stationing of Jupiter missiles in Italy and Turkey – a provocative move which seemed aimed at giving the US first strike capability against the USSR. As an article in *The Atlantic* explains:

"The Jupiter's' destabilizing effect was widely recognized among defense experts within and outside the US government and even by congressional leaders. For instance, Senator Albert Gore Sr., an ally of the administration, told Secretary of State Dean Rusk that they were a "provocation" in a closed session of the Senate Foreign Relations Committee in February 1961 (more than a year and a half before the missile crisis), adding, "I wonder what our attitude would be" if the Soviets deployed nuclear-armed missiles to Cuba. Senator Claiborne Pell raised an identical argument in a memo passed on to Kennedy in May 1961.

Given America's powerful nuclear superiority, as well as the deployment of the Jupiter missiles, Moscow suspected that Washington viewed a nuclear first strike as an attractive option. They were right to be suspicious. The archives reveal that in fact the Kennedy administration had strongly considered this option during the Berlin crisis in 1961."
See, "The Real Cuban Missile Crisis," Benjamin Schwarz, *The Atlantic* (Jan/Feb. 2013). Retrieved at: https://www.theatlantic.com/magazine/archive/2013/01/the-real-cuban-missile-crisis/309190/

73. Background Information:
Stanley Kubrick (1928-1999), American film director, screenwriter, and producer regarded as one of the most influential directors in modern cinema. Most notable films: *The Shining; 2001: A Space Odyssey; A Clockwork Orange; Dr. Strangelove;* and *Full Metal Jacket,* which examines the dehumanizing effects of the Vietnam War on soldiers. The film was released just one year after Oliver Stone's *Platoon.* See, http://www.imdb.com/name/nm0000040/bio?ref_=nm_ov_bio_sm

Kubrick's 1964 film *Dr. Strangelove* or: *How I Learned to Stop Worrying and Love the Bomb* satirizes

Cold War hysteria over nuclear conflict between the United States and the Soviet Union. See, http://www.imdb.com/title/tt0057012

74. Background Information:
See, "The Real Cuban Missile Crisis," Ibid.

75. Background Information:
See, "Hillary, Putin's No Hitler," Timothy Stanley, CNN (March 5, 2014). Retrieved at: http://www.cnn.com/2014/03/05/opinion/stanley-hillary-clinton-hitler/

76. Background Information:
It is true, as Stone states, that General Curtis LeMay was a proponent of striking the USSR and beginning WWIII while the Soviet Union was still relatively weak. See, "Waiting for WWIII," Joshua Rothman, *The New Yorker* (Oct. 16, 2012). Retrieved at: http://www.newyorker.com/books/double-take/waiting-for-world-war-iii

77. Background Information:
Oliver Stone is here referring to the alternative account of the killing of Osama bin Laden by Pulitzer-prize winning journalist, Seymour M. Hersh, entitled, *The Killing of Osama Bin Laden* (Verso 2016).

78. Background Information:
For a detailed account of the economic and social disaster which followed the collapse of the USSR – a disaster even greater than that of the US's Great Depression – see, Cohen, Stephen F. *Soviet Fates and Lost Alternatives* (Columbia University Press 2011).

79. Background Information:
The four parties represented in the Russian Parliament which Putin refers to are: Putin's United Russia Party, the Communist Party of the Russian Federation, the Liberal Democratic Party of Russia and A Just Russia. See, "Russia Parliament Elections: How the Parties Line Up," BBC (March 6, 2012). Retrieved at: http://www.bbc.com/news/world-europe-15939801

80. Background Information:
Of course, this just happened again in 2016 with Donald J. Trump losing the popular vote but winning the Electoral College vote and therefore the Presidency.

81. Claim: "Now concerning the rights of sexual minorities. During the Soviet times, there was a criminal responsibility for homosexuals, and right now there is none. We eliminated that part of the criminal code back in the 1990s."

For an explanation of Russia's legal policies towards the LBGT community and their impact on that community, see, "Russia's Mixed Messages on LGBT," Stephen Ennis, BBC (April 29, 2016). Retrieved at: http://www.bbc.com/news/world-europe-36132060 The article explains that, as of the date of its publication, no member of the LGBT community had actually been imprisoned in Russia under the newly-passed law forbidding "homosexual propaganda."

82. Background Information:
Putin appears to be referring here to the Supreme Court's 2015 decision legalizing gay marriage in all 50 states. This was a 5-4 decision in the case of *Obergefell v. Hodges, 576 US __ (2015). In truth, the Supreme Court had invalidated all state laws criminalizing homosexual activity 12 years sooner in the case of* Lawrence v. Texas, 539 US 558 (2003).

83. Background Information:
The "gay propaganda law" was signed into law by President Putin on June 30, 2013. While

the stated purpose is to protect children from homosexual content, activists counter that the law is used against the LGBT community in general. See, "Russia: Court Rules Against LGBT Activist," *Human Rights Watch* (February 3, 2016). Retrieved at: https://www.hrw.org/news/2016/02/03/russia-court-rules-against-lgbt-activist

84. Claim: "So I was very much surprised to hear criticism from the United States, because some legislation in the United States provides criminal responsibility for homosexuals."

Contradicting: As indicated above in fn. 82, Putin is in fact incorrect that homosexual activity is still criminalized in the US. Such criminalization, while lasting into this century, was finally ended with the Supreme Court's 2003 decision in Lawrence v. Texas.

85. Background Information:
Putin is right on the money in terms of his estimate that Muslims make up about 12% of the Russian population, and shall make up about 20% by the year 2030. He is also correct that the absolute number of Muslims in Russia continues to grow, and indeed to far outpace the general population growth in Russia. Indeed, contrary to Putin's claims, the overall population of Russia is actually in decline. See, "Russia's Growing Muslim Population," Strafor Enterprises (Aug. 8, 2013). Retrieved at: https://www.stratfor.com/image/russias-growing-muslim-population

86. Ibid.

87. Background Information:
Putin is correct that Russia signed the Kyoto Protocol which the US was one of the few countries in the world that refused to sign. See, "The Only Nations That Haven't Signed 1997's Global Climate Treaty are Afghanistan, Sudan & the USA," Brian Merchant, Treehugger.com (Nov. 28, 2011). Retrieved at: https://www.treehugger.com/climate-change/only-nations-havent-signed-1997s-global-climate-treaty-are-afghanistan-us.html

88. Background Information:
Putin's estimate of the US National Debt is right on. It is now at around $19 trillion and growing, and amounts to 102% of GDP. See, "5 Things Most People Don't Understand About The National Debt," Taylor Tepper, *Time* (April 22, 2016). Retrieved at: http://time.com/money/4293910/national-debt-investors/

89. Background Information:
Putin's estimate of Russia's debt ratio is a bit low, but still, he is not far off. At present, Russia's national debt amounts to about 15% of GDP. See, https://debtclock.tv/world/russia/

90. Correction:
Oliver Stone actually greatly overestimates Russia's National Debt which is only $150 billion (and not $1 trillion). Ibid.

91. Background Information:
Putin is optimistic about the strength and stability of the Russian economy, however, oil prices in 2016 dropped well below the $50 per barrel level that had been assumed for government planning. At $30 per barrel, the Finance Ministry had to begin considering different scenarios for 2016. See, "Moody's Warns Russian Deficiit Goal in Doubt as Oil Jolts Budget," Anna Andrianova, Bloomberg (February 12, 2016). Retrieved at: https://www.bloomberg.com/news/articles/2016-02-12/moody-s-warns-russian-deficit-goal-in-doubt-as-oil-jolts-budget

92. Claim: "You're paying, what is it, 83 percent of the Chechnyan budget?"

Supporting: Oliver Stone is quite correct that Russia is providing over 80%, and up to 90%, of Chechnya's budget. "Russian Anger Grows Over Chechnya Subsidies," Michael Schwirtz, *New York Times* (Oct. 8, 2011). Retrieved at: http://www.nytimes.com/2011/10/09/world/europe/chechnyas-costs-stir-anger-as-russia-approaches-elections.html

93. Claim: "OS: Well, worker unrest is an issue. People haven't been paid in some regions. A great amount has been written about it in the West. People have not been paid sometimes one, two, three months.

VP: Well, there are these technical issues related to the arrears in payment—paying the salary, but it's minimum. There are no real problems with paying the salary. There are only issues related to irresponsibility, to negligence, to making decision too late, but economically and from the point of view of the budget, there are no problems whatsoever."

Contradicting: It does appear, as Oliver Stone relates, and contrary to what Putin says, that there is a problem with some workers not getting paid in Russia. See, "Unpaid Workers Unite in Protest Against Putin," Andrew E. Kramer, *New York Times* (April 21, 2015). Retrieved at: https://www.nytimes.com/2015/04/22/world/europe/russian-workers-take-aim-at-putin-as-economy-exacts-its-toll.html?_r=0

94. Background Information:
It is true that Russia has quite recently received very high praise from the IMF for its economic policies. See, "Russia's economy moves back to positive zone of growth – IMF Chief," *Tass News Agency* (April 17, 2017). Retrieved at: http://tass.com/economy/941775

95. Background Information
For a good description of the origins of the war in the Caucasus, see,
"Chechnya, Russia and 20 years of Conflict," Ibid.
"Miscalculations Paved Path to Chechen War," Ibid.

96. Background Information:
It is true, as Putin claims, that both the IMF and World Bank eventually decided to give loans to Russia based upon the humanitarian issues related to the war in Chechnya. See, Retrieved at: "Chechnya Conflict: Recent Developments," CRS *Report for Congress* (May 3, 2000). https://www.hsdl.org/?view&did=451457 It is also true, as Putin claims, that it is generally the case that the IMF does not generally take political/human rights issues into account in deciding whether to give loans. "Russia: Partisan War in Chechnya On the Eve of WWII Commemoration," *Human Rights Watch* (May, 1995). Retrieved at: https://www.hrw.org/reports/1995/Russiaa.htm

97. Background Information:
It is undisputed that Russia has paid off all of the debts of the former Soviet Union as Putin claims. See, "Russia to pay off Soviet debt with $125 mln for Bosnia and Herzegovina," Reuters (March 21, 2017). Retrieved at: http://www.reuters.com/article/russia-bosnia-debt-idUSR4N-1F102X

98. Background Information:
For full transcript of Putin's 2007 speech in Munich, See, "Putin's Prepared Remarks at 43rd Munich Conference on Security Policy," Ibid.

99. Background Information:
So many US military leaders have referred to Russia as the number one threat to the US that

it's hard to know who Putin is referring to here. In any case, Retired General James "Mad Dog" Mattis, now Secretary of Defense, has recently reiterated this claim. See, "Trump's Pentagon nominee says Russia is No. 1 security threat to US," *Associated Press* (Jan. 12, 2017). Retrieved at: http://www.cbc.ca/news/world/pompeo-mattis-confirmation-hearings-1.3932152

100. Background Information:
It is true, as Oliver Stone claims, that Obama quadrupled US military spending for Europe, and that this increase was largely directed towards Eastern Europe. See, "US 'to quadruple defense budget for Europe,'" BBC (Feb. 2, 2016). Retrieved at: http://www.bbc.com/news/world-us-canada-35476180

101. Ibid.

102. Claim: "Further escalation is already happening because the United States is deploying its antiballistic missile system in Eastern Europe and we on many occasions proposed real variants, real scenarios for cooperation."

See, "US Withdraws From ABM Treaty; Global Response Muted," Ibid.

103. Background Information:
It is true, as Putin claims, that the US has rejected both Russia's and China's proposals to ban the militarization of space. "US Opposes New Draft Treaty from China and Russia Banning Space Weapons," Bill Gertz, *Washington Free Beacon* (June 19, 2014). Retrieved at: http://freebeacon.com/national-security/u-s-opposes-new-draft-treaty-from-china-and-russia-banning-space-weapons/

104. Background Information
As Putin alludes, he and Obama worked together to finalize a deal with Iran to limit its nuclear capability. See, "Barack Obama Praises Putin for help clinching Iran deal," Roland Oliphant, *The Telegraph* (July 15, 2015). Retrieved at: http://www.telegraph.co.uk/news/worldnews/barackobama/11740700/Barack-Obama-praises-Putin-for-help-clinching-Iran-deal.html

105. Claim: "And this year, in 2016, the US is going to allocate more than $600 billion US dollars to defense. It's just too much—more than the total defense expenditure of all the other countries of the world."

The numbers don't add up: US military budget is indeed six hundred billion dollars, but this is much less than the total amount of defense spending by the rest of the world combined. See, "Here's how US defense spending stacks up against the rest of the world," John W. Schoen, CNBC (May 2, 2017). Retrieved at: http://www.cnbc.com/2017/05/02/how-us-defense-spending-stacks-up-against-the-rest-of-the-world.html

106. Background Information:
It is true as Oliver Stone claims, that Charles de Gaulle pulled France out of NATO in 1967. France would return decades later. See, "1967: De Gaulle pulls France out of NATO's integrated military structure," Dr. Jamie Shea, NATO (March 3, 2009) Retrieved at: http://www.nato.int/cps/en/natohq/opinions_139272.htm

107. Background Information:
For a good description of how US NGOs, as well as the US government, interfered in Ukraine and helped bring about the 2014 coup, see, "Brokering Power: US Role in Ukraine Coup Hard to Overlook," *RTNews* (Feb. 19, 2015). Retrieved at: https://www.rt.com/news/233439-us-meddling-ukraine-crisis/

108. Claim: "All suspicions on that account were never justified—there was no evidence. And yet there were suspicions. And to alleviate those suspicions, Iran agreed to this nuclear deal, signed an accord, I believe in order to normalize its relations with the United States, with other countries of the world, which were expressing their concerns on that matter."

See, "Barack Obama Praises Putin for help clinching Iran deal," Ibid.

109. Background Information:
See, "Russia's Ultimate Lethal Weapon," Pepe Escobar, Counterpunch (September 18, 2015). Retrieved at: http://www.counterpunch.org/2015/09/18/russias-ultimate-lethal-weapon/

110. Background Information:
Tsar Alexander III (reigned from March 12, 1881 - November 1, 1894) with his wife Dowager Empress Maria Feodorovna (Princess Dagmar of Denmark) See, http://www.alexanderpalace.org/palace/mariabio.html

111. Background Information:
Charlie Rose interview, (September 29, 2015) https://charlierose.com/videos/22696

112. Background Information: "And it was sent out that he understands well many problems that the country is facing, and he is not just willing to engage in a dialogue with the opposition groups - even the armed opposition - but he's willing to work together with them to elaborate a new constitution."

See, "Assad says he can form new Syria government with opposition," Jack Stubbs and Lisa Barrington, *Reuters* (March 31, 2016). Retrieved at: http://www.reuters.com/article/us-mideast-crisis-syria-idUSKCN0WW1YO

113. Background Information:
See, "4.5mn Russian tourists won't visit Turkey this year," *RT* (January15, 2016). Retrieved at: https://www.rt.com/business/329075-turkey-lose-russian-tourists/

114. Background Information:
Turkish construction companies are heavily invested in Russia, having been awarded a wide variety of projects from shopping malls to facilities for the Sochi Olympics. See, "Why Turkey Aims for 'Zero Problems' With Russia's War in Syria," Behlul Ozkan, *Huffington Post*. Retrieved at: http://www.huffingtonpost.com/behlal-azkan/turkey-russia-syria_b_8265848.html

115. Background Information:
Turkey was G20 Chair in 2015 in the resort city of Antalya on 15-16 November 2015. "G20 is the premier platform for international economic cooperation. G20 was born out of the necessity to develop joint responses against challenges brought by economic crises of 1997, and 1998. First meeting of G20 countries was held in 1999 at the level of Finance Ministers and Central Bank Governors." http://www.mfa.gov.tr/g-20-en.en.mfa

116. Correction: "And when out of the blue a Russian plane was downed, at that approach of the Syrian-Turkish border it didn't even come up during our discussions."
President Putin incorrectly recalled the timeline of events leading up to the G20 Summit since it was held in Antalya, Turkey on November 15-16, 2015, whereas the Russian plane was shot down on November 24, 2015.

117. Background Information:
Oliver Stone asks in what month of 2015 did Russia enter Syria militarily, and Putin replies

that he is uncertain of the month, but believes that it was in the summer. The fact is that Russia sent troops to Syria in early September 2015. See, "Exclusive: Russian troops join combat in Syria - sources," Gabriela Baczynska, Tom Perry, Laila Bassam, Phil Stewart, *Reuters* (September 10, 2015). Retrieved at: http://www.reuters.com/article/us-mideast-crisis-syria-exclusive-idUSKCN0R91H720150910

118. Claim: "I think it was Israel's defense minister and Greece's defense minister publicly said that they were seeing that radical groups were supplying oil to the Turkish territory."

Supporting: See, "Israeli defense minister accuses Turkey of buying IS oil," BBC (January 26, 2016). Retrieved at: http://www.bbc.com/news/world-europe-35415956

119. Background Information:
It's true as Oliver Stone claims that John Kerry accused Russia of "targeting legitimate opposition groups," See, "John Kerry condemns Russia's 'repeated aggression' in Syria and Ukraine" *The Guardian* (February 13, 2016). Retrieved at: https://www.theguardian.com/us-news/2016/feb/13/john-kerry-condemns-russias-repeated-aggression-in-syria-and-ukraine

120. Claim: " As in Kunduz where American planes hit a hospital run by Doctors Without Borders."

Supporting:
See, "US military struggles to explain how it wound up bombing Doctors Without Borders hospital," Thomas Gibbons-Neff, *Washington Post* (October 5, 2015). Retrieved at: https://www.washingtonpost.com/news/checkpoint/wp/2015/10/05/afghan-forces-requested-air-strike-that-hit-hospital-in-kunduz/

121. Claim: Oliver Stone points out that the Chinese embassy was bombed by the West.
Supporting: See, "Nato bombed Chinese embassy deliberately," John Sweeney, Jens Holsoe and Ed Vulliamy, *The Guardian* (October 16, 1999). Retrieved at: https://www.theguardian.com/world/1999/oct/17/balkans

122. Claim: Oliver Stone asks about a Russian SU40 plane that was shot down by a Turkish F-16. Putin corrects him that it was a Russian SU24 that was shot down, but also says that the pilots were shot at.

Supporting: See, "Turkey shooting down plane was 'planned provocation' says Russia, as rescued pilot claims he had no warning - latest," Isabelle Fraser and Raziye Akkoc, *The Telegraph* (November 26, 2015). Retrieved at: http://www.telegraph.co.uk/news/worldnews/middleeast/syria/12015465/Turkey-shoots-down-Russia-jet-live.html

123. Background Information:
Russia did indeed inform the American military before their planes took to the air. See, "US Agrees With Russia on Rules in Syrian Sky," Neil MacFarquhar, the *New York Times* (October 20, 2015). Retrieved at: https://www.nytimes.com/2015/10/21/world/middleeast/us-and-russia-agree-to-regulate-all-flights-over-syria.html

124. Claim: Putin says that Russia is operating in Syria at the invitation of the Syrian government and thus, legitimately.

Supporting: "Russia Begins Airstrikes In Syria After Assad's Request," Bill Chappell, NPR (September 30, 2015). Retrieved at: http://www.npr.org/sections/thetwo-way/2015/09/30/444679327/russia-begins-conducting-airstrikes-in-syria-at-assads-request

125. Claim: Putin cites 70 to 120 airstrikes per day by Russian planes in Syria, compared to only three to five per day by the international coalition led by the United States.

The numbers vary over time, but appear to be in the ballpark. See, "Russia Is Launching Twice as Many Airstrikes as the US in Syria" David Axe," *The Daily Beast* (February 16, 2016). Retrieved at: http://www.thedailybeast.com/articles/2016/02/23/russia-is-launching-twice-as-many-airstrikes-as-the-u-s-in-syria

126. Correction: 120 times per day for 60 days is 7,200 airstrikes

127. Claim: "The projected number of terrorists participating in ISIS is estimated at 80,000. 30,000 of them are foreign mercenaries from 80 countries of the world."

The estimated number of ISIS terrorists range according to source, from 20-30,000, and from 80-100,000. As per, Putin's estimate, see, "Russian Intel: ISIS Has 80,000 Jihadis in Iraq and Syria," Jordan Schachtel, *Breitbart* (November 11, 2015). Retrieved at: http://www.breitbart.com/national-security/2015/11/11/russian-intel-isis-80000-jihadis-iraq-syria/

Regarding foreign mercenaries in ISIS, see: "Thousands Enter Syria to Join ISIS Despite Global Efforts," Eric Schmitt, Somini Sengupta, September 26, 2015. Retrieved at: https://www.nytimes.com/2015/09/27/world/middleeast/thousands-enter-syria-to-join-isis-despite-global-efforts.html?_r=0

128. Background Information:
Robert McNamara was, according to the *New York Times* "the forceful and cerebral defense secretary who helped lead the nation into the maelstrom of Vietnam and spent the rest of his life wrestling with the war's moral consequences." and "the most influential defense secretary of the 20th century. Serving Presidents John F. Kennedy and Lyndon B. Johnson from 1961 to 1968." See, "Robert S. McNamara, Architect of a Futile War, Dies at 93," Tim Weiner, (July 6, 2009). Retrieved at: http://www.nytimes.com/2009/07/07/us/07mcnamara.html?pagewanted=all

129. Correction: According to the House of Saud official website, King Abdulaziz, founder of the modern Kingdom of Saudi Arabia, never traveled beyond the Arab world.

See, http://houseofsaud.com/saudi-royal-family-history/

130. Claim: "There was a great danger of a war erupting and I believe that back then President Obama made the right decision. And he and I managed to agree on coordinated actions"

President Obama was widely criticized for making the decision not to attack Syria after the nerve agent sarin was used on a Damascus suburb. However, there was also support for the president showing restraint. See, "When Putin Bailed Out Obama," former CIA analyst Ray McGovern, *Consortium News* (August 31, 2016). Retrieved at: https://consortiumnews.com/2016/08/31/when-putin-bailed-out-obama/

131. Background Information:
See, "Russia Expands Sanctions Against Turkey After Downing of Jet," Andrew E. Kramer, the *New York Times* (December 30, 2015). Retrieved at: https://www.nytimes.com/2015/12/31/world/europe/russia-putin-turkey-sanctions.html

132. Background Information:
"So you have double sanctions - you have sanctions against Turkey and the US sanctions

against you." See, "US Imposes Sanctions Over Russia's Intervention in Ukraine," Julie Hirshchfeld Davis, the *New York Times* (December 22, 2015). Retrieved at: https://www.nytimes.com/2015/12/23/world/europe/us-russia-ukraine-sanctions.html

133. Claim: "Dick Cheney, vice president - said in his meeting we . . . about the Middle East and the Near East being the "keys to the kingdom.""

Unverifiable Claim

134. Background Information:
Quote attributed to Sheikh Zaki Yamani, Saudi Arabian Oil Minister from 1962 to 1986. "The Stone Age did not end for lack of stone, and the Oil Age will end long before the world runs out of oil." See, "The end of the Oil Age" *The Economist* (October 23, 2003). Retrieved at: http://www.economist.com/node/2155717

135. Claim: "it was not our initiative that back in 2014, NATO stopped all contact with us in framework of the Russia-NATO council"

Supporting: See, "Ukraine crisis: Nato suspends Russia co-operation," BBC (April 2, 2014). Retrieved at: http://www.bbc.com/news/world-europe-26838894

136. Background Information:
"The Warsaw Pact was an organization of Central and Eastern European communist states. It was established on May 1, 1955, in Warsaw, Poland to counter the perceived threat from the creation of the NATO alliance, specifically the prospect of the integration of a 're-militarized' West Germany into NATO, which took place on May 9, 1955, via ratification of the Paris Peace Treaties. The communist states of Central and Eastern Europe were signatories except Yugoslavia. The members of the Warsaw Pact pledged to defend each other if one or more of the members were attacked. The pact lasted throughout the Cold War. It began to fall apart in 1989, following the collapse of the Eastern Bloc and political changes in the Soviet Union." *New World Encyclopedia*

See, http://www.newworldencyclopedia.org/entry/Warsaw_Pact

137. Background Information:
Renouncing his Georgian citizenship to avoid "guaranteed imprisonment" Saakashvili was granted Ukrainian citizenship and appointed governor of Odessa. See, "Georgia ex-leader Saakashvili gives up citizenship for Ukraine," BBC (June 1, 2015). Retrieved at: http://www.bbc.com/news/world-europe-32969052

138. Claim: "And we had to respond, because one of the first actions they took was to kill our peacekeepers from our peacekeeping battalion . . . "

Supporting: When Georgian forces launched their assault on South Ossetia, they did in fact kill and injure a number of Russian peacekeepers. See. "Russian troops and tanks pour into South Ossetia" Helen Womack, Tom Parfitt, Ian Black, *The Guardian* (August 8, 2008). Retrieved at: https://www.theguardian.com/world/2008/aug/09/russia.georgia

139. Background Information:
The St. Petersburg Marrinski Theatre Orchestra, led by acclaimed conductor Valery Gergiev, held a concert dedicated to the victims of terrorist groups at the ancient ruins of Palmyra in Syria. See, "Russian orchestra plays concert in ancient Syrian ruins of Palmyra," Fred Pleitgen, CNN (May 6, 2016). Retrieved at: http://www.cnn.com/2016/05/05/middleeast/syria-palmyra-russia-concert/

140. Background Information:
After the collapse of a previous Minsk Protocol to stop the fighting in Donbass region of Ukraine, new peace negotiations were held on February 11, 2015 in eastern Ukraine in the Belarusian capital Minsk. Points of the Minsk Agreement ranged from immediate and full bilateral ceasefire, withdrawal of heavy weapons by both sides, effective monitoring and verification, begin a dialogue on the holding of local elections, pardon and amnesty by banning prosecution of figures involved in the Donetsk and Luhansk conflict, release of all hostages and other illegally detained people, unimpeded delivery of humanitarian aid, restoration of full social and economic links, full Ukrainian government control restored, withdrawal of foreign armed groups, weapons and mercenaries, and constitutional reform in Ukraine, with adoption of a new constitution by the end of 2015.

See, "Ukraine ceasefire: New Minsk agreement key points," BBC (February 12, 2015). Retrieved at: http://www.bbc.com/news/world-europe-31436513

141. Claim: " But back then, our American friends, our European friends told us that the prime minister—back then it was Mr. Yatsenyuk and President Poroshenko had to pull their efforts together, they had to work together and we know how it ended"

Supporting: Putin refers here to the legacy of the Poroshenko-Yatsenyuk government which ended with Prime Minister Yatsenyuk's resignation. See, "The Toxic Coddling of Petro Poroshenko," Lev Golinkin, *Foreign Policy* (April 13, 2016). Retrieved at: http://foreignpolicy.com/2016/04/13/the-toxic-coddling-of-kiev-ukraine-poroshenko-yatsenuk/

142. Claim: Oliver Stone asks for confirmation whether Russia spent $51 billion to prepare for the Sochi Olympics. Putin replies that he doesn't want to give the wrong number, and would tell him later.

Supporting: According to the *Washington Post*, the consensus figure is $50 billion, with qualifications. See, "Did the Winter Olympics in Sochi really cost $50 billion? A closer look at that figure," Paul Farhi, the *Washington Post* (February 10, 2014). Retrieved at: https://www.washingtonpost.com/lifestyle/style/did-the-winter-olympics-in-sochi-really-cost-50-billion-a-closer-look-at-that-figure/2014/02/10/a29e37b4-9260-11e3-b46a-5a3d0d2130da_story.html

143. Background Information:
See, "In Russia, how one mainly Muslim region beat back radicalism," Fred Weir, Christian Science Monitor (August 22, 2016). Retrieved at: http://www.csmonitor.com/World/Europe/2016/0822/In-Russia-how-one-mainly-Muslim-region-beat-back-radicalism

144. Claim: "the United States spends, this is published, $75 billion on intelligence, $52 billion of which is civilian"

Supporting: According to publicly disclosed figures detailed in a report by the Congressional Research Service, Oliver Stone's numbers are correct. See, "Intelligence Community Spending: Trends and Issues." Anne Daugherty Miles, (November 8, 2016) Retrieved at: https://fas.org/sgp/crs/intel/R44381.pdf

145. Claim: "And [as we've discussed], the United States spends more than all other countries in the world combined."

See, "Here's how US defense spending stacks up against the rest of the world," Ibid.

146. Background Information:
After September 11, 2001, Putin offered the US support in terms of intelligence information

as well coordinating with central Asian nations to allow US forces to use former Soviet Union military bases. See, "9/11 a 'turning point' for Putin," Jill Dougherty CNN (September 10, 2002). Retrieved at: http://www.edition.cnn.com/2002/WORLD/europe/09/10/ar911.russia.putin/index.html

147. Claim: " But instead of that we saw the West expanding their political power and influence in those territories which we considered sensitive and important for us to ensure our global strategic security."

After the collapse of the Soviet Union, NATO began a progressively eastward expansion. the See, "Did the West Break Its Promise to Moscow?" Uwe Klussmann, Matthias Schepp, Klaus Wiegrefe, *Der Spiegel* (November 26, 2009). Retrieved at: http://www.spiegel.de/international/world/nato-s-eastward-expansion-did-the-west-break-its-promise-to-moscow-a-663315.html

148. Background Information:
After the financial crisis of 2008, world economies scrambled to recover. Russia's approach was unique to its own economy. See, "Russia's Response to the Global Financial Crisis," Pekka Sutela, *Carnegie Endowment for International Peace* (July 29, 2010) Retrieved at: carnegieendowment.org/files/russia_crisis.pdf

149. Background Information:
See, "Vladimir Putin finds his thrill on 'Blueberry Hill,'" Shaun Walker, *Independent* (December 13, 2010). Retrieved at: http://www.independent.co.uk/news/world/europe/vladimir-putin-finds-his-thrill-on-blueberry-hill-2158697.html

150. Claim: "the former head of the KGB had opened to the US partners the whole system of surveillance in the American Embassy in Moscow"

Supporting: In December 1991, Vadim Bakatin, head of the KGB, turned over blueprints and bugging devices used to bug the US Embassy in Moscow. See, "KGB Gives US Devices and Plans Used to Bug Embassy," Los Angeles Times (December 14, 1991). Retrieved at: http://articles.latimes.com/1991-12-14/news/mn-197_1_eavesdropping-devices

151. Claim: "On many occasions, repeatedly, I told the US, the European partners, the Georgian leadership—I asked them to prevent the escalation of this conflict."

Supporting: In his editorial in the Financial Times, Russian Foreign Affairs Minister, Sergei Lavrov, notes that "hours before the Georgian invasion, Russia had been working to secure a UN Security Council statement calling for a renunciation of force by both Georgia and South Ossetians." See, "Why Russia's response to Georgia was right," Sergei Lavrov, *Financial Times* (August 12, 2008). Retrieved at: https://www.ft.com/content/7863e71a-689e-11dd-a4e5-0000779fd18c

152. Claim: Referring to Georgian President Saakashvili, Putin remarks that his counterparts were saying "What do you expect, he's mad?"

Supporting: See, "I Would Call Saakashvili Insane," Benjamin Bidder, *Spiegel Online* (May 14, 2009). Retrieved at: http://www.spiegel.de/international/world/georgian-opposition-leader-zurabishvili-i-would-call-saakashvili-insane-a-624807.html

153. Background Information:
During his ten years as president of Georgia, Eduard Shevardnadze was plagued with accusations of running a corrupt government and economy, while at the same time he expressed

a desire for Georgia to join NATO. See, "Shevardnadze Resigns as Georgian President" Fox News (November 24, 2003). Retrieved at: http://www.foxnews.com/story/2003/11/24/she-vardnadze-resigns-as-georgian-president.html

154. Background Information:
The US was not pleased with Russia's decision to offer Edward Snowden temporary asylum after he leaked classified information. See, "Defiant Russia Grants Snowden Year's Asylum," Steven Lee Myers, Andrew E. Kramer, the *New York Times* (August 1, 2013). Retrieved at: http://www.nytimes.com/2013/08/02/world/europe/edward-snowden-russia.html

155. Claim: Ukrainian opposition leader Viktor Yushchenko repeatedly asserted that he had been poisoned by political rivals.

Supporting: *See,* "Yushchenko Poisoned, Doctors Say" *Deutsche Welle* (December 12, 2004). Retrieved at: http://www.dw.com/en/yushchenko-poisoned-doctors-say/a-1425561

156. Background Information:
See: Ukraine protests after Yanukovych EU deal rejection," Oksana Grytsenko, BBC (November 30, 2013). Retrieved at: http://www.bbc.com/news/world-europe-25162563

157. Claim: " Mr. Yanukovych didn't leave to go abroad. He was in the country when his residence was taken."

Supporting: President Yanukovych left Kiev for Ukraine's second largest city Kharkiv, that was considered his eastern political base. See, "Ukraine crisis: Viktor Yanukovych leaves Kiev for support base," Bonnie Malkin, *The Telegraph* (February 22, 2014). Retrieved at: http://www.telegraph.co.uk/news/worldnews/europe/ukraine/10655335/Ukraine-crisis-Viktor-Yanu-kovych-leaves-Kiev-for-support-base.html

158. Background Information:
Putin notes that losing the base in Sebastopol was not a threat because the new base at Novorossiysk was being commissioned. See, "Russia To Unveil New $1.4 Billion Black Sea Fleet Base Near Crimea," Damien Sharkov, Newsweek (July 28, 2016). Retrieved at: http://www.newsweek.com/russia-unveil-new-14-bn-black-sea-fleet-base-four-years-484974

159. Claim: "The expression of this free will, whose overwhelming majority had voted for independence and for joining Russia."

Supporting: See, "Crimeans vote over 90 percent to quit Ukraine and join Russia," Ibid

160. Background Information:
On February 18, 2008, the United States formally recognized Kosovo as a sovereign and independent state. See, "US Recognizes Kosovo as Independent State," Secretary Condoleezza Rice, US Department of State (February 18, 2008). Retrieved at: https://2001-2009.state.gov/secretary/rm/2008/02/100973.htm

161. Background Information:
Speculation about Putin's wealth is rampant. Oliver Stone asks Putin about claims that he is "the single richest person in the world." Putin replies that he does not have such wealth as attributed to him. In the realm of public opinion, the question appears to remain unresolved. We provide two references to this claim.

See, "Is Vladimir Putin hiding a $200 billion fortune? (And if so, does it matter?)," Adam Taylor, *Washington Post*, (February 20, 2015). https://www.washingtonpost.com/news/worldviews/wp/2015/02/20/is-vladimir-putin-hiding-a-200-billion-fortune-and-if-so-does-it-matter/

See, "Former Kremlin banker: Putin 'is the richest person in the world until he leaves power,'" Elena Holodny, Business Insider (July 28, 2015). Retrieved at: http://www.businessinsider.com/former-kremlin-banker-putin-is-the-richest-person-in-the-world-until-he-leaves-power-2015-7

162. Background Information:
The seven bankers refer to Russian tycoons, who financed Boris Yeltsin's campaign for re-election as president. The nickname, semibankirshchina, or rule of the seven bankers, refers to a group of seven noblemen, who ran Russia in the 17the century for a brief period. See, "Russia bows to the 'rule of the seven bankers'," *Irish Times* (August 29, 1998). Retrieved at: http://www.irishtimes.com/culture/russia-bows-to-the-rule-of-the-seven-bankers-1.187734

163. Background Information:
On June 7, 2016, 11.5 millions documents were leaked, detailing how Mossack Fonseca, a Panamanian law firm, effectively aided over 14,000 clients to create offshore businesses and bank accounts to avoid, dodge, or completely conceal taxes. These "papers" highlight how the world's rich and famous secure and hide their wealth. See, https://panamapapers.icij.org/20160403-panama-papers-global-overview.html

164. Background Information:
Born in Moscow in 1821, Dostoyevsky changed the course of literature by deeply examining philosophy, religion, and existentialism in his works that focused on the internal struggle of the poor, working-class Russian. His notable works include *Crime and Punishment*, *The Brothers Karamazov*, and *Notes from the Underground*. He died in St. Petersburg in 1881. See, *Fyodor, Dostoevsky*. Bloom, Harold. Infobase Publishing. 2009.

165. Claim: "But, you know, even Trump has said the Russians hacked the election"
Supporting: See, "Donald Trump Concedes Russia's Interference in Election," Julie Hirschfeld Davis, Maggie Haberman, the *New York Times* (January 11, 2017). Retrieved at: https://www.nytimes.com/2017/01/11/us/politics/trumps-press-conference-highlights-russia.html

166. Background Information:
In discussing the statement by Donald Trump that Russia hacked the US elections, Putin replies that Trump had earlier said that anyone anywhere, including a person lying in bed with a laptop, could initiate a hacking attack. See, "Hackers Are Mad That Donald Trump Body-Shamed Them at the Presidential Debate," Katie Reilly, *Fortune* (September 26, 2016). Retrieved at: http://fortune.com/2016/09/26/presidential-debate-hackers-body-shamed/

167. Claim: "the US spends more on defense than all the other countries in the world combined spends on their defense—more than six hundred billion US dollars."

See, "Here's how US defense spending stacks up against the rest of the world," Ibid.

168. Claim: "But in 2012 this interference was particularly aggressive."

Dueling Accusations: While some US officials condemned the results of the 2012 elections in Russia, the Kremlin contended that the US was financing opposition groups, as well as coordinating with demonstrators in Moscow. See, "Despite Kremlin's Signals, US Ties Remain Strained After Russian Election," David M. Herszenhorn, Steven Lee Myers, the *New York*

Times (March 6, 2012). Retrieved at: http://www.nytimes.com/2012/03/07/world/europe/ties-with-us-remain-strained-after-russian-election.html

169. Background Information:
Although US Deputy Defense Secretary, William Lynn, refused to say whether the US was involved in the development of the virus, Stuxnet, that targeted Iran's Natanz nuclear plant, it is believed that a US-Israeli operation was behind the attack. See, "US was 'key player in cyber-attacks on Iran's nuclear programme,'" Peter Beaumont, Nick Hopkins, *The Guardian* (June 1, 2012). Retrieved at: https://www.theguardian.com/world/2012/jun/01/obama-sped-up-cyberattack-iran

170. Background Information:
Oliver Stone's 2016 film, Snowden, follows Edward Snowden in the lead-up and aftermath of his decision to leak classified information to the press. See, "In 'Snowden," the national security whistleblower gets the Oliver Stone treatment," Ann Hornaday, the *Washington Post* (September 15, 2016). Retrieved at: https://www.washingtonpost.com/goingout-guide/movies/in-snowden-the-national-security-whistleblower-gets-the-oliver-stone-treatment/2016/09/15/8f2ebde4-78e9-11e6-ac8e-cf8e0dd91dc7_story.html

171. Background Information:
Although Oliver Stone mentioned six major banks being attacked, sources note that five Russian banks underwent a Botnet attack. See, "5 major Russian banks repel massive DDoS attack" *RTNews* (November 10, 2016). Retrieved at: https://www.rt.com/news/366172-russian-banks-ddos-attack/

172. Claim: "We will attack Russia in the same manner as they attacked us in this election."

Supporting: When asked whether the US was preparing to send a message to Russia for interfering in the US elections, Vice President Joe Biden replied: "We're sending a message . . . We have the capacity to do it . . . He'll know it . . . And under the circumstances that have the greatest impact." See, "Biden Hints at US Response to Russia for Cyberattacks," David E. Sanger, the *New York Times* (October 15, 2016). Retrieved at: https://www.nytimes.com/2016/10/16/us/politics/biden-hints-at-us-response-to-cyberattacks-blamed-on-russia.html

173. Background Information:

On June 24, 2016, Russia's lower house of parliament voted 325 to 1 to adopt a package of amendments targeting terrorist activities and any perceived support of such activities. Human rights activists claim that the anti-terrorism measures will roll back personal freedoms and privacy. See, "Russia passes 'Big Brother' anti-terror laws," Alec Luhn, *The Guardian* June 26 2016. Retrieved at: https://www.theguardian.com/world/2016/jun/26/russia-passes-big-brother-anti-terror-laws

174. Claim: "And they've got connections of their own in Russia. And they prepare terrorist attacks."

Supporting: A number of factors add up to the likelihood of future terrorist attacks in Russia. See, "Attacks on Russia Will Only Increase," Colin P. Clarke, *The Atlantic* (April 4, 2017). Retrieved at: https://www.theatlantic.com/international/archive/2017/04/russia-st-petersburg-isis-syria/521766/

175. Background Information:
See, "US launches long-awaited European missile defense shield," Ryan Browne, CNN (May

12, 2016). Retrieved at: http://www.cnn.com/2016/05/11/politics/nato-missile-defense-romania-poland/

176. Background Information:
See, "Chechen soldiers among Russian military police in Aleppo to 'ease interaction with locals,'" *RTNews* (January 30, 2017). Retrieved at: https://www.rt.com/news/375551-chechen-soldiers-patrolling-aleppo/

177. Confirmation:
The distance from Moscow to Damascus is 3,170 km by auto, 2,476 km by plane.

178. Background Information:
See, "Fethullah Gülen: who is the man Turkey's president blames for coup attempt?" Peter Beaumont, *The Guardian* July 16, 2016. Retrieved at: https://www.theguardian.com/world/2016/jul/16/fethullah-gulen-who-is-the-man-blamed-by-turkeys-president-for-coup-attempt

179. Claim: "The US ship Donald Cook was apparently coming right into the Black Sea when it made a U-turn and didn't carry through its mission."

See, "A strange recent history of Russian jets buzzing Navy ships," Thomas Gibbons-Neff, *The Washington Post* (April 14, 2016). Retrieved at: https://www.washingtonpost.com/news/checkpoint/wp/2016/04/14/a-strange-recent-history-of-russian-jets-buzzing-navy-ships/

180. Claim: "is this when Victoria Nuland, the Undersecretary of State, had that conversation with the American ambassador and said, "Fuck the EU"?"

Supporting: Leaked audio and transcripts of US Secretary of State Victoria Nuland's conversation with US Ambassador to Ukraine, Geoffrey Pyatt do indeed record the f-word.

See, "Ukraine crisis: Transcript of leaked Nuland-Pyatt call," BBC (February 7, 2014). Retrieved at: http://www.bbc.com/news/world-europe-26079957

181. Background Information:
The USS Donald Cook's current homeport is Rota, Spain. See, "USS Donald Cook Departs Norfolk for Permanent Station in Rota, Spain," Retrieved at: http://www.navy.mil/submit/display.asp?story_id=78889

182. Background Information:
See, "The Russian Economy Inches Forward: Will That Suffice to Turn the Tide?" *Russia Economic Report - The World Bank* (November 9, 2016). Retrieved at: http://www.worldbank.org/en/country/russia/publication/rer

INDEX

*Note: items in **bold** are topics discussed at length

Abkhazia, 52, 185
Afghanistan, 3, 32, 33, 35-38, 143, 174, 175, 179
Al Qaeda, 33, 34, 36
al-Assad, Bashar, 2, 132, 140, 146, 160, 161, 234, 239
al-Nusra front, 140
Aleppo, 233, 234
Anti-Ballistic Missile System (ABM), 41- 44, 51, 72, 77, 80, 98, 115, 117, 118, 177, 179, 187, 194, 195, 232,
Assange, Julian, 214
Azerbaijan, 179
Baker, James, 40
Barr, Aaron, 114
Berezovsky, Boris, 16, 17, 19, 200
Berlin Wall, 31
Biden, Joseph, 223
Big Brother Law, 226
Bin Laden, Osama, 33, 36-37, 93, 94
Bolshevik Revolution, 7, 95, 118, 148
Bonaparte, Napoleon, 25-26
Buk (air defense system of the Ukrainian armed forces), 70
Botnet attack, 222
Brezhnev, era of, 246
Bush, George W., 52, 115, 180

Caliphate, 131, 152
Casey, Bill, 33
Castro, Fidel, 21, 22, 199, 203
Caucasus, 33, 52, 111, 173, 179, 234, 245
Central Bank of Russia, 110, 180
Chavez, Cesar, 199, 205
Chechen wars, 15, 17, 19, 37,
Chechnya, 33, 37, 109, 172, 173, 174
Cheney, Richard, 39, 148
China, 89, 90, 91, 92, 144, 206, 229
Churchill, Winston, 25, 46
Clinton, Hillary, 82, 114
Clinton, William, 39, 40, 41, 42, 156, 209
Cold War, 1, 2, 25, 33, 40, 46, 47, 72, 78, 81, 83, 156, 183, 221
Communism, 2, 47
Communist Party, 95, 223
Crimea, 65, 69, 76, 77, 191, 195, 196, 197, 240
Cromwell, Oliver, 25
Cuba Missile Crisis, 23, 81, 239
Cypress, 202
Dacha, 7, 87
Dagestan, 38, 112, 172
Damascus, 235, 238
de Gaulle, Charles, 120

Deep State, 210
Doctors Without Borders
Donbass, 66-67, 70, 71, 81, 82, 192, 197
Dostoevsky, Fyodor, 210
East German Stasi
Eastern bloc, 156
el-Sisi, Abdel Fattah, 131
Electoral College, 48, 122, 210, 211,
   215, 219, 225, 237
Erdogan, Recep Tayyip, 134, 135, 138,
   235, 236
European Union (EU), 63, 64, 92, 118,
   192
Federal Security Bureau, 13
Federal Security Service, 13
Fracking, 150-151
Free Trade Area of the CIS, 63
French socialist Utopian, 112
French War, 8
FSB, 13, 184
Fuchs, Klaus, 45
G20, 134, 136, 217, 237
Gaddafi, Muammar, 32
Gaidar, Yegor, 29
Georgia, 52, 156, 184, 185, 188
Georgian situation, 51
Georgian war, 174
Gergiev, Valery
Gershman, Paul, 71
Glazyev, Sergey, 148
Golden Fleece, 178
Google, 228
Gorbachev, Mikhail, 1, 2, 10, 12, 14,
   30, 31, 40, 55, 163, 164, 188, 244
Guantanamo Bay, 123
Gülen, 236
Hannibal, Barca, 213
Hersh, Sy, 93
Hiroshima, Japan, 82, 224
Hitler, Adolf , 26, 82, 114
Hussein, Saddam, 31, 46, 150
Iceberg Theory, 22
Imperialism, 48
Intercontinental Ballistic Missiles
   (ICMBs), 78, 117

International Committee of Arma-
   ments Control, 117
International Court of Justice, 69, 196
International Monetary Fund (IMF),
   110, 111, 112
Iraq War, 30-32, 35, 38, 39, 45, 46, 51,
   69, 148, 149
ISIS, the Islamic State of Iraq and
   Syria, 31, 36, 46, 132, 135, 136,
   140, 141-143
Islamic fundamentalism, 33, 34
Islamic terrorism, 36, 46
Israel, 67, 133, 135, 143, 149, 152, 159,
   218
Judo, philosophy of, 7, 23, 24, 27, 85,
   130, 131, 166-167
Kadyrov, Ramzan, 172, 173,
Kayagin, Alexander, 50
Kennedy, John F. 23, 80, 81, 82,
   assassination papers, 183
Kerry, John, 75, 79, 136, 145, 161, 219
KGB, 1, 8, 9, 11, 18, 54, 55, 56, 169,
   183
Khodorkovsky, Mikhail, 19
Khrushchev, Nikita, 14, 23, 80, 81
Kiev, 65, 66, 67, 68, 74, 82, 158, 160,
   189, 191, 197
Kirill (Patriarch of Moscow), or Vladi-
   mir Mikhailovich Gundyayev, 87
Kosovo
   crisis, 69
   independence of, 69, 196
   the bombing of Belgrade, 178
Krasnodar, 77
Kremlin, 88, 163, 183, 187, 213, 225
Krylov, Ivan, 159
Kuan Yew, Lee, 206
Kubrick, Stanley, 81, 195
Kuchma, Leonid, 72, 189
Kunduz, Afghanistan, 136
Kurds (Kurdish peoples), 134
Kuwait, Invasion of, 30-31
Kyoto Protocol, 100
Lagarde, Christine (Madame), 110
Lavrov, Sergey, 75
LeMay, Curtis, 82

Leningrad, 5, 6, 7, 8, 9, 14, 87

Leontief, Wassily, 27

LGBT Community, 97

Libya, 37, 131, 160, 234

Maidan massacre, 73, 74

Mao Tse Tung, 203

Marcus Porcius Cato (the Elder), 113

McCain, John, 71, 212

McNamara, Robert, 141

Mecca, 160

Medea, 160

Medvedev, Dmitry, 21, 184, 186, 203

Military Industrial Security Complex, 118, 210

Minsk Agreements, 66, 67, 74, 158, 197

Morgan, J.P., 199

Nagasaki, Japan, 82, 224

National Endowment for Democracy, 71

National Security Agency (NSA), 55, 171, 212, 215, 220, 227

National Security Council (NSC), 103, 218

Neocons, 56, 146, 183

Nevsky Pyatchok, 6

Nichaiev, Andrei, 29

Nikolaevich, Mikheil 188

Non-governmental organization (NGO), 71, 120, 219

North Sea, 98, 99

Novorossiysk, 77, 193

Nuland, Victoria, 71, 240

Obama, Barack, 50-54, 74, 75, 117, 123, 138, 146, 161, 188-189, 209, 211, 217, 219, 223, 225, 237, 238, 246

    nuclear deal in Iran, 114

Oblest, Moscow, 7

October Socialist Revolution, 52

Odessa, 73, 160

Odysseus, 178

Oligarchs, 3, 16, 17, 19, 24, 73, 162, 199-201

Onassis, Aristotle, 199

Orange Revolution, 174

Organization of Islamic Conference, 218

Ossetia, 52, 184, 185, 187, 188

Pakistan, 93-94

Palestine, 67

Palmyra, 158, 161

Panama Papers, 202

Perestroika, 9

Permanent Court of Arbitration, 229

Persian Gulf, 145

Poland, 44, 74, 115, 194, 223

Politburo of the Communist Party of the Soviet Union, 223

Poroshenko, Petro, 64, 66, 67, 159

Privatization, 17, 19, 20, 24, 28, 29, 63

Putin, Vladimir

    on war, 78

    on religion, 86

    on family, 88

    on China, 89

    on Bin Laden, 93

    on power, 94

    on Democracy and Freedom, 95

    on the Arctic, 98

    on Muslims, 99

    on Kyoto Protocol, 100

    on being Anti-American, 100

    on work management and national security, 103

    on economy, 107

    on economics, 126

    on Syria, 130

    on Russian relations with Turkey, 133

    on Saudi Arabia, 142

    on Security of Russia, 154

    on Ukraine, 158

    on Russian surveillance, 169

    on Chechnya, 172

    on Putin's first Presidency, 178

    on Georgia, Ukraine, and Crimea, 184

    on the 2016 Election, 209

    on cyber warfare, 219

    on international relations, 229

on Syria and defense, 233
on sovereignty, 244
Reagan, Ronald, 30, 33, 79, 82, 105, 106, 107
Right Sector, 74
Ritneva River, 6
Riyadh, Saudi Arabia, 151
Rockefeller, John D., 199
Romania, 44, 115, 194, 232
Rose, Charlie, 128, 190
Rosenberg, Julius and Ethel, 45
Rousseff, Dilma, 127
Russian Federation, 12, 52, 76, 97, 109, 112, 172, 180, 185, 204, 240-241
Russian War, 8
Saakashvili, Mikheil, 51, 52, 73, 157, 184, 185, 187, 188
Sanders, Bernie, 123
Sebastopol, 193
Second Chechen War, 15, 17, 37
Second Punic War, 213
Security Council of Russia, 103
September 11th attacks 32
Sharon, Ariel, 152
Shevardnadze, Eduard, 188
Siege of Leningrad, 5, 6
Silk Road, 92, 133
Simonyan, Margarita, 91
Snowden, Edward, 50-54, 56-59, 61, 62, 91, 188, 220-222, 227
Sobchak, Anatoly, 11, 12, 13, 16, 17
Sochi, 72, 77, 133, 161, 162, 163, 178, 235
Somalia, 234
Soros, George, 71
South Ossetia, 52
Sovereignty, 45, 46, 60, 83, 119, 120, 121, 161, 221, 237, 244-247
Soviet Union, 1-3, 7, 9, 12-13, 17, 25-26, 30, 33-34, 40-41, 44-47, 81, 94, 115-116, 118, 120, 142, 156, 170, 172, 175, 183-184, 192-193, 199, 203, 223
Special Services, 56, 103, 104, 169, 170, 171, 179, 227, 228
St. Andrew Hall, 127

St. Petersburg, 6, 7, 11, 12, 16, 18, 28, 86, 199, 237
Stalin, Joseph, 7, 14, 25, 26, 46, 47, 96, 119, 170, 172, 203
Star Wars (Strategic Defense Initiative), 79
Stone, Sharon, 179, 182
Stuxnet, 220, 222, 224
Sunni tribes, 140, 218, 233
Supreme Court of the United States, 96
Suvorov, Alexander Vasilyevich, 231
Syria, 2, 32, 36, 46, 50, 114, 130-132, 134-136, 138-142, 145, 146, 158, 160, 161, 194, 216-218, 228, 233, 234, 235, 237, 238, 239
Tajikistan, 33
Tatars, 69, 196
Tbilisi, 16, 17
The Arctic, 98
The Pentagon, 114, 115, 117, 154, 220, 238
Tiger economy, 206
Timoshenko, Stephen, 189
Tolstoy, Leo, 113
TOPOL (ballistic missile), 78
Trans-Siberian Railroad, 92
Truman, Harry S., 46, 47, 198
Trump, Donald J., 3, 123, 209, 210-218, 225
Tsarism, 199
Tsipras, Alexis, 91
Turkey, 81, 133-138, 141, 147, 233-237
Ukraine, 2, 56, 60, 62-68, 71-74, 76, 81, 82, 90, 112, 115, 120-121, 158-159, 171-172, 181, 190-196, 217, 219, 243
UN Security Council, 31
United Nations Charter, 69, 139, 150
USS Donald Cook, 239-241
Verkhovna Rada, 67
Vietnam War, 30
Wall Street, 111, 118, 148, 179, 180, 182-183
Wallace, Mike, 23
Warsaw Treaty, 156

Weapons of Mass Destruction (WMD), 39, 113, 122

Western bloc, 120, 121, 156

WikiLeaks, 214

Wilson, Woodrow, 46

World Trade Organization (WTO), 64

World War II (Second World War), 6-8, 25, 47, 81, 118-120, 172, 213

Yanukovych, Viktor, 63, 65, 72, 73, 74, 189, 190, 191, 239, 240

Yatsenyuk, Arseniy, 159, 192

Yeltsin, Boris, 1, 12-16, 28-29, 33, 56, 164

Yugoslavia, 179

Yushchenko, Viktor, 189, 190